# E-Service Digital Innovation

*Edited by Kyeong Kang and Fatuma Namisango*

Published in London, United Kingdom

E-Service Digital Innovation
http://dx.doi.org/10.5772/intechopen.102275
Edited by Kyeong Kang and Fatuma Namisango

Contributors
Abdulrahman Ahmad N. Alkenani, Adam Malešević, Mapula Hildah Lefophane, Md Imtiaz Ahmed, Mercy Samuel, Siddharth Gupta, Sheldon Liang, Hong Liu, Melanie Van Stry, Nguyen Quoc Hung Luu, Darci de Borba, Sandra Schön, Martin Ebner, Sarah Edelsbrunner, Kyeong Kang, Lifu Li, Fatuma Namisango



First published in London, United Kingdom, 2023 by IntechOpen
IntechOpen is the global imprint of INTECHOPEN LIMITED, registered in England and Wales, registration number: 11086078, 5 Princes Gate Court, London, SW7 2QJ, United Kingdom

British Library Cataloguing-in-Publication Data
A catalogue record for this book is available from the British Library

Additional hard and PDF copies can be obtained from orders@intechopen.com

E-Service Digital Innovation
Edited by Kyeong Kang and Fatuma Namisango
p. cm.
Print ISBN 978-1-80356-572-9
Online ISBN 978-1-80356-573-6
eBook (PDF) ISBN 978-1-80356-574-3

For EU product safety concerns:
IN TECH d.o.o., Prolaz Marije Krucifikse Kozulić 3, 51000 Rijeka, Croatia,
info@intechopen.com or visit our website at intechopen.com.

# Meet the editors

Dr. Kyeong Kang is a distinguished academic luminary based in Australia, holding a Ph.D. in Computing Sciences from the University of Technology, Sydney (UTS), Australia. Specializing in the intricate field of social-technical studies, she showcases a profound understanding of the cultural intricacies woven into information systems. Serving as a devoted faculty member at UTS, Dr. Kang mentors Ph.D. candidates, guiding them through the nuances of their research odysseys. Her academic advisor role at UTS has shaped the university's research trajectory. With a passion for bridging academia and industry, Dr. Kang leads various research endeavors tailored to real-world challenges. Her scholarly pursuits encompass a vast range, from digital service innovation and system design to the rich tapestry of socio-cultural dynamics in system co-creation. Her relentless commitment to advancing knowledge and innovation cements her reputation as a leading voice in the international academic community.

Dr. Fatuma Namisango is Lecturer of Information Technology in the School of Information Technology, College of STEM, Murdoch University, Australia. She has a Ph.D. in Information Systems from the University of Technology Sydney (UTS), Australia. She teaches business analysis and system development approaches, managing information in organizations, and managing IT projects. Her research focuses on cross-cultural issues in information systems, human factors in computing, social information systems, technology affordances and constraints, socio-materiality and new ways of working and living, human information behaviors, and sustainability in IS education. Dr. Namisangohas has published her work in the *International Journal of Information Management*, *Computers in Human Behavior*, *Information Systems Frontiers*, and *Journal of Service Theory and Practice*.

# Contents


**Preface** **IX**

**Section 1**
Digital Services and Societal Structures **1**

**Chapter 1** **3**
Dissimilar Social Settings Impact on User Motivations and Activities on Live-Streaming Digital Platforms
*by Kyeong Kang, Lifu Li and Fatuma Namisango*

**Chapter 2** **21**
Research Directions for Value Co-Destruction in Banking Digital Transformation
*by Darci de Borba*

**Chapter 3** **39**
Perspective Chapter: Digital Business Model – The Present, Future, and the Vision
*by Abdulrahman Ahmad N. Alkenani*

**Chapter 4** **55**
Rural Consumers' Willingness to Pay for Online Grocery Delivery Services during COVID-19 Pandemic: Preliminary Evidence from South Africa
*by Mapula Hildah Lefophane*

**Section 2**
Digital Transformation of Education **79**

**Chapter 5** **81**
Perspective Chapter: Building an Online Ecosystem for English Teaching and Learning in the Times of Covid-19 Pandemic and Beyond
*by Nguyen Quoc Hung Luu*

**Chapter 6** **93**
Perspective Chapter: Digitization of Traditional Higher Education Touchpoints
*by Adam Malešević*

**Chapter 7** 133
Supporting Learning and Teaching with Good Design: Report and Lessons Learned from Learning Experience Design in Higher Education
*by Martin Ebner, Sarah Edelsbrunner and Sandra Schön*

**Section 3**
Application of Digital Innovation 145

**Chapter 8** 147
Perspective Chapter: Data Monetization Model for Sustaining Smart City Initiatives
*by Mercy Samuel and Siddharth Gupta*

**Chapter 9** 165
Understanding the Artificial Intelligence Implementation for Allocating an Order to a Seller among Multiple Sellers Who Sell the Same Product
*by Md Imtiaz Ahmed*

**Chapter 10** 177
UnIX-CARE: Universal Interface and Experience via Collaborative Archive Repository Express
*by Sheldon Liang, Melanie Van Stry and Hong Liu*

# Preface

In the transformative landscape of digital innovation, the intersection of technology and service has never been more critical. *E-Service Digital Innovation* is a seminal text meticulously crafted to cater to the intricate needs of academics, researchers, and practitioners navigating digital services' evolving realms. This book offers a profound and holistic understanding, examining the multifaceted dimensions of digital innovation through a scholarly lens while providing pragmatic insights for real-world application.

At the onset, we delve into the intricacies of user motivation, dissecting the complex tapestry of psychological drivers and behavioral patterns that underpin user engagement with digital services. This foundational understanding is paramount for academics and researchers aiming to unravel the nuances of user interaction and devise strategies that resonate with the end users' intrinsic and extrinsic motivations.

In social settings and value co-creation, this book critically examines the symbiotic relationship between digital services and societal structures. We explore how digital innovations act as catalysts for social change while being shaped by the fabric of society they seek to transform. The discourse extends to unravel how value is co-created in digital ecosystems, fostering a collaborative environment where organizations and users collectively contribute to the enrichment of digital services.

The transformative journey of banking through digital means is presented with a comprehensive analysis, showcasing the radical shifts in financial services and the strategic imperatives for institutions in the digital age. This sets a robust foundation for the subsequent exploration of digital business models, where we dissect the varied strategies employed by organizations to navigate the digital economy.

As we venture into the future with Industry 5.0, this book positions itself at the forefront of academic discourse, exploring the confluence of smart technologies, human ingenuity, and innovative practices redefining the manufacturing and production landscape.

Artificial Intelligence (AI) and blockchain are presented not merely as technological phenomena but as transformative agents rewriting business and societal engagement rules. The chapters dedicated to these domains provide a balanced, critical, and ethically grounded exploration, ensuring that readers are equipped with a comprehensive understanding of the opportunities, challenges, and responsibilities that accompany these technologies.

The resilience of organizations in the face of volatility and uncertainty is addressed in the chapter on business continuity, providing a repository of strategies, best practices, and scholarly discourse to navigate tumultuous times. In juxtaposition, exploring digital adoption in rural settings provides a nuanced and context-rich understanding of these regions' unique challenges and opportunities.

The digital transformation of education is examined through the lenses of online learning and learning ecosystems, setting the stage for an in-depth exploration of e-service in higher education. This book further integrates student relationship management, offering strategies and frameworks to cultivate meaningful and enriching interactions between educational institutions and their students.

Instructional learning design is addressed with scholarly rigor, ensuring educators and practitioners have the knowledge and tools to deliver digital education effectively. The chapter on data monetization offers a critical examination of the strategies and ethical considerations surrounding the financial exploitation of data, ensuring that readers are well-versed in the nuanced dynamics of this domain.

The Internet of Things (IoT) and the concept of self-financing cities are presented as avant-garde applications of digital innovation, showcasing the transformative potential of technology in urban planning and governance. Exploring AI in e-commerce provides a rich discourse on how AI revolutionizes retail, enhances customer experiences, and creates new business paradigms.

The collaborative archive repository express and online publishing chapters address the transformative impact of digital technologies on data management, sharing, and the publishing industry. These chapters provide valuable insights and frameworks for academics, researchers, and practitioners navigating the complexities of collaborative intelligence and the digital publishing landscape.

*E-Service Digital Innovation* is a magnum opus, a scholarly tour de force that seamlessly blends academic rigor with practical wisdom, ensuring that readers are not just observers but active participants in the digital transformation journey. It invites readers to immerse themselves in the depth of its content, engage with its critical discourses, and emerge with a profound understanding of e-service digital innovation, ready to contribute to and shape the digital future.

**Kyeong Kang**
School of Professional Practice and Leadership,
Faculty of Engineering and IT,
University of Technology Sydney,
Sydney, Australia

**Fatuma Namisango**
Murdoch University,
Perth, Australia

Section 1

# Digital Services and Societal Structures

Chapter 1

# Dissimilar Social Settings Impact on User Motivations and Activities on Live-Streaming Digital Platforms

*Kyeong Kang, Lifu Li and Fatuma Namisango*

## Abstract

This chapter delves into the motivations and activities of users within various social contexts on live digital platforms. It introduces an innovative research model that employs the well-established Achievement Motivation Theory to investigate how three fundamental needs relate to the motivation of live streamers during their live-streaming activities. The study aims to illuminate the underlying drivers that influence live streamers' engagement and behavior within the dynamic landscape of live digital content. Live-streaming digital platforms have become prominent channels for user engagement and content creation, enabling individuals to broadcast live videos and connect with audiences in real time. However, user motivations and behaviors on these platforms can significantly differ based on their social settings. This research explores the impact of diverse social backgrounds on user motivations and activities on live-streaming digital platforms, shedding light on the intricacies that shape user behavior across various contexts. Influence of Social Settings: Social settings encompass cultural norms, societal values, economic conditions, and technological infrastructure. These factors shape users' attitudes, preferences, and aspirations on live-streaming platforms, ultimately influencing their motivations and activities. Drawing on the Achievement Motivation Theory by McClelland, this chapter examines motivating factors for live-streaming activities, focusing on the need for achievement, power, and affiliation. The study employs variance-based structural equation modeling (SEM), specifically partial least squares (PLS), to analyze these elements. The findings highlight the positive impact of these factors on live streamers' motivation to create live-streaming content, offering theoretical insights and practical implications for scholars and practitioners engaged in live-streaming activities. This research aids in understanding the live-streamer community within the rapidly evolving landscape of live digital platforms.

**Keywords:** live digital platforms, live-streaming, user motivation, social setting, content creation

## 1. Introduction

In the realm of business digital platforms, a comprehensive comprehension of user motivations and behaviours within diverse social contexts on live digital platforms stands as a pivotal catalyst for the enhancement and augmentation of digital platform services. The intrinsic value of these services is profoundly influenced by the intricacies governing user engagement and activities in the digital landscape. As such, an in-depth exploration of these facets not only serves as an academic endeavour but also as a pragmatic pursuit with profound implications for businesses operating within the digital domain.

The contemporary business landscape is indelibly intertwined with the proliferation of digital platforms, where individuals harness the power of live-streaming technologies to engage with audiences in real time. However, the dynamics of user motivations and activities on these platforms exhibit significant variations contingent upon the social settings in which they operate. The amalgamation of cultural norms, societal values, economic conditions, and technological infrastructure collectively blends user attitudes, preferences, and aspirations, thereby exerting a profound influence on their interactions within live digital environments.

This chapter embarks on a scholarly exploration of this intricate terrain, invoking a synthesis of theoretical frameworks, empirical analyses, and methodological rigor to unravel the multifaceted dimensions of user motivation and behaviour. By shedding light on the dynamic interplay between social contexts and user engagement within the digital sphere, this inquiry aspires to proffer not only a deeper academic understanding but also a pragmatic roadmap for businesses aspiring to optimize their digital platform services.

In the ensuing pages, we embark on a journey that delves into the depths of user motivations and activities, navigating the complex terrain of live digital platforms and their profound implications for the contemporary business ecosystem.

A novel research model is proposed, which employs an existing Achievement Motivation Theory [1] to investigate the relationship between three fundamental needs and the motivation of live streamers during their live-streaming activities. The study aims to shed light on the underlying drivers influencing the live streamers' engagement and behavior in the dynamic realm of live digital content.

Live-streaming digital platforms have become a prominent medium for user engagement and content creation, allowing individuals to broadcast live videos and connect with audiences in real time. However, the motivations and activities of users on these platforms can vary significantly depending on the social settings in which they operate. This study explores how dissimilar social settings impact user motivations and activities on live-streaming digital platforms, shedding light on the nuances that influence user behavior in different contexts, such as the Influence of Social Settings, developed vs. less-developed regions, urban vs. rural communities, individualistic vs. collectivist cultures, technological accessibility and gender and social norms.

**The influence of social settings:** Social settings encompass a range of factors, including cultural norms, societal values, economic conditions, and technological infrastructure. These elements can shape users' attitudes, preferences, and aspirations on live-streaming platforms, ultimately affecting their motivations and activities.

**Developed vs. less-developed regions:** In more economically developed regions, users may be driven by achievement-oriented motivations, seeking recognition and success through high-quality content and large viewer bases. On the other hand, in less-developed areas, users might prioritize affiliation-oriented motivations, aiming to build close-knit communities and foster meaningful connections with their audiences.

**Urban vs. rural communities:** Users from urban areas may be more inclined to explore diverse content creation opportunities, embracing technology to its fullest potential. In contrast, users from rural communities may focus on content that reflects their local culture and traditions, emphasizing a strong sense of belonging and identity.

**Individualistic vs. collectivist cultures:** Users may be motivated by personal aspirations to stand out and showcase their unique talents in individualistic cultures. In contrast, users from collectivist cultures may prioritize group harmony and cooperation, leading to collaborative and community-centered content.

**Technological accessibility:** The availability and accessibility of technology can significantly impact user motivations and activities. In regions with advanced technical infrastructure, users may be more likely to engage in live-streaming for professional purposes. At the same time, those with limited access may primarily use it for social interaction and entertainment.

**Gender and social norms:** Social norms and expectations surrounding gender roles can also shape user motivations and activities. In some settings, there might be specific expectations or limitations on what content male and female users are encouraged or allowed to produce.

With the rapid development of live-streaming digital platforms, online users are willing to engage in live-streaming activities and create unique content. Drawing on the McClelland achievement motivation theory, this chapter discusses the motivating factors for live-streaming activities from three perspectives: the need for achievement, the need for power, and the need for affiliation. We analyzed the above elements using a variance-based structural equation modeling (SEM) technique, partial least squares (PLS). All factors positively affect live streamers' motivation to produce live-streaming content. Our findings present theoretical and practical implications for scholars and practitioners in live-streaming activities. The research results are helpful for related scholars and departments to understand the live-streamer group and pay more attention to live-streaming activities.

## 2. Introduction of investigation

A study examines how the three core achievement needs, affiliation, and power influence live streamers' motivation on live digital platforms. By reading this relationship, we seek to provide insights into the factors that inspire and sustain live-streaming engagement among content creators.

Live digital platforms have witnessed a remarkable surge in popularity, with live-streaming emerging as a dominant mode of communication and content creation. With various live-streaming options, understanding the motivations driving live streamers becomes crucial for platform providers and content creators. The present research delves into the psychological underpinnings of live-streaming motivation to address this gap, employing the McClelland Achievement Motivation Theory as the theoretical framework.

Live-streaming is an online activity that allows live streamers to reach and interact with online viewers over the Internet [2]. Unlike traditional social media platforms, the main advantage of live-streaming is that live streamers can get real-time feedback. With the improvement of live-streaming technology and the popularity of smartphones, more and more online users consume and actively produce information, aiming to enhance their social influence and develop the e-business [3]. Meanwhile, live-streaming platforms are gradually replacing traditional social media platforms and attracting many user groups. For example, the number of active live-streaming users in China has increased from 230 to 330 million between 2018 and 2019, and 27% of online shoppers claim they will purchase products directly through live-streaming platforms [4, 5]. Given the technical convenience and huge user base, more and more Chinese users are willing to engage in live-streaming activities on live-streaming platforms.

Previous studies have identified the importance of live-streaming functions and analyzed online users' watching motivation on live-streaming platforms [6–8]. However, insufficient focus on live streamer groups and discussing their live-streaming motivation. Unlike online viewers, live streamers have specific needs to create live-streaming content, such as meeting their financial needs and enhancing social value [3]. Specifically, young entrepreneurs establish business activities on live-streaming platforms to reduce investment costs, and ethnic minority group users produce cultural content to promote cultural diversity and build their careers [9–12]. Different live streamer groups have unique goals for developing live-streaming content. Still, limited scholars focus on this specific phenomenon. Considering this, the main research question is: What *factors affect live streamers' motivation to produce live-streaming content?*

Based on the research question, this chapter draws on the McClelland achievement motivation theory, also known as the three needs theory, to design specific influencing factors and explore live streamers' live-streaming motivation [1]. The approach can be applied to discover and predict behavior and performance based on an individual's needs [13]. According to the McClelland achievement motivation theory, personal motivation can be influenced by the needs for achievement, affiliation, and power [1]. However, previous research [14–16] applied the McClelland achievement motivation theory to analyze individuals' and organizational behaviors, almost none of them applied it to focus on live-streaming activities and discuss live streamers' live-streaming motivation. Considering the sense of accomplishment, the live-streaming activity can bring, using the theory could provide some theoretical support for the framework exploration. The study proposes a research model and specific hypotheses which apply the McClelland achievement motivation theory to analyze the relationship between three needs and live streamers' live-streaming motivation.

The McClelland Achievement Motivation Theory [1] posits that individuals are driven by three primary needs: achievement, affiliation, and power. Achievement refers to the desire for excellence, the aspiration to accomplish challenging tasks, and the pursuit of success. Affiliation entails the need for social interactions, forming connections, and fostering positive relationships. Power reflects the yearning for control, influence, and authority over others.

## 3. Study background

### 3.1 Live-streaming motivation

"Live-streaming" can be defined as a synchronous function, and live streamers on live-streaming platforms can create live videos and interact in real time with online viewers [17]. Visual interaction is integral to the live-streaming engagement field [18]. Convenient functions provided by live-streaming platforms have unique attractiveness for live streamers, such as real-time video interaction, Danmuku, virtual gift-sending systems, and online store functions [19, 20]. Because of the advanced peer-to-peer technology, online users can be not only receivers of information but also creators of information, known as live streamers. For instance, young live streamers can produce novel content to make online friends, and online merchants tend to build trust with online consumers and advertise their products [21]. Different needs of live streamers can be met through live-streaming activities. The significance of the current study is to focus on live streamers' live-streaming motivation based on the McClelland achievement motivation theory.

### 3.2 McClelland achievement motivation theory

The achievement motivation theory can be applied to explain and predict motivation based on an individual's need for achievement, power, and affiliation [22]. It has been widely adopted in many academic areas, such as distance learning and entrepreneurial persistence [23, 24]. Limited studies apply it to analyze individual live-streaming activities, i.e., live-streaming motivation. It supports that personal motives are related to achievement, affiliation, and power motives. The need for achievement refers to live streamers' success in competition with some standard of excellence, such as building their fan group and establishing their own careers [16]. The need for power means live streamers prefer to influence online viewers and seek positions of authority [25].

Regarding affiliation needs, it refers to live streamers' needs to develop, maintain, and restore warm personal relationships with online viewers [25]. Based on the McClelland achievement motivation theory, three different needs significantly link individuals' motivation. Considering that limited scholars apply the approach to discuss live-streaming motivation, this paper needs to examine the relationship between three needs and live streamers' live-streaming motivation.

## 4. Hypothesis development

Based on the McClelland achievement motivation theory [1], we argue that three needs, including achievement, affiliation, and power, significantly affect live-streaming motivation. This chapter proposes three hypotheses to explore the motivators for live-streaming, as shown in **Figure 1** below.

### 4.1 Need for achievement

As defined by Moore et al. [16], the need for achievement refers to the drive for success and excellence compared to a particular standard. In the context of live-streaming platforms, live streamers can fulfill this need through technical convenience, which allows them to attain social recognition and economic status by creating distinctive content or establishing online start-ups, as pointed out by Li and Kang [26]. A prime example of this phenomenon is live-streaming commerce, where the barriers to entry for starting a business are reduced, enabling live streamers to easily engage with online consumers and discuss product information directly on live-streaming platforms [27, 28]. This symbiotic relationship between live streamers and consumers facilitates the fulfillment of the need for achievement, as live streamers can achieve success and excellence by effectively reaching and engaging with their audience, leading to greater social value and economic opportunities.

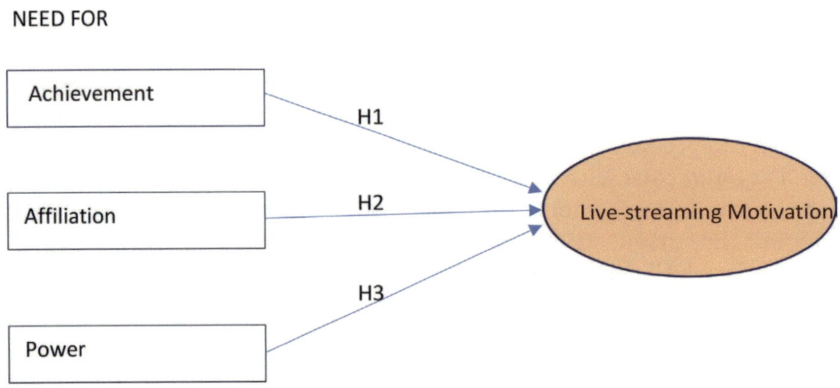


**Figure 1.**
*Research model.*

The new business model would help live streamers achieve higher economic status and implement their career goals. Thus, we hypothesize that:

**Hypothesis 1:** The need for achievement positively affects live streamers' live-streaming motivation.

### 4.2 Need for power

Based on the definition proposed by Lussier and Achua [25], the need for power means live streamers tend to influence online viewers and seek positions of authority through live-streaming Fields [25]. By creating unique live-streaming content, live streamers can attract online viewers' attention and build trust with them [29]. The trust created with online viewers helps live streamers pass on personal ideas and influence viewers' judgment [4, 30]. This process can satisfy live streamers' need for power, and hence we hypothesize that:

**Hypothesis 2:** The need for power positively affects live streamers' live-streaming motivation.

### 4.3 Need for affiliation

Affiliation need relates to live streamers' needs to develop, maintain, and restore warm personal relationships with others [25]. Because of the real-time interactive technology and convenient online communication functions, it is simple for live streamers to understand online viewers' experiences and narrow the emotional distance from them [31]. Meanwhile, other convenient functions, such as group chat, gift-sending system, and fan group functions, can be helpful for live streamers to communicate with online viewers and maintain a strong relationship with them [9, 32]. Therefore, we hypothesize that:

**Hypothesis 3:** The need for affiliation positively affects live streamers' live-streaming motivation.

### 4.4 Live-streaming motivation

Live-streaming motivation refers to the driving factors that inspire individuals to engage in live-streaming activities on digital platforms. Live-streaming has become a popular medium for content creators to broadcast real-time videos and interact with their audience dynamically and interactively. Understanding the motivations behind live-streaming is crucial to comprehend why individuals participate in content creation and communication. Motivations for live-streaming can vary widely among different individuals and content creators.

It is essential to recognize that motivations for live-streaming can be multifaceted and may evolve. Individuals may have a combination of motivations that drive them to engage in live-streaming activities. Understanding these motivations helps platforms, marketers, and content creators tailor their strategies to meet streamers' and viewers' needs and expectations, leading to a more vibrant and engaging live-streaming community.

## 5. Research approach

To achieve the research objectives, the study adopted a quantitative approach as Evans and Mathur's [33] field study. First, a comprehensive literature review was conducted to establish the theoretical foundation and gather relevant insights from previous studies. Subsequently, quantitative data was collected through an online survey from a diverse sample of live streamers comprising different content categories and platforms. The survey comprised validated scales to measure achievement motivation, affiliation motivation, power motivation, and live-streaming motivation.

We collected data from a diverse sample of live streamers across different digital platforms to examine the motivating factors for live-streaming activities. A well-structured survey instrument was developed, incorporating validated scales to assess the need for achievement, power, and affiliation. The survey also included measures of live-streaming motivation. With the aid of variance-based structural equation modeling, namely partial least squares (PLS), we analyzed the relationships among these variables.

It is suitable for researchers to collect data during the COVID-19 pandemic, as identified by previous studies [26]. Furthermore, the study chooses Chinese live streamers as research samples because the development of live-streaming platforms is fast in China. For instance, as China's most popular live-streaming platform, TikTok (Douyin) has attracted more than 500 million active users and has become the third most downloaded app [34, 35]. Considering the rapid development of live-streaming platforms in China, this study selects the Chinese live-streaming environment as the research context.

### 5.1 Measurement items

All constructs measured in this study are based on existing literature. For instance, according to the research proposed by Schönbrodt and Gerstenberg [36], the need for achievement, power, and affiliation have been measured by three question items, respectively. Meanwhile, based on three questions Field, live-streaming motivation is examined [37]. Except for basic information statistics, such as gender, age, EMG background, and living regions, major question items are shown in **Table 1**. The paper utilizes the Likert 7-point scale with a range from the lowest score = 1 to the highest score = 7 to measure participants' answers [38].

| Variable | Item | Measurement | Adopted from |
|---|---|---|---|
| Need for achievement | NA1<br>NA2<br>NA3 | Continuously engage in new, exciting, and challenging goals and projects.<br>I am attracted to situations that allow me to test my abilities.<br>My goal is to do at least a little bit more than anyone else has done before | Schönbrodt and Gerstenberg [36] |
| Need for power | NP1<br>NP2<br>NP3 | I like to have the final say.<br>I would like to be an executive with power over others.<br>I feel confident when directing the activities of others. | Schönbrodt and Gerstenberg [36] |
| Need for affiliation | NF1<br>NF2<br>NF3 | Engage in a lot of activities with other people.<br>Encounters with other people make me happy.<br>I like to make as many friends as I can. | Schönbrodt and Gerstenberg [36] |
| Live-streaming motivation | LS1<br>LS2<br>LS3 | I am ready to do anything to be a live streamer.<br>I will make every effort to start live-streaming.<br>I have the firm intention to create live-streaming content someday. | Ho and Yang [37] |

**Table 1.**
*Questionnaire items.*

### 5.2 Data collection

The current study used the questionnaire design platform wjx.cn because the online questionnaire is distributed on Chinese social media platforms. Its academic functions and the Chinese language option are comfortable for Chinese users to fill in. Filtering questions have been designed before the formal questionnaire, including their live-streaming platform using experience and live-streaming content-producing experience. From October 2022 to November 2022, online questionnaires were distributed on Chinese social media platforms like WeChat, Sina Weibo, and QQ. One hundred fifty-four replies have been received, and inappropriate responses have been deleted, including incomplete answers and the same IP address. Finally, 130 questionnaires are valid for this study, and the rate of the valid questionnaire is 84.42%.

## 6. Data analysis

The variance-based Structural Equation Modeling (SEM) and partial least squares (PLS) path modeling is applied to examine the research model and analyze hypotheses [39, 40]. The measurement and structural model analysis is conducted through the SmartPLS 3, which fits the research purpose. Meanwhile, implementing PLS-SEM analysis on SmartPLS can better understand the research model, and it has relaxed data requirements, which has been identified by previous studies [41, 42].

### 6.1 Descriptive statistics

Among these 130 respondents (**Table 2**), 46.15% are female, and 53.85% are male. Regarding their age, 49.23% are between 21 and 30, and 34.62% are between 31 and 40. Regarding participants' platform-using experiences, 46.15% have 2–3 years of user experience, and 39.23% have 1–2 years of user experience, as shown in **Table 2**.

| Demographic variables | Category | Frequency | Percentage (%) |
|---|---|---|---|
| Gender | Female | 60 | 46.15 |
| | Male | 70 | 53.85 |
| Age | ≤20 | 12 | 9.23 |
| | 21–30 | 64 | 49.23 |
| | 31–40 | 45 | 34.62 |
| | ≥40 | 9 | 6.92 |
| Platform using experience | Less than half-year | 9 | 6.92 |
| | 1–2 year | 51 | 39.23 |
| | 2–3 year | 60 | 46.15 |
| | Above 3 years | 10 | 7.69 |

**Table 2.**
*The basic information of respondents (N = 130).*

### 6.2 Measurement model

The study must involve reliability, convergent validity, and discriminant validity evaluations to check the measurement model [43]. Firstly, as per the previous research [40], three criteria, including average variance extracted (AVE), composite reliability (CR), and Cronbach's Alpha, need to be utilized to evaluate the reliability of the research model. In detail, AVE should be greater than 0.50, CR should be higher than 0.70, and Cronbach's Alpha should be more incredible than 0.70 [44]. **Table 3** shows that all data results meet the requirements, meaning acceptable reliabilities.

The convergent validity and discriminant validity were evaluated. As **Table 3** presents, the factor loadings within their intended constructs are highly correlated,

| Item | Indicator | Loading | AVE | Composite reliability | Cronbach's Alpha |
|---|---|---|---|---|---|
| LS | LS1 | 0.850 | 0.766 | 0.907 | 0.847 |
| | LS2 | 0.913 | | | |
| | LS3 | 0.860 | | | |
| NA | NA1 | 0.904 | 0.779 | 0.914 | 0.857 |
| | NA2 | 0.919 | | | |
| | NA3 | 0.823 | | | |
| NF | NF1 | 0.836 | 0.749 | 0.899 | 0.832 |
| | NF2 | 0.900 | | | |
| | NF3 | 0.858 | | | |
| NP | NP1 | 0.861 | 0.794 | 0.920 | 0.869 |
| | NP2 | 0.942 | | | |
| | NP3 | 0.867 | | | |

**Table 3.**
*The results of factor loadings, AVE, CR, and Cronbach's Alpha.*

presenting that the measurement model meets the requirement of convergent validity and discriminant validity [45–47]. The range of marked items shown in **Table 3** is from 0.823 to 0.942, which is higher than 0.708, indicating that the model meets the convergent validity [44]. Meanwhile, AVE can be used to analyze convergent validity. As **Table 3** shows, the AVE results are higher than the proposed AVE value of 0.50, demonstrating the convergent validity of this research model [48].

In addition to the convergent validity, the discriminant validity should be tested by checking the Fornell-Larcker criterion. The AVE square root on the diagonals (**Table 4**) can be utilized to evaluate whether the discriminant validity of the model is acceptable [46, 49]. As per this criterion, a key condition is that the square root of the average variance extracted by a particular construct should exceed the correlation between that construct and any other constructs within the model. As shown in **Table 4**, the AVE square root on the diagonals is significantly higher than other correlations, claiming that the discriminant validity meets related requirements. Meanwhile, values of the HTMT ratio remain lower than 0.90, as recommended in the literature for discriminant validity confirmation [44]. Hence, all constructs get discriminant validity.

In **Table 4**, the bold values represent correlations between constructs. Specifically, the bold numbers in the upper part of the table (Fornell-Larcker criterion) represent correlations between constructs, while the bold values in the lower part of the table (HTMT criterion) also indicate correlations but follow a different measurement criterion. These bold values are significant because they reveal the strength and direction of the relationships between the various constructs being studied. Researchers often highlight these bold values to draw attention to key findings and to assess discriminant validity between constructs.

Our findings, as presented in **Table 4**, reveal that the AVE square root values along the diagonal significantly surpass the correlations with other constructs. This observation strongly supports the assertion that our model indeed fulfills the prerequisites for discriminant validity as per the relevant criteria.

Furthermore, we ensure that our results align with the established recommendations in the literature by verifying that the values of the Heterotrait-Monotrait (HTMT) ratio consistently remain below the threshold of 0.90, as advised for

| **Fornell-Larcker criterion** | | | | |
|---|---|---|---|---|
| | **LS** | **NA** | **NF** | **NP** |
| LS | **0.875** | | | |
| NA | 0.748 | **0.883** | | |
| NF | 0.730 | 0.656 | **0.865** | |
| NP | 0.771 | 0.701 | 0.679 | **0.891** |
| **HTMT criterion** | | | | |
| | **LS** | **NA** | **NF** | **NP** |
| LS | | | | |
| NA | 0.877 | | | |
| NF | 0.867 | 0.772 | | |
| NP | 0.888 | 0.808 | 0.797 | |

**Table 4.**
*Discriminant validity is based on the Fornell-Larcker criterion and HTMT criterion.*

| Relationship | Original sample (O) | Standard deviation (STDEV) | T statistics (\|O/ STDEV\|) | P values |
|---|---|---|---|---|
| NA- > LS | 0.310 | 0.098 | 3.151 | 0.002 |
| NF- > LS | 0.279 | 0.092 | 3.027 | 0.003 |
| NP- > LS | 0.364 | 0.105 | 3.452 | 0.001 |

**Table 5.**
*Hypotheses results.*

confirming discriminant validity [44]. Consequently, we can confidently affirm that all constructs within our study unequivocally exhibit discriminant validity.

### 6.3 Structural model evaluation

When self-report questionnaires are applied to collect data simultaneously from the same participants, a standard method variance (CMV) can be problematic [50]. We tested CMV using the variance inflation factor (VIF) [44, 51]. The occurrence of a VIF higher than 3.3 can be proposed as an indication of pathological collinearity. Thus, the value of VIF must be below 3.3 to be free from the multicollinearity problem [44]. The data analysis shows that the VIF scores for all constructs are between 2.104 and 2.356, which are significantly lower than 3.3. Hence, the study can support that there are no collinearity problems detected.

### 6.4 Hypothesis testing

We assessed path significance and t-statistical test using the bootstrapping technique on SmartPLS 3 [52]. As **Table 5** presents, all hypotheses can be supported because t-statistics results are notably higher than 1.96 and P values are less than 0.01 [52]. Specifically, according to the data analysis in **Table 5**, the need for achievement positively affects live streamers' live-streaming motivation ($\beta = 0.310$, $t = 3.151$, $p < 0.01$), which supports H1. The need for power positively affects live streamers' live-streaming motivation ($\beta = 0.364$, $t = 3.452$, $p < 0.001$), supporting H2. Meanwhile, the need for affiliation positively affects live streamers' live-streaming motivation ($\beta = 0.279$, $t = 3.027$, $p < 0.01$), supporting H3.

## 7. Discussion of findings

We proposed three factors that motivate live-streaming activities for live streamers rather than online viewers, as often discussed in previous studies. Our hypotheses were based on the McClelland achievement motivation theory, which posits the need for achievement, affiliation, and power to influence individual engagement in activities. Our findings revealed that all three needs—achievement, affiliation, and power—positively affect live streamers' live-streaming motivation. Generally, our findings confirm McClelland's achievement motivation theory's relevance and usefulness in studying motivation for behavior in digital platforms.

While all three factors positively influence live-streaming motivation, our findings suggest that power could be a stronger motivator for live streamers, followed by achievement and affiliation. This observation aligns with Heser, Banse, and Imhoff

[53], who also noted that the need for power was a stronger motivator for social networking activities such as friending and uploading pictures. However, Alshaibani and Qusti [14] found the need for achievement to be a stronger motivator for using WhatsApp. The variation in findings across studies suggests that the three motivators could differ based on the online platform used. Such differences should be because different platforms are designed to support different needs and have presented several affordances.

Specifically, live streamers focus on their achievements, such as economic goals and social status, while producing live-streaming content. Meanwhile, interesting live-streaming content can attract a large fan base, potentially influencing their viewing interest and purchasing motivation. Thus, working in the live-streaming industry can satisfy live streamers' needs for power. Finally, because of live-streaming technology, live streamers can communicate with online reviewers in real time, meeting their social requirements. Therefore, the need for affiliation positively affects live streamers' live-streaming motivation.

## 8. Theoretical and practical implications

Although previous research applied the McClelland achievement motivation theory to analyze individuals' and organizational behaviors [15, 16], almost none discussed live streamers' motivation to produce live-streaming content. With the rapid development of the live-streaming industry, more and more online users are willing to share information through live-streaming platforms and engage in live-streaming activities. Meanwhile, based on the McClelland achievement motivation theory, the study combines it with live-streaming backgrounds and proposes specific hypotheses. It is helpful for future studies to systematically analyze the live-streaming phenomenon and discover live streamers' live-streaming motivation.

Regarding the practical implications, the study results are helpful for related scholars and departments to understand the live streamer group. For instance, engaging in live-streaming activities can help live streamers build a close relationship with online viewers and satisfy their needs for affiliation. Real-time interaction with online viewers is beneficial for live streamers to meet new friends and build online communities, for instance, during the COVID-19 pandemic and the strict quarantine policies. Engaging in live-streaming activities could meet live streamers' affiliation and achievement needs and release anxiety during the pandemic. Consequently, focusing on the live-streaming industry could be fruitful because its development can promote economic development and meet online users' spiritual needs. Given the similarities between live-streaming motivation and other online activities motivation, the findings could also be used to focus on some specific research areas, such as online marketing and distance teaching activities.

## 9. Discussion, study limitations

The survey analysis results indicated the need for achievement, power, and affiliation significantly and positively influence live streamers' motivation to engage in live-streaming activities and produce content. Live streamers with a higher need for achievement were more driven to create challenging and exceptional content. In comparison, those with a higher need for power exhibited a greater desire to take charge of their content creation process and influence their audience. Additionally, streamers with a higher need for affiliation focused on building strong bonds with their viewers and creating a sense of community.

Although the research model has been established based on the McClelland achievement motivation theory, several details should be improved in future studies. Firstly, the McClelland achievement motivation theory must fully explain the motivation process and display how it occurs in various activities. Hence, related scholars should consider its limitation and combine it with other behavior research theories, that is, the stimulus-organism-response (S-O-R) theory. Meanwhile, the multi-group analysis should be developed in future studies based on live streamers' genders, ages, and educational backgrounds. Different groups could focus on different needs.

Moreover, the data is collected from Chinese users. However, influenced by social and cultural backgrounds, there would be some differences between Eastern and Western users. The cultural differences should be analyzed in future studies, and more influencing factors related to the social and cultural backgrounds should be discussed, including uncertainty-avoidance thinking, power distance, and collectivism [54, 55]. Finally, the online questionnaire participants are from the TikTok platform, and they could pay more attention to the need for affiliation rather than achievement. This is because the TikTok platform is designed based on entertainment, which differs from the Taobao Live platform which focuses on live-streaming commerce. Future studies should present the uniqueness of platforms and discover the specific behavior of users from different platforms.

## 10. Conclusion

This chapter highlights the importance of McClelland's [1] achievement motivation theory in understanding the motivating factors behind live-streaming activities. Using variance-based structural equation modeling, our study reveals that the need for achievement, power, and affiliation positively impact live streamers' motivation to create live-streaming content. The implications of these findings extend to scholars and practitioners alike, emphasizing the significance of live-streaming activities in the digital realm and underscoring the need for further research and attention to this dynamic and evolving domain.

The study draws on the McClelland achievement motivation theory to analyze live streamers' live-streaming motivation. Unlike existing research, it designs influencing factors from three aspects, including the need for achievement, the need for power, and the need for affiliation. Through the data analysis, all of them positively affect live streamers' motivation to produce live-streaming content. The research results are helpful for related scholars and departments to understand the live-streamer group and pay more attention to the live-streaming activities.

## Author details

Kyeong Kang[1]*, Lifu Li[1] and Fatuma Namisango[2]

1 School of Professional Practice and Leadership, Faculty of Engineering and IT, University of Technology Sydney, NSW, Australia

2 Murdoch University, Australia

*Address all correspondence to: kyeong.kang@uts.edu.au

## References

[1] McClelland D. Achievement motivation theory. In: Organizational Behavior: Essential Theories of Motivation and Leadership. London: M. E. Sharpe Inc; 2005. pp. 46-60

[2] Wang X, Wu D. Understanding user engagement mechanisms on a live-streaming platform. In: Paper Presented at the International Conference on Human-Computer Interaction. Orando: Springer Nature; 2019

[3] Gros D, Wanner B, Hackenholt A, Zawadzki P, Knautz K. World of streaming. Motivation and gratification on Twitch. In: Paper Presented at the International Conference on Social Computing and Social Media. Vol.36. No. 6. Vancouver: Springer Nature; 2017. pp. 2611-2631

[4] Li L, Kang K. Understanding the real-time interaction between middle-aged consumers and online experts based on the COM-B model. Journal of Marketing Analytics. June 2024;**3**(2)

[5] Li L, Kang K, Zhao A, Feng Y. The impact of social presence and facilitation factors on online consumers' impulse buying in live shopping–celebrity endorsement as a moderating factor. In: Information Technology & People. UK: Emerald Publishing Limited; 2022b

[6] Li L, Kang K, Feng Y, Zhao A. Factors affecting online consumers' cultural presence and cultural immersion experiences in live-streaming shopping. Journal of Marketing Analytics. (Switzerland AG: Springer Nature). 2022a:1-14

[7] Li L, Kang K, Sohaib O. Analysing younger online viewers' motivation to watch video game live-streaming through a positive perspective. Journal of Economic Analysis. 2023a;**2**(2):56-69

[8] Xu Y, Ye Y. Who watches live-streaming in China? Examining viewers' behaviors, personality traits, and motivations. Frontiers in Psychology. 2020;**11**:1607

[9] Li L, Kang K. Exploring the relationships between cultural content and viewers' watching interest: A study of Tiktok videos produced by Chinese ethnic minority groups. In: Paper Presented at the 18th International Conference on e-Business. 2021b

[10] Li L, Kang K. Why ethnic minority groups' online-startups are booming in China's tight cultural ecosystem? Journal of Entrepreneurship in Emerging Economies. (UK: Emerald Publishing Limited). 2021c;**15**(2):278-300

[11] Li L, Kang K. Ethnic minority group college students' liberal and conservative attitudes to online start-ups: Regional difference perspective. Journal of Entrepreneurship in Emerging Economies. (UK: Emerald Publishing Limited). 2023. (ahead-of print). Available from: https://www.emerald.com/insight/content/doi/10.1108/JEEE-02-2023-0035/full/html.

[12] Li L, Kang K, Sohaib O. Investigating factors affecting Chinese tertiary students' online-startup motivation based on the COM-B behaviour changing theory. Journal of Entrepreneurship in Emerging Economies. 2021;**15**(3):566-588

[13] McClelland D. Achievement motivation theory. In: Organizational

Behavior 1. UK, London: Routledge; 2015. pp. 46-60

[14] Alshaibani MH, Qusti ES. The role of smartphone app "WhatsApp" on achievement motivation and social intelligence among female undergraduate students. Perspectives in Psychiatric Care. 2021;**57**(2):597

[15] Lăzăroiu G. Work motivation and organizational behavior. Contemporary Readings in Law and Social Justice. 2015;7(2):66-75

[16] Moore LL, Grabsch DK, Rotter C. Using achievement motivation theory to explain student participation in a residential leadership learning community. Journal of Leadership Education. 2010;**9**(2):22-34

[17] Scheibe K. The impact of gamification in social live-streaming services. In: Paper Presented at the International Conference on Social Computing and Social Media. LasVegas: Springer Nature; 2018

[18] Lin Y, Yao D, Chen X. Happiness begets money: Emotion and engagement in live streaming. Journal of Marketing Research. 2021;**58**(3):417-438

[19] Li L, Feng Y, Zhao A. An interaction–immersion model in live-streaming commerce: The moderating role of streamer attractiveness. Journal of Marketing Analytics. (Switzerland AG: Springer Nature). May 2023:1-16

[20] Li L, Kang K. The Role of Cultural Attractors in Live-Streaming Content: Regional Cultural Perspective Using Multi-Group Analysis. Taipei: Bepress; 2022b

[21] Zimmer F, Scheibe K. What drives streamers? Users' characteristics and motivations on social live-streaming services. In: Paper Presented at the Proceedings of the 52nd Hawaii International Conference on System Sciences. Hawaii: Hamilton Library; 2019

[22] McClelland DC, Koestner R, Weinberger J. How do self-attributed and implicit motives differ? Psychological Review. 1989;**96**(4):690

[23] Sabiu IT, Abdullah A, Amin A, Tahir IM. An empirical analysis of the need for achievement motivation in predicting entrepreneurial persistence in Bumiputra entrepreneurs in Terengganu, Malaysia. International Journal of Business and Globalisation. 2018;**20**(2):190-202

[24] Siok TH, Sim MS, Rahmat NH. Motivation to learn online: An analysis from Mcclelland's theory of needs. International Journal of Academic Research in Business and Social Sciences. 2023;**13**(3):215-234

[25] Lussier R, Achua C. Leadership: Theory, Application, Skill Development. 3rd ed. Mason, OH: Thomson Learning; 2007

[26] Li L, Kang K. Impact of opportunity and capability on e-entrepreneurial motivation: A comparison of urban and rural perspectives. Journal of Entrepreneurship in Emerging Economies. 2022. (ahead-of-print). DOI: 10.1108/JEEE-06-2022-0178

[27] Li L, Kang, K. Analyzing Shopping Behavior of the Middle-Aged Users in Tiktok Live-Streaming Platform. Salt Lake City: Bepress; 2020

[28] Xu P, Cui B-j, Lyu B. Influence of streamer's social capital on purchase intention in live-streaming E-commerce. Frontiers in Psychology. (London: Frontier Media). 2022;**12**:6194

[29] Liu GH, Sun M, Lee NC-A. How Can Live Streamers Enhance Viewer

Engagement in eCommerce Streaming? Hawaii: Hamilton Library; 2021

[30] Zhong Y, Zhang Y, Luo M, Wei J, Liao S, Tan K-L, et al. I give discounts, I share information, I interact with viewers: A predictive analysis on factors enhancing college students' purchase intention in a live-streaming shopping environment. In: Young Consumers. Malaysia: Emerald Group Publishing Limited; 2022

[31] Wongkitrungrueng A, Assarut N. The role of live-streaming in building consumer trust and engagement with social commerce sellers. Journal of Business Research. 2020;**117**:543-556

[32] Li L, Kang K. Effect of the social and cultural control on young eastern ethnic minority groups' online-startup motivation. Entrepreneurship Research Journal. 2021a. Published online by De Gruyter December 24, 2021. DOI: 10.1515/erj-2021-0262

[33] Evans JR, Mathur A. The value of online surveys. Internet Research. 2005;**15**(2):195-219

[34] Chaffey, D. Global Social Media Research Summary 2019. 2019. Available from: https://www.smartinsights.com/social-media-marketing/social-media-strategy/new-global-social-media-research/

[35] Zhou Q. Understanding User Behaviors of Creative Practice on Short Video Sharing Platforms–A Case Study of TikTok and Bilibili. Ann Arbor, MI: University of Cincinnati, University of Cincinnab ProQuest Dissertabons Publishing; 2019

[36] Schönbrodt FD, Gerstenberg FX. An IRT analysis of motive questionnaires: The unified motive scales. Journal of Research in Personality. (Görngen). 2012;**46**(6):725-742

[37] Ho C-T, Yang C-H. A study on behavior intention to use live-streaming video platform based on TAM model. In: Paper Presented at the Proceedings of the Asian Conference on Psychology and Behavioral Sciences. Nagoya: IAFOR; 2015

[38] Dawes J. Do data characteristics change according to the number of scale points used? An experiment using 5-point, 7-point and 10-point scales. International Journal of Market Research. 2008;**50**(1):61-104

[39] Chin WW. Commentary: Issues and opinion on structural equation modeling. 1998a

[40] Chin WW, Marcolin BL, Newsted PR. A partial least squares latent variable modeling approach for measuring interaction effects: Results from a Monte Carlo simulation study and an electronic-mail emotion/adoption study. Information Systems Research. 2003;**14**(2):189-217

[41] Hair J, Hollingsworth CL, Randolph AB, Chong AYL. An updated and expanded assessment of PLS-SEM in information systems research. Industrial Management & Data Systems. 2017;**117**(3):442-458

[42] Sarstedt M, Cheah J-H. Partial least squares structural equation modeling using SmartPLS: A software review. Journal of Marketing Analytics. 2019;7(3):196-202

[43] Hair JF, Black WC, Babin BJ, Anderson RE, Tatham RL. Multivariate Data Analysis. Vol. 5. Upper Saddle River, NJ: Prentice Hall; 1998

[44] Hair JF, Risher JJ, Sarstedt M, Ringle CM. When to use and how to report the results of PLS-SEM. European Business Review. 2019a;**31**(1):2-24

[45] Alkutbi S, Alrajawy I, Nusari M, Khalifa GS, Abuelhassan AE. Impact of ease of use and usefulness on the driver intention to continue using car navigation systems in the United Arab Emirates. International Journal of Management and Human Science (IJMHS). 2019;**3**(1):1-9

[46] Chin WW. Commentary: Issues and opinion on structural equation modeling. JSTOR. 1998b;**22**(1):vii-xvi

[47] Wang N, Sun Y, Shen X-L, Zhang X. A value-justice model of knowledge integration in wikis: The moderating role of knowledge equivocality. International Journal of Information Management. 2018;**43**:64-75

[48] Hair JF, Black WC, Babin BJ, Anderson RE. Multivariate Data Analysis: International Version. New Jersey: Pearson; 2010

[49] Fornell C, Larcker DF. Evaluating structural equation models with unobservable variables and measurement error. Journal of Marketing Research. 1981;**18**(1):39-50

[50] Zainol ZB, Yahaya R, Osman J. Application of relationship investment model in predicting student engagement towards HEIs. Journal of Relationship Marketing. 2018;**17**(1):71-93

[51] Kock N. Common method bias in PLS-SEM: A full collinearity assessment approach. International Journal of e-Collaboration (IJeC). 2015;**11**(4):1-10

[52] Hair JF Jr, Hult GTM, Ringle C, Sarstedt M. A Primer on Partial Least Squares Structural Equation Modeling (PLS-SEM). Sage publications; 2016

[53] Heser K, Banse R, Imhoff R. Affiliation or power. Swiss Journal of Psychology. 2015;**74**(1):37-47. DOI: 10.1024/1421-0185/a000144

[54] Hofstede G. Dimensionalizing cultures: The Hofstede model in context. Online Readings in Psychology and Culture. 2011;**2**(1):8

[55] Li L, Kang K, Sohaib O. The impact of group support on college student's online business motivation: The uncertainty avoidance thinking as a moderating factor. Business Perspectives and Research. 2023b. 22785337231163946

Chapter 2

# Research Directions for Value Co-Destruction in Banking Digital Transformation

*Darci de Borba*

## Abstract

Digital transformation imposes an invisible legacy on managers: the destruction of value. Technology's ability to make services intangible can lead to irreparable losses of value to businesses, resulting in a decline in economic potential and imposing a dictatorship of gratuitousness. To research how this happens and propose solutions, I analyze the trend of value co-destruction (VCD) in banking digital transformation. The ability to understand and predict such changes is important to guide the planning, implementation, and evaluation processes of business decisions, since the application of expert systems in decision support is common. Value creation is a central concept in business literature since companies create value through their operations and the delivery of services and products that meet the desires of their customers. However, the value can also be destroyed, causing the bankruptcy of companies and significant changes in the market. Through a semi-systematic review of the literature, I seek the theoretical guidelines of VCD in the context of online banking services. We found 112 articles related to the theme, and part of the systematic analysis of these articles is arranged in this work. The main objective of this theoretical essay is to evidence research propositions for analysis of VCD in the context of digital banking transformation.

**Keywords:** value co-creation, value co-destruction, dominant service logic, banking, digital transformation, expert systems

## 1. Introduction

Digital transformation has recognized capacity to generate opportunities, while, as a social and economic trend, it forces public and private companies to adapt to the changes imposed by the diffusion of emerging technologies [1]. Its challenges affect individuals, organizations, ecosystems, and society. The ability to understand, conduct, and predict such changes is important to guide the processes of planning, implementation, and evaluation of business decisions [2].

As an interdisciplinary theme, digital transformation has a broad definition according to the context of the study. In the work Verhoef [3], digital transformation is understood as the process of using information technology (IT) to facilitate change, create value, restructure businesses to gain competitive advantage, create business opportunities, create new business models, interconnect products, and link production systems to global networks. The way IT contributes or impairs the creation of value in business has aroused the interest of researchers [4–6]. Investments in IT have intensified in recent times, growth not accompanied by empirical research on the effects of digital transformation through the insertion of online services and, consequently, the potential loss of value resulting [7].

Organizations create value through their operations, services, products, and business models that meet the desires of their customers [8]. However, Vargo and Lusch [9] propose the use of the term value co-creation (VCC), justifying that value is built by the customer, in the use of the service. VCC is defined as the process in which consumers team up with service providers or other consumers to generate user-perceived benefits in the consumption process. That is, it assumes that value creation takes place through the service in use [10].

Many studies on VCC are supported by the theoretical lens of the service-dominant logic (SDL), which is defined from the dynamics of value co-creation through the integration of resources in a specific context, and not embedded by the company in the production process or in the execution of the service [9, 11]. Plé and Cáceres [12] criticized marketing's failure to understand the processes related to value creation more broadly [11] and how its potential results can also be negative [13]. Value co-destruction (VCD) is conceptualized as the decrease in value that occurs when the customer uses the product and also when value is realized collaboratively during the interaction between customer and seller [14]. Starting from the premise that interactions can result in value co-creation, they considered it logical for the existence of value co-destruction (VCD) through the same interaction processes and the misuse of services by customers [12, 15].

The technology has helped companies to create value, since it allows them to expand the services capillarity and personalization, and branding capacity. For example, the use of artificial intelligence and machine learning can generate economies of scale, improve process efficiency, and enhance business penetration, but such technologies can also destroy business value and sometimes with serious and irreversible consequences [7, 16–20]. Organizations have the task of balancing the potential and limitations of technologies in order to generate adequate value propositions, which becomes a critical aspect for any business model [21]. Echeverri and Skålén [22] recognize that interactive value formation does not just occur during dyadic interactions between customers and suppliers, as many VCD studies informed. Therefore, VCD and VCC can be performed through the interactions between several types of actors.

Value creation is a central concept in business literature [23]. Organizations create value through their operations that deliver services and products to meet the wishes of their users [8]. Digital transformation assists companies in creating value, considering their contribution to personalization, capillarity, integration, and optimization [24]. However, organizations have the task of considering the potentialities and limitations of technologies in order to generate appropriate value propositions, which becomes a critical aspect for the business model [21].

The main objective of this theoretical essay is to evidence research propositions for analysis of VCD in the context of digital banking transformation. To enable the delivery of the general objective described, it is necessary to: 1) delimit the concepts related to digital transformation and VCD; 2) understand how the VCD process is configured; 3) define the mechanisms related to VCD; and 4) gather characteristics of the financial services segment in the context of digital transformation.

## 2. Service-dominant logic

Value creation has been the subject of several studies over time. Despite the numerous studies, there is no consensus on the way the value is formed. In the midst of conceptual differences, it is possible to identify three competing theoretical structures [25, 26]. The first movement comprises the value as embedded in the product or services when made available to users. From this perspective, the value is defined in monetary measures, comparing costs and revenues. The separation is very clear: consumers on the outside and the value created within the company [26, 27]. This logic did not consider the effects of relationship networks, political positions, personal influence, and other adjacent issues.

Interactive value formation describes value creation in buyer-vendor interaction. In this sense, the integration of resources such as content and the service system is defined as context [28]. The literature brings us different perspectives on the service, among them: 1) service-dominant logic (SDL) [9], 2) service logic [29], and 3) client-dominant logic [30]. In all these lenses, the formation of value arises from the provider-user interaction, however, differs in the definition of how value, and especially VCC, relates to services and actors [28].

Service logic understands value creation as a result of the value created by the provider and then complemented in direct user interaction [29]. SDL considers all value as co-creation [9] including that indirect interaction between provider and user. Finally, the logic of the dominant client considers that the value is created by the user from the offer reached by the provider, that is, it is independent of the interaction between customer and seller [30].

Among the perspectives presented, SDL was chosen as the theoretical lens because it is considered more complete in its multifaceted perspective, which includes the formation of interactive [28], VCC [11], VCD [12, 14], the integration of resources [29]. It was also considered the adequacy that the lens presents in applications in service systems [7, 31] and their suitability for digital services analysis [31–34].

### 2.1 Co-creation of value

Vargo and Lusch [9] proposed the revision of the logic prevailing at the time focused on tangible resources. The new perspective focused on intangible resources, co-creation of value and relationships, elected the provision of services as a fundamental way for exchanges. The origin of the term VCC comes from Vargo and Lusch [9, 11], who considered all users as co-creators of value. VCC has gained prominence in management research, precisely by proposing the alternative view to the concept of value embedded in the product and arguing that providers co-create the value of services and products in collaboration with their users [11]. This view was complemented by Grönroos [29], who described the activities of users as agents of economic value creation, emphasizing, however, that VCC requires two or more economic factors, such as users, suppliers, employees, and other resources. In this sense, it is pertinent to consider that the adoption of online services, such as financial services, places the user as a co-creator of value, reducing the company's control over the value proposition of the business [35].

### 2.2 Value co-destruction

VCD is a concept proposed by Plé and Cáceres [12] in addition to the work of Vargo and Lusch [11]. The authors recognized that interactions between the parties can result in VCC; however, by the same logic, it is possible to consider that the value can also be co-destroyed. The fundamental premise of the concept is that it would not be possible to guarantee the absence of error in services, thus it was possible to affirm that the VCD results from the misuse of resources during interactions in service systems [29, 36] or inappropriate relationship practices [12, 14].

Both concepts, VCC and VCD, are linked to the service-dominant logic theory (SDL), which, among other things, emerged as an alternative way of thinking about the creation and exchange of value. SDL initially proposed that value creation emerged from the use of the service, something the authors called value in use [9]. Later, other studies questioned some gaps in the theory, among them, the relationship of resources with the creation of value [29], the lack of recognition of the potential negative effects that interaction could generate [12, 14], the lack of consideration of other stakeholders [37, 38], and the participation of employees of supplier companies [39]. In this sense, the construction of value is not linked to factors directly related to commercially traded products or services, the focus is on the experiences, logic, and the ability of the user to extract value from the products and other resources [26].

The evolution of production in the researched theme was followed by important advances, as highlighted in **Figure 1**. Until 2010, the main elements of the theme, that is, VCC, VCD, and SDL were postulated. Between 2011 and 2016, theoretical support mechanisms were developed, such as the VCD process, VCD relationship between companies, and VCD background. From 2015, contexts related to IT and digital transformation motivated empirical works.

## 3. Digital transformation in banks

The financial services segment is strongly marked by competition, intensively in knowledge and technological [40], a position that generates market pressures for the provision of online self-service [7]. Financial technology companies (fintechs) are

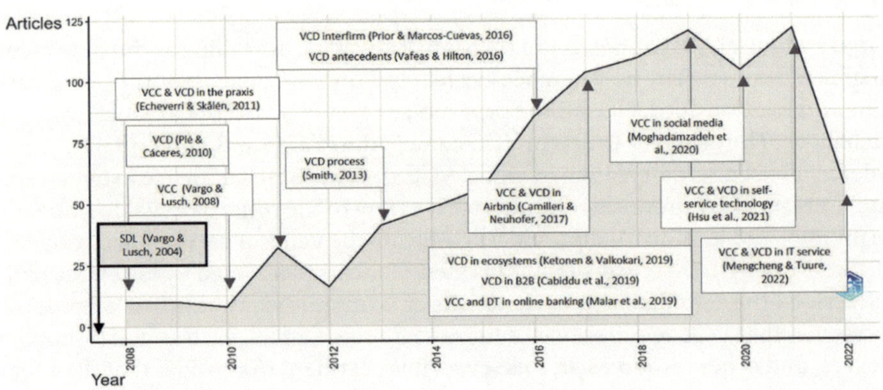


**Figure 1.**
*Annual scientific production.*

gaining market ground, in part by countering the high prices of services operators by traditional banks [41] but also taking advantage of the lethargy of traditional institutions that, by not knowing the profound effects of engaging users in value creation, promote digital transformation cautiously [42].

The move toward disruptive technology taken by fintechs is not unique to the financial services industry. However, due to the ability to act on gigantic user bases, predictability of the evolution of the sector and a regulatory basis already consolidated, digital transformation in the sector lacks urgency in the dimensioning of damages and, mainly, in the survey of alternatives to mediate the effects of co-destruction [41]. The abrupt loss of value in the financial services segment can generate damage, since these are structures that condense economic factors and balance the financial dynamics that sustain and give flow to economic assets. Thus, a mass deterioration of these economic agents can generate chain losses and profoundly compromise the economy of a society, such as the recent case of Lehman Brothers [43].

Despite this, research published in a recent report by McKinsey [44] evaluated the level of digital maturity in several sectors in Brazil. The best positioned sectors in the study are financial services, retail, and telecommunications and technology, they scored on the average of the other sectors: advanced industries, basic industries, transportation and infrastructure, and consumer goods. The research adopted the following dimensions in the evaluation: strategy, capacities, organization, and culture and used a scale of 100 points in which the financial sector scored 75, the highest in the Brazilian context and the second largest in the world. Specifically, the financial services sector is the one with the highest degree of maturity in models and tools and has greater regularity in all dimensions. The sector is composed of insurers, payment companies, and banks.

The banking subsector has the highest digital maturity in Brazil, lagging only in the strategy dimension, in which the entities of means of payment are superior. The perception of the potential for change identified in the financial services sector was highlighted in the research, as well as the *extensive experience in analytics*, whose percentage of companies in the practice of models and tools stood at 82%, against 35% in the other sectors. Specifically in the capabilities dimension, the financial services sector stood out for the dissemination of themes of user experience, digitization of processes, and implementation of the agile method [44]. In this sense, it is relevant to understand how digital transformation can affect the financial services sector and what alternatives managers can use to prevent potential losses and co-destruction of value [7, 45].

### 3.1 Expert systems in banks

There are many different expert systems already in use, especially in banks, which have slightly different characteristics. Such systems provide knowledge from different domains that are mutually dependent. Domains often have similar subsets of knowledge [46]. Expert systems are technological systems with substantial domain knowledge that can find solutions that resemble those that would be found by human beings faced with significant problems [47]. Expert systems have several applications, such as virtual assistants [48], artificial intelligence [49], geo-information management [50], and among others. In the banking segment, it is common to apply expert systems in decision support. In banking planning, it is of vital importance for the decision-maker to understand the dynamic behavior of the system he must control. However, your ultimate goal is rather to make a decision that takes this system to a certain position [51]. Another common application is in virtual customer service and in the provision of digital services previously offered by human attendants [52]. The VCD is triggered when expert systems are applied to the service, since, in such situations, the interference of users is more and definitive in the construction of value [53].

## 4. Value co-destruction in banking digital transformation

Society is increasingly digital, and it is evident that digitization delivers benefits to consumers, industries, and service providers, in addition to enabling entrepreneurship in various social layers, generating opportunities through facilitated access to the business environment provided by technology [20, 54, 55]. In the context of large companies, the digitization of society requires facing several challenges, such as greater control of the consumer market that tends to take unexpected directions and increase concentration, especially in the service sector [56–58]. Leading companies in digital maturity in the world have performance in EBITA up to five times higher compared with other companies [44].

The introduction of online financial services presents risks and challenges that are not yet dominated by organizational managers, in addition to the lack of research covering VCC in the context of digital transformation in financial services [7]. In the field of fintechs, there are difficulties in monetization since users refuse to pay for digital financial services [59]. This hinders the development of business models and highlights the difficulty of organizations in creating value for a digital service. Considering that the service was charged before it was digital, we can infer that there was destruction of value. It is important to note that the advent of web 3.0 places collaboration and co-creation of value in a changing and decentralized [45]. However, there is a lack of a clear definition of value and co-creation, its dimensions, and antecedents. Given the various assumptions proposed by the researchers, the concept of co-creation is still complex and has gaps, making theoretical application difficult [60]. The arguments presented illustrate the research problem identified.

The inconsistency in SDL accused by Plé and Cáceres [12] about the lack of consideration of the negative aspects in VCC denotes that such aspects are related to the misuse, whether accidental or intentional, of system resources, causing unexpected results that can destroy value. However, there are no specific frameworks that assist in the treatment, prevention or modification of such conditions that can lead to VCD. Another aspect that was mentioned in the seminal work of Vargo and Lusch [9] and was not contemplated in the aspirations of the VCD or even better developed in later research is the role of knowledge as an obstacle to the creation of value [5, 36].

Studies on VCC and VCD in SDL focused on specific sectors, such as tourism [6, 16, 45, 61–63], transportation [14, 33, 64], ecosystems [39, 65, 66], and social media [19, 20, 55, 61, 67, 68]; in addition to other scattered surveys across multiple sectors. However, few studies have been dedicated to the challenges of digital transformation, especially in the financial services segment, which has advanced in digitization, and its operations affect several other sectors [44].

The gap identified by this study is the lack of further deepening in the understanding of the structures that permeate the VCD and a framework that guides the treatment of issues related to VCD in the situation of digital transformation. The choice of the financial services segment seeks to take advantage of the opportunity to explore such structures in an industry with recognized digital maturity, large number of competitors, and an extensive user base.

## 5. Method

The systematic review of the literature aims to demonstrate the state of the art of research related to digital transformation, VCC, and VCD in the scope of SDL. The evidence will serve as a basis for critical discussion, identification of gaps, and research propositions. The research objective in this work is to explore VCD in the financial services segment in the context of digital transformation. However, as research on the subject is incipient, both in financial services and in digital transformation, articles from research in other contexts were sought that can help in the broad understanding of the theoretical lens and its nuances.

### 5.1 Procedures of systematic review of the literature

The review implemented in this work is a semi-systematic review of the literature, as defined by Snyder [69]. The systematic review has a narrow focus, analyzes quantitative articles, and seeks to contribute to evidence of the effects. The semi-systematic review has a broader focus, explores quantitative, qualitative, or theoretical research, and contributes to the demonstration of the state of knowledge in the field. The research procedures occur in a standardized and schematized way, to promote a broad understanding of the theoretical and empirical developments and thus identify patterns, gaps, and research trends. The research procedures are [69]: 1) project: definition of search terms, databases, inclusion and exclusion criteria; 2) conduction: systematic search of articles for sample construction, selection of articles by reading the title and abstract, selection of articles by full reading, and selection by the impact of the journal or document; 3) analysis: definition of research questions to guide the search for information, codification of excerpts, classification of findings and writing of analyses; and 4) to structure and write the review: statement of the purpose of the review, writing of the report with the findings, and manifestation of the contribution of the review.

The search terms for phase 1 were defined from the *reading of top journals of* the search field that were selected by search in Google Scholar from the number of citations. The list with the terms and references follows: co-creation [7], [12, 70–72]; co-destruction [7, 12, 70]; interactive value [70]; service-dominant logic [12, 70]; digital transformation [7, 73]; and value destruction [7, 74, 75].

The research bases chosen were Scopus (SCO), Web of Science (WOS), and Proquest (PRO). The definition of the bases had as criteria: possibility of configuration of filters, reduction of overlap, and support for exporting the list of articles.

From the list of terms, several *search strings were tested until you found the one that* gathered the necessary diversity of material within the field delimitation, as *follows: (Co-creation OR Cocreation OR "Value Construction") AND (Codestruction OR Co-destruction OR "Value Destruction") AND ("Interactive value*" OR "Dominant-Logic")*; resulting in 34 articles in the SCO, 43 articles in WOS, and 35 articles in THE PRO, totaling 112 articles.

In all cases, the filters used were searched by topic (title, summary, and keywords), articles only, without date limit, and English language. Thirty-one duplicate articles were removed from the sample, 19 that were considered out of scope after reading the abstract, 1 for inadequate material, 2 that were considered out of scope after reading the full article, and 1 because the article was not available. The articles considered more relevant, by the number of citations, are in **Table 1**. The content of the articles will be discussed throughout the literature review.

| Article title and reference | | H Index *1 | SJR*1 | Cit. *2 |
|---|---|---|---|---|
| 1. Co-creation and co-destruction: A practice-theory based study of interactive value formation | [14] | 72 | 1699 | 997 |
| 2. Not always co-creation: Introducing interactional co-destruction of value in service-dominant logic | [12] | 111 | 1599 | 836 |
| 3. Value co-creation and co-destruction in the Airbnb sharing economy | [76] | 100 | 2288 | 280 |
| 4. The value co-destruction process: A customer resource perspective | [36] | 110 | 1483 | 273 |
| 5. Co-Production, Interdependence And Publicness Extending Public Service-dominant Logic | [77] | 78 | 1974 | 190 |
| 6. Studying customers' resource integration by service employees in interactional value co-creation | [15] | 111 | 1599 | 158 |
| 7. Value co-destruction in interfirm relationships: The impact of actor engagement styles | [78] | 72 | 1699 | 138 |
| 8. Consumer showrooming: Value co-destruction | [79] | 104 | 2261 | 137 |
| 9. Antecedents to value diminution: A dyadic perspective | [80] | 72 | 1699 | 115 |
| 10. Transformative service research and service dominant logic: Quo Vaditis? | [67] | 104 | 2261 | 115 |

*Notes: *1 The h index and SJR values were obtained in consultation with the Scimago website (https://www.scimagojr.com/) on 06/05/2022. *2The number of citations was obtained in a consultation conducted on the Google Scholar website (https://scholar.google.com.br/) on 05/25/2022.*

**Table 1.**
*Most relevant articles by the number of citations in Google scholar.*

## 6. Presentation of data and discussion

The sample of articles was submitted to quantitative analyses to determine the degree of relevance of titles, sources, and authors. **Figure 2** shows the quantities of articles along the publication interval of the sample documents, as well as the sum of the number of citations in each period. As for the number of citations, the years 2010 and 2011 are highlighted, the citations are concentrated in *two specific articles "Co-creation and co-destruction: A practice-theory based study of interactive value formation"* [14] and *"Not always co-creation: Introducing interactional co-destruction of value in service-dominant logic"* [12]. The common point in the two studies is the treatment they gave to the VCD, which, at the time of the publications, had not yet been explored in depth. The work of Plé and Cáceres [12] is referenced as a pioneer in the introduction of VCD in the context of the SDL theory originally proposed by Vargo and Lusch [9]. The relevance given to these seminal works in the VCD demonstrates the interest that the theme raises in the literature. As for bibliographic production, the highlight was 2021 with 14 articles. The period between 2019 and 2022 corresponds to 63.79% of the production of the period and, in 2022, there are already seven articles published.

The financial services segment is recognized for the high level of maturity in the development of technologies [44]. Digital transformation plays a relevant role in the context of financial services; much of this recognition is due to the opportunities it is able to generate through information technology [1]. Technology lays the foundation for emerging business models, proposing a redesigned value creation and capture logic. The point is that technology is not just a business tool, it has the potential to

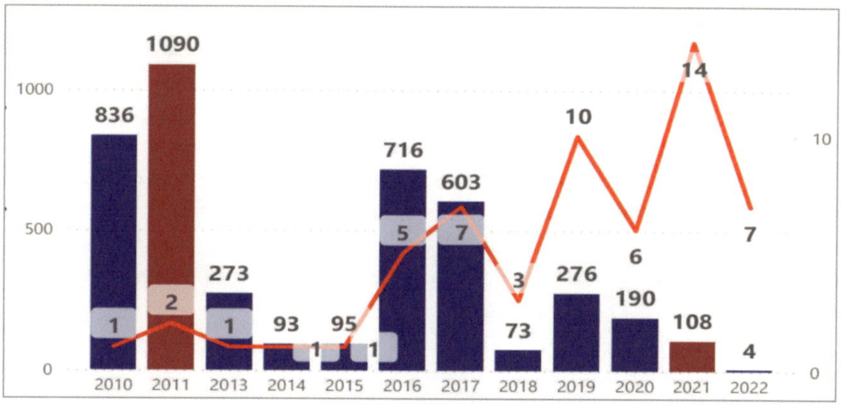


**Figure 2.**
*Number of articles and number of citations per year of publication.*

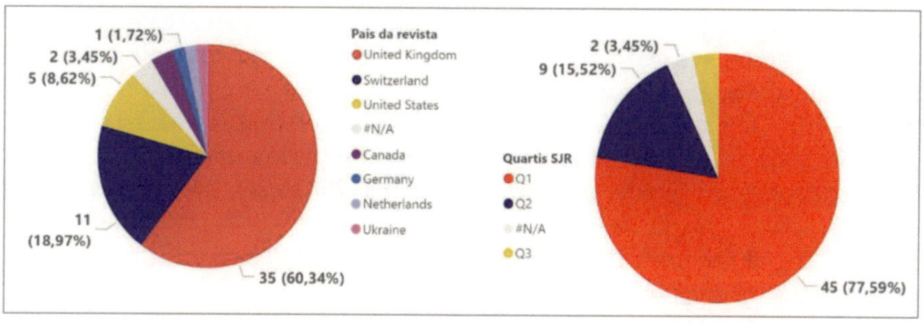


**Figure 3.**
*Number of articles per country of the journal and quartile of the SJR.*

modify relationships, raise standards, and change market rules [2]. The myopic perception of this process focuses only on the possibilities of obtaining competitive advantage as a way to create and add more value to users, to convert the supposed increase in value perception into profits [3].

The accelerated shift to digital channels in the banking sector is likely to continue, and this changes the way traditional financial institutions relate to customers, but also the options available to customers. Fintechs and large technology organizations are creating solutions aimed at the growing digital banking public, and this raises the challenge to different levels [81, 82]. Digital transformation efforts vary widely based on an organization's business objectives.

The graphs in **Figure 3** tell you about font characteristics. More than 60% of the articles were published in UK journals, wherein two articles with the highest sample citation, and already listed in **Table 1**, are concentrated in *the magazines "Marketing Theory"* and *"Journal of Services Marketing."* Another 19% of the articles were published in Swedish journals, all distributed in the journals *"Sustainability"* and *"Administrative Sciences."*

Regarding quartiles, most of the sample (77.59%) is concentrated in journals at level Q1 that has an H Index between 24 and 153. Quartile Q2 has H Index between 23 and 106. Thus, the graph in **Figure 2** attests to the relevance of the sample by the degree of impact of the sources. This information was searched on the Scimago (https://www.scimagojr.com) website.

Some authors discuss other characteristic elements of the financial services segment that may aggravate the effects of VCD. In the work of Gilliam [53], they found information asymmetry as partially responsible for the apparent difficulty of banks in creating co-creative services. On the one hand, bankers cannot understand the attributions of consumers, and on the other, users have difficulty understanding financial services with breadth and depth. This is particularly interesting if we consider that the banking industry is one of the oldest and most highly used, but still needs to confront bilateral asymmetries.

## 7. Final remarks

SDL classified the resources as operational and operating. In goods logic, you are a resource operating alongside other tangible resources. In SDL logic, the user is an asset player, so knowledge, motivation, and skills are valued as inputs of value creation [9]. Operating resources, such as products and revenue, are tangible and static and need actions to generate value. Operating resources, including the actors' knowledge and skills, are intangible and dynamic, so they generate value through interactions [39]. The present literature review identified that research in VCD in digital banking transformation has potential for exploitation in two lines: 1) one highlights the role of resources and service systems [29, 45, 83, 84]; and 2) another focuses on practices [22, 85, 86].

The mapping of the topic through semi-systematic analysis confirmed the need for in-depth studies involving the relationships between the SDL and the concepts of VCD, and digital transformation, which can produce new insights. The following is a brief list of the main proposals research directions:

1. identification of antecedents associated with VCD in digital transformation [3];

2. a literature review to investigate the current theoretical field support for digital transformation demands and other antecedents related to digital services [87];

3. investigate which of the main expert systems are involved in the VCC and VCD process and which are the critical points that managers should focus on;

4. identification of practical lessons learned in the banking context, which already experiences digital transformation, seeking to list and compare variables and antecedents [7, 12, 88];

5. more robust investigations on VCC and VCD in the B2B context [14]; and

6. longitudinal survey to assess VCD constancy over time.

*DOI: http://dx.doi.org/10.5772/intechopen.107534*

## Author details

Darci de Borba
University of Vale do Rio dos Sinos, Porto Alegre, Brazil

*Address all correspondence to: darci17@gmail.com

## References

[1] Alsafi T, Fan I-S. Investigation of cloud computing barriers: A case study in Saudi Arabian SMEs. Journal of Information Systems Engineering and Management. 2020;**5**(4):em0129. DOI: 10.29333/jisem/8534

[2] A. Omar, V. Weerakkody, and U. Sivarajah, "Digitally enabled service transformation in UK public sector: A case analysis of universal credit," International Journal of Information Management, vol. 37, no. 4, pp. 350-356, Aug. 2017, DOI: 10.1016/j.ijinfomgt.2017.04.001.

[3] P. C. Verhoef et al., "Digital transformation: A multidisciplinary reflection and research agenda," Journal of Business Research, vol. 122, pp. 889-901, Jan. 2021, doi: 10.1016/j.jbusres.2019.09.022.

[4] Chen CY, Chou YL, Lee CS. Social innovation, employee value cocreation, and organizational citizenship behavior in a sport-related social enterprise: Mediating effect of corporate social responsibility. Sustain. 2021;**13**(22):12582. DOI: 10.3390/su132212582

[5] Bonina C, Koskinen K, Eaton B, Gawer A. Digital platforms for development: Foundations and research agenda. Information Systems Journal. 2021;**31**(6):869-902. DOI: 10.1111/isj.12326

[6] Sthapit E, Björk P. Towards a better understanding of interactive value formation: Three value outcomes perspective. Current Issues in Tourism. 2020;**23**(6):693-706. DOI: 10.1080/13683500.2018.1520821

[7] Malar DA, Arvidsson V, Holmstrom J. Digital transformation in banking: Exploring value Co-creation in online banking Services in India. Journal of Global Information Technology Management. 2019;**22**(1):7-24. DOI: 10.1080/1097198X.2019.1567216

[8] Bowman C, Ambrosini V. Value creation versus value capture: Towards a coherent definition of value in strategy. British Journal of Management. 2000;**11**:1, 1-15. DOI: 10.1111/1467-8551.00147

[9] Vargo SL, Lusch RF. Evolving to a new dominant logic for marketing. Journal of Marketing. 2004;**68**(1):1-17. DOI: 10.1509/jmkg.68.1.1.24036

[10] Francisco R. Ensaio Teórico. Acta Universitatis Agriculturae Silviculturae Mendelianae Brun. 2010;**53**(9):1689-1699. DOI: 10.1088/1751-8113/44/8/085201

[11] Vargo SL, Lusch RF. Service-dominant logic: Continuing the evolution. Journal of the Academy of Marketing Science. 2008;**36**(1):1-10. DOI: 10.1007/s11747-007-0069-6

[12] Plé L, Cáceres RC. Not always co-creation: Introducing interactional co-destruction of value in service-dominant logic. Journal of Services Marketing. 2010;**24**(6):430-437. DOI: 10.1108/08876041011072546

[13] R. B. Woodruff and D. J. Flint, "Toward customer value theory for marketing's new dominant logic," Towar. a Serv. Log. Mark. Dialog, debate, Dir. Armonk ME Sharpe, 2006.

[14] Echeverri P, Skålén P. Co-creation and co-destruction: A practice-theory based study of interactive value formation. Marketing Theory. 2011;**11**(3):351-373. DOI: 10.1177/1470593111408181

[15] Plé L. Studying customers' resource integration by service employees in interactional value co-creation. Journal of Services Marketing. 2016;**30**(2):152-164. DOI: 10.1108/JSM-02-2015-0065

[16] Arıca R, Polat I, Cobanoglu C, Çorbacı A, Chen PJ, Hsu MJ. Value co-destruction and negative e-WOM behavior: The mediating role of tourist citizenship. Tourism Review. 2022;**77**:1116-1134. DOI: 10.1108/TR-05-2021-0219

[17] Kamalpour M, Eden R, Syed RA, Buys L, Tariq A, Watson J. What older adults do in online communities when they co-create and co-destruct value. International Journal of Quality and Service Sciences. 2021;**13**(3):433-455. DOI: 10.1108/IJQSS-03-2020-0043

[18] Luyen T, Shabbir H, Dean D. A multidimensional practice-based framework of interactive value formation. Journal of Service Research. 2022;**25**(2):281-300. DOI: 10.1177/10946705211025606

[19] Minina A, Masè S, Smith J. Commodifying love: Value conflict in online dating. Journal of Marketing Management. 2022;**38**(1-2):98-126. DOI: 10.1080/0267257X.2022.2033815

[20] Moghadamzadeh A, Ebrahimi P, Radfard S, Salamzadeh A, Khajeheian D. Investigating the role of customer co-creation behavior on social media platforms in rendering innovative services. Sustain. 2020;**12**(17):6926. DOI: 10.3390/SU12176926

[21] G. Molling and A. Zanela Klein, "Value proposition of IoT-based products and services: a framework proposal," Electron. Mark., no. 0123456789, 2022, doi: 10.1007/s12525-022-00548-w.

[22] Echeverri P, Skålén P. Value co-destruction: Review and conceptualization of interactive value formation. Marketing Theory. 2021;**21**(2):227-249. DOI: 10.1177/1470593120983390

[23] Järvi H, Kähkönen A-K, Torvinen H. When value co-creation fails: Reasons that lead to value co-destruction. Scandinavian Journal of Management. 2018;**34**(1):63-77. DOI: 10.1016/j.scaman.2018.01.002

[24] Cennamo C, Dagnino GB, Di Minin A, Lanzolla G. Managing digital transformation: Scope of transformation and modalities of value Co-generation and delivery. California Management Review. 2020;**62**(4):5-16. DOI: 10.1177/0008125620942136

[25] Payne AF, Storbacka K, Frow P. Managing the co-creation of value. Journal of the Academy of Marketing Science. 2008;**36**(1):83-96. DOI: 10.1007/s11747-007-0070-0

[26] Cabiddu F, Moreno F, Sebastiano L. Toxic collaborations: Co-destroying value in the B2B context. Journal of Service Research. 2019;**22**(3):241-255. DOI: 10.1177/1094670519835311

[27] Prahalad CK, Ramaswamy V. Co-creation experiences: The next practice in value creation. Journal of Interactive Marketing. 2004;**18**(3):5-14. DOI: 10.1002/dir.20015

[28] Makkonen H, Olkkonen R. Interactive value formation in interorganizational relationships: Dynamic interchange between value co-creation, no-creation, and co-destruction. Marketing Theory. 2017;**17**(4):517-535. DOI: 10.1177/1470593117699661

[29] Grönroos C. Value co-creation in service logic: A critical analysis. Marketing Theory. 2011;**11**(3):279-301. DOI: 10.1177/1470593111408177

[30] Heinonen K, Strandvik T, Mickelsson KJ, Edvardsson B, Sundström E, Andersson P. A customer-dominant logic of service. Journal of Service Management. 2010;**21**(4):531-548. DOI: 10.1108/09564231011066088

[31] Mengcheng L, Tuure T. Information technology–supported value Co-creation and Co-destruction via social interaction and resource integration in service systems. The Journal of Strategic Information Systems. 2022;**31**(2):101719. DOI: 10.1016/J.JSIS.2022.101719

[32] Sebastian IM, Moloney KG, Ross JW, Fonstad NO, Beath C, Mocker M. How big old companies navigate digital transformation. MIS Quarterly Executive. 2017;**16**(3):197-213. DOI: 10.4324/9780429286797-6

[33] Schulz T, Zimmermann S, Böhm M, Gewald H, Krcmar H. Value co-creation and co-destruction in service ecosystems: The case of the reach now app. Technological Forecasting and Social Change. 2021;**170**:120926. DOI: 10.1016/j.techfore.2021.120926

[34] Blaschke M, Riss U, Haki K, Aier S. Design principles for digital value co-creation networks: A service-dominant logic perspective. Electronic Markets. 2019;**29**(3):443-472. DOI: 10.1007/s12525-019-00356-9

[35] Kahli R, Grover V. Business value of IT: An essay on expanding research directions to keep up with the times. Journal of the Association for Information Systems. 2008;**9**(1):23-39. DOI: 10.17705/1jais.00147

[36] Smith AM. The value co-destruction process: A customer resource perspective. European Journal of Marketing. 2013;**47**(11-12):1889-1909. DOI: 10.1108/EJM-08-2011-0420

[37] Hsieh YHY-H, Chen W-TWT. Measuring the value variation of a service system: A Markov-switching model estimation. The Journal of Business and Industrial Marketing. 2017;**32**(8):1159-1171. DOI: 10.1108/JBIM-11-2016-0263

[38] Hsu PF, Nguyen TK, Huang JY. Value co-creation and co-destruction in self-service technology: A customer's perspective. Electronic Commerce Research and Applications. 2021;**46**(101):101029. DOI: 10.1016/j.elerap.2021.101029

[39] Chen H-W, Lin F-R. Evolving obligatory passage points to sustain service systems: The case of traditional market revitalization in Hsinchu City, Taiwan. Sustainability. 2018;**10**(7):2540. DOI: 10.3390/su10072540

[40] De Borba D, Chaves MS, Oliveira M. Knowledge sharing in the banking sector: A systematic literature review and research agenda. Int. J. Knowl. Manag. Stud. 2022;**13**(1):55. DOI: 10.1504/IJKMS.2022.119260

[41] Mihet R, Philippon T. The economics of big data and artificial intelligence. International Financial Review. 2019;**20**:29-43. DOI: 10.1108/S1569-376720190000020006

[42] Oladejo M, Akanbi T. Bankers perceptions of electronic banking in Nigeria: A review of post consolidation experience. Research Journal of Finance and Accounting. 2012;**3**(2):1-12

[43] Iborra M, Safón V, Dolz C. What explains the resilience of SMEs? Ambidexterity capability and strategic consistency. Long Range Planning. 2020;**53**(6):101947. DOI: 10.1016/j.lrp.2019.101947

[44] Martins H, Dias Y, Castilho P, Leite D. Transformações Digitais

no Brasil: Insights Sobre o nível de Maturidade Digital das Empresas no país. Brasil: McKinsey&Company; 2019. pp. 3-32. Available from: https://www.mckinsey.com/br/our-insights/transformacoes-digitais-no-brasil

[45] Hamidi F, Gharneh NS, Khajeheian D. A conceptual framework for value co-creation in servicenterprises (case of tourism agencies). Sustain. 2020;**12**(1):1-21. DOI: 10.3390/su12010213

[46] Stefan K, Andreas S, Gunter S. Problem solving in federative environments: The fresco concept of cooperative agents. Lectute Notes in Computer Science (including Subser. Lect. Notes Artif. Intell. Lect. Notes Bioinformatics). 1992;**611 LNAI**:185-203. DOI: 10.1007/3-540-55616-8_48

[47] Drnevich PL, Croson DC. Information technology and business-level strategy: Toward an integrated theoretical perspective. MIS Quarterly: Management Information Systems. 2013;**37**(2):483-509. DOI: 10.25300/MISQ/2013/37.2.08

[48] Chirkov ON, Tsipina NV, Slinchuk SA, Vorobyev EI. Automated expert support complex based on a machine learning semantic processor. Journal of Physics Conference Series. 1691;**1**:2020. DOI: 10.1088/1742-6596/1691/1/012062

[49] Karimi T, Fathi MR, Yahyazade Y. Developing a risk management model for banking software development projects based on fuzzy inference system. Journal of Optimization in Industrial Engineering. 2020;**13**(2):267-278. DOI: 10.22094/JOIE.2020.1883892.1700

[50] Abramov VM, Sikarev IA, Chusov AN, Tatarnikova TM, Shilin MB. Digital transformation of expert systems design within geoinformation management in Arctic. Journal of Physics Conference Series. 2001;**1**:2021. DOI: 10.1088/1742-6596/2001/1/012014

[51] Touraïvane T. Constraint programming and industrial applications. Lecture Notes in Computer Science. 1995;**976**:640-642. DOI: 10.1007/3-540-60299-2_41

[52] Karthikumar SK, Chitra P. Implementing cooperative bacterial foraging optimisation algorithm based resources and VM management in IaaS cloud. International Journal of Knowledge Management Studies. 2019;**10**(1):69-83. DOI: 10.1504/IJKMS.2019.097127

[53] D. A. Gilliam, T. Preston, C. C. Rockwell, and J. R. Hall, "Comparative analysis of attributions from customer experiences and journeys,"64, 672-698, International Journal of Market Research, p. 147078532110602, 2021, doi: 10.1177/14707853211060262.

[54] Derave T, Sales TP, Gailly F, Poels G. Sharing platform ontology development: Proof-of-concept. Sustain. 2022;**14**:4. DOI: 10.3390/su14042076

[55] Pulkkinen J, Jussila J, Partanen A, Trotskii I, Laiho A. Smart mobility: Services, platforms and ecosystems. Technology Innovation and Management Review. 2019;**9**(9):15-24. DOI: 10.22215/TIMREVIEW/1265

[56] Shin S-C, Ho J-W, Yuryevich Pak V. Digital transformation through e-government innovation in Uzbekistan; Digital Transformation through e-Government Innovation in Uzbekistan. IEEE Conference Proceedings. 2020;**2020**:632-639

[57] Malchenko Y, Gogua M, Golovacheva K, Smirnova M,

Alkanova O. A critical review of digital capability frameworks: A consumer perspective. Digital Policy Regulation and Governance. 2020;**22**(4):269-288. DOI: 10.1108/DPRG-02-2020-0028

[58] Borokhovich KA, Lee AA, Simkins BJ. A framework for journal assessment: The case of the journal of banking & finance. Journal of Banking & Finance. 2011;**35**(1):1-6. DOI: 10.1016/j.jbankfin.2010.07.006

[59] Braido G, Klein A, Papaleo G. Facilitators and barriers faced by mobile payment fintechs in the brazilian context. Brazilian Business Review. 2021;**18**(1):22-44. DOI: 10.15728/BBR.2021.18.1.2

[60] Marco-Stefan Kleber D, Volkova T. Value Co-creation drivers and components in dynamic markets. Marketing Branding Research. 2017;**4**(3):249-263. DOI: 10.33844/mbr.2017.60225

[61] Bordian M, Gil-saura I. Do imc and ecological knowledge drive value co-creation? The new way to loyalty in hospitality. Sustain. 2021;**13**(19):10785. DOI: 10.3390/su131910785

[62] Freire RR, Veríssimo JMC. Mapping co-creation and co-destruction in tourism: A bibliographic coupling analysis. Anatolia. 2021;**32**(2):207-217. DOI: 10.1080/13032917.2020.1855594

[63] Solakis K, Peña-Vinces JC, Lopéz-Bonilla JM. DART model from a customer's perspective: An exploratory study in the hospitality industry of Greece. Problems and Perspectives in Management. 2017;**15**(2):536-548. DOI: 10.21511/ppm.15(si).2017.07

[64] Trittin-Ulbrich H, Scherer AG, Munro I, Whelan G. Exploring the dark and unexpected sides of digitalization: Toward a critical agenda. Organization. 2021;**28**(1):8-25. DOI: 10.1177/1350508420968184

[65] Fuentes M, Smyth H, Davies A. Co-creation of value outcomes: A client perspective on service provision in projects. International Journal of Project Management. 2019;**37**(5):696-715. DOI: 10.1016/j.ijproman.2019.01.003

[66] Hogg J, Werner K, Griese KM. Conceptualising event value co-destruction and developing a future agenda for events research. International Journal of Event and Festival Management. 2021;**12**(3):346-363. DOI: 10.1108/IJEFM-01-2021-0006

[67] Kuppelwieser VG, Finsterwalder J. Transformative service research and service dominant logic: Quo Vaditis? Journal of Retailing and Consumer Services. 2016;**28**:91-98. DOI: 10.1016/j.jretconser.2015.08.011

[68] Zuboff S. Big other: Surveillance capitalism and the prospects of an information civilization. Journal of Information Technology. 2015;**30**(1):75-89. DOI: 10.1057/jit.2015.5

[69] Snyder H. Literature review as a research methodology: An overview and guidelines. Journal of Business Research. 2019;**104**(July):333-339. DOI: 10.1016/j.jbusres.2019.07.039

[70] Echeverri P, Skålén P. Co-creation and co-destruction. Marketing Theory. 2011;**11**(3):351-373

[71] Wataya E, Shaw R. Measuring the value and the role of soft assets in smart city development. Cities. 2019;**94**(February):106-115. DOI: 10.1016/j.cities.2019.04.019

[72] Pee LG, Kankanhalli A. A model of organisational knowledge management maturity based on people, process, and

technology. Journal of Information and Knowledge Management. 2009;**8**(2):79-99. DOI: 10.1142/S0219649209002270

[73] Carlos EDA. Desafios culturais, metodológicos e tecnológicos da transformação digital: um estudo de caso no mercado bancário brasileiro. Rev. Inovação, Proj. e Tecnol. 2020;**8**(2):181-197. DOI: 10.5585/iptec.v8i2.18415

[74] Canhoto AI, Clear F. Artificial intelligence and machine learning as business tools: A framework for diagnosing value destruction potential. Business Horizons. 2020;**63**(2):183-193. DOI: 10.1016/j.bushor.2019.11.003

[75] Mahajan G. Critically exploring value destruction to create more value. Journal of Creative Value. 2019;**5**(1):3-10. DOI: 10.1177/2394964319841944

[76] Camilleri J, Neuhofer B. Value co-creation and co-destruction in the Airbnb sharing economy. International Journal of Contemporary Hospitality Management. 2017;**29**(9):2322-2340. DOI: 10.1108/IJCHM-09-2016-0492

[77] Alford J. Co-production, interdependence and publicness: Extending public service-dominant logic. Public Management Review. 2016;**18**(5):673-691. DOI: 10.1080/14719037.2015.1111659

[78] Prior DD, Marcos-Cuevas J. Value co-destruction in interfirm relationships: The impact of actor engagement styles. Marketing Theory. 2016;**16**(4):533-552. DOI: 10.1177/1470593116649792

[79] Daunt KL, Harris LC. Consumer showrooming: Value co-destruction. Journal of Retailing and Consumer Services. 2017;**38**(May):166-176. DOI: 10.1016/j.jretconser.2017.05.013

[80] Vafeas M, Hughes T, Hilton T. Antecedents to value diminution: A dyadic perspective. Marketing Theory. 2016;**16**(4):469-491. DOI: 10.1177/1470593116652005

[81] Holotiuk F, Klus MF, Lohwasser TS, Moormann J. Motives to form alliances for digital innovation: The case of banks and fintechs. In: 31st In Bled eConference. Slovenia: AIS Electronic Library (AISeL); 2018. pp. 301-315. DOI: 10.18690/978-961-286-170-4.20

[82] Mcdaniel G. Marketing Research. International Student Version. Airlington: John Wiley Sons; 2018. Available from: https://www.wiley.com/en-br/Marketing+Research%2C+11th+Edition-p-9781119392019

[83] Grönroos C, Voima P. Critical service logic: Making sense of value creation and co-creation. Journal of the Academy of Marketing Science. 2013;**41**(2):133-150. DOI: 10.1007/s11747-012-0308-3

[84] Pulkkinen J, Jussila J, Partanen A, Trotskii I, Laiho A. SmartMobility: Services, platforms and ecosystems. Technology Innovation and Management Review. 2019;**9**(9):15-24

[85] Ramos-Mejía M, Jauregui-Becker JM, Koers-Stuiver M, Franco-Garcia ML. Cycles of action and reflection as the basis of transformative innovation. Management Research Review. 2019;**42**(1):141-154. DOI: 10.1108/MRR-02-2018-0063

[86] Van Riel ACR, Zhang JJ, McGinnis LP, Nejad MG, Bujisic M, Phillips PA. A framework for sustainable service system configuration: Exploring value paradoxes with examples from the hospitality industry. Journal of Service Management. 2019;**30**(3):349-368. DOI: 10.1108/JOSM-12-2018-0396

[87] Calhau, Codá R, Silva Farias J. Interactive value formation: Exploring the literature on dark side of the service experience from the perspective of value Co-destruction (VCD). Services Marketing Quarterly. 2021:**43**(4):520-540. DOI: 10.1080/15332969.2021.1997505

[88] De Borba D, Chaves MS. An integrative analysis of knowledge management implementation frameworks: A proposed research agenda. Revista Alcance. 2021;**28**(2):258-277. DOI: 10.14210/alcance.v28n2(mai/ago).p. 258-277

Chapter 3

# Perspective Chapter: Digital Business Model – The Present, Future, and the Vision

*Abdulrahman Ahmad N. Alkenani*


## Abstract

An imperative contemporary management dilemma in moments of rapidly evolving regarding the ongoing digital transformation of business and society in general is recognizing and trying to translate these adjustments into digital business model innovation (DBMI). Academia has plenty to show in exchange of assisting with this managerial problem, but studies in the field still seem to be hazy in terms of what DBMI is, the present, future, and vision. Therefore, this article aimed to review the present situation of DBMI, its future, and its vision in the general context. The secondary databases were used to collect the relevant articles, and the outcome of the study found that DBMI has attained prolonged growth in different businesses especially in COVID-19 period. This scenario would not be changed in future because of increasing digital impact on several businesses. Therefore, it is recommended for all types of businesses to adopt digital business model innovation to attain competitive advantage.


**Keywords:** digital business model innovation, innovation, future of DBMI, vision of DBMI, managerial challenges

## 1. Introduction

Almost all industries are being impacted by digitalization, which is creating opportunities and challenges for established firms, large born digitals, and smaller start-ups [1, 2]. Through the proliferation of digital technologies, such as those related to the Internet of Things, and the acceptance and use of affordable mobile devices and personal computers, both industry players and consumers are becoming increasingly smart [3–5]. The competition has increased with the introduction of dynamic changes in the business environment. This is fueled by agile start-ups that leverage the low entry barriers in digital markets to enter industries that were once dominated by veterans [6–8].

With increasing penetration of digital technologies, the availability of data has increased in multiple folds. This scenario makes the data analytics and ML capabilities, crucial competitive advantages for business sustainability [9]. Such instances, when the impact of digitization in business has gained much attention, transform the functioning of businesses oriented to digital formats and not as a secondary support activity. Further, digital assets have gained much attention in organizations and businesses [10, 11]. In this crucial time, managers understood the importance of digital technology and prioritized the digital transformation of their business functions in their leadership agendas [12]. Despite this, a lot of such migrations fail since businesses fail to unleash the advantages of significant investments in digital technologies [13]. One of the primary reasons for this digital paradox is that investments in digital technologies alone, while potentially leading to technological superiority, do not guarantee success [2, 14].

Nonetheless, given its significance in firm digital transformation, DBMI research is still in its infancy, and the phenomenon is poorly understood [1, 4, 15, 16]. The primary issue to be addressed here is the absence of construct clarity in terms of DBMI concept [5] since DBMI was not defined earlier [17, 18]. Scholars have repeatedly identified a lack of coherent nomenclature [19, 20] or the continual uncertainty [21, 22], emphasizing that consternation about the DBMI concept is critical [17]. A high level of construct clarity for DBMI is thus required to advance the understanding of DBMI and allow further knowledge accumulation to assist managers and practitioners in their digital transformation endeavors [23, 24]. Scholars, on the other hand, have made few attempts to define the concept of DBMI [25]. Considering these facts, the present article aimed to fill the gap by reviewing the current and future trend of DBMI. Hence, the article conducts review collection from reputed journals. The article was structured into the following ways as the initial section will collect the relevant reviews, later section will follow methods, findings, and discussion, and the final section will conclude the article.

## 2. Literature

### 2.1 Business model innovation

During this financial change, managers, executives, and entrepreneurs are in the hunt for latest sources of competitive benefit, which is distinct from the previously explored product area and process innovation as stated by [26]. The term "business model innovation" is split into two kinds: business model design and business model reconfiguration [27]. Business model reconfiguration includes the alteration of the present company trade model, while the trade model design denotes the process of designing the novel trade model for newly developed companies [27].

The rationale to follow BMI is it's holistic as well as systemic thinking. On having an observation of **Figure 1** [29] rather than focusing on separated changes or

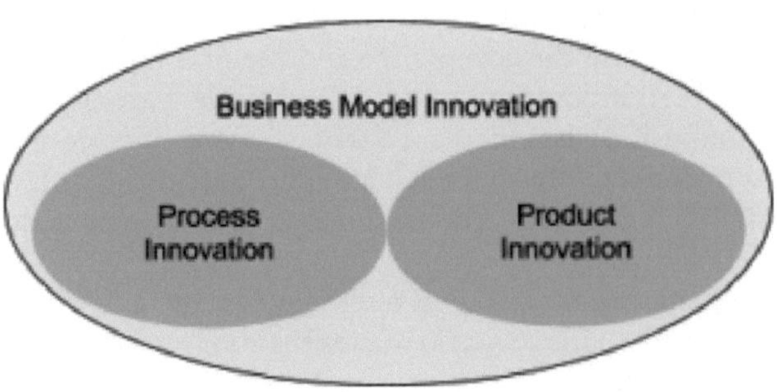


**Figure 1.**
*An illustration of business model innovation and its holistic perspective [28].*

hindering personal choice, the strategic leadership is to acquire the total design of activity system prior to optimizing the information.

Utmost level of focus is kept on the business model innovation in the recent period of years, this report has opted to employ a definition from a recent report within the industry, and it was quite effective as well. The description is considered to be credible since the literature research encloses many study papers from effectively renowned authors simultaneously enclosing both contrary outlooks of disruptive trade model innovation and incremental innovation.

### 2.2 Relevance of business model innovation for a firm

A customer-centric trade model is mainly about serving its consumer in an efficient way. To do the same, the organization must understand the consumer and implement the model as per these knowledge and understandings. Consequently, business model management involves the changes of present model, modifying it to the changes in the industry along with the new insights regarding the consumers. The efforts are made, rearranged and renewed trade models are to be taken to consideration as trade model innovations while the market implementation turns new-to-the-organization. To elevate the consumer's empathy, companies are using various tools, which are generally associated with the design thinking [30]. These kinds of tools involve the journey maps [31] and empathy maps [32] while the latter is mainly gused to catch the outlook and viewpoint of the consumer.

Collin et al. [33]; Jansson and Andervin [34]; Dufva and Dufva [35] examined that a vital transformative force, which tends to influence our society in an extensive way, is none other than digitalization; the societal impacts, which root from the application of digital technological developments. These waves of change not alone bring new products, services, or technology but as well change the basic human behavior.

As per the study of OECD [36], digitalization tends to affect in a virtual manner and the chances are wide and expanded, but simultaneously it is not completely imaginable. The opportunities that emerge from digitalization are promptly persuaded by several numbers of factors. The new radical business models are the outcome along with the optimizations in resource usage and production, automation, etc. [4].

### 2.3 Digital Business Model Innovation (DBMI)

Undoubtedly, digital transformation is more of a managerial issue than a technological one [37]. To prosper from digital technologies and stay competitive in this complicated digital business context, firms must design, develop, and implement digital business model innovation [38]. Digital business model innovation entails changes in a company's value proposition, value delivery, and/or value capture [4]. The importance of treating digital business model innovation as a stand-alone treatment from prior kinds of business model innovation has been actually supported in the literature [2, 3, 39, 40].

Digital business model is an evolution of business continuity plan by itself in which companies innovate and improve themselves on a daily basis to ensure their product and service offerings attract, build, and sustain a loyal customer network. Business owners experience a prism of challenges such as dynamic customer demands, increasing physical and digital safety concerns, competitive markets, vibrant work environment, and the need for sustainability practices [41]. With Industry 5.0,

Artificial Intelligence, Blockchain technology, Virtual Reality, and IoT round the corner, digital business models focus on enhancing value proposition and providing a competitive edge for the firms.

The current section will further discuss on advanced digital business models, evolution of digital business models in the aftermath of COVID-19 and its future.

### 2.4 Evolution of digital business models

In recent years, the phenomenon of digital transformation (DT) has grown in popularity [42, 43]. Digital transformation, also known as "digitalization," is defined as "the incorporation of digital technologies into business processes" [44]. The use of digital technologies allows for the integration of products and services across functional, organizational, and geographic boundaries [45]. As a result, because they have the "power" to disrupt the status quo and drive technological change, digital technologies accelerate the pace of change and lead to significant transformation in a variety of industries [46, 47].

Digital technologies have transformed how industries operate [48], ushering in the concept of "Industry 4.0" or the "smart factory" [49]. Strategy researchers listed out the three essential features of digital technologies such as digital artifacts, digital platforms, and digital infrastructures [40]. These elements produce opportunities for layered modular architecture and empower firms with strategic choice of pursuing a digital innovation strategy [50]. As a result, digitalization blurs the boundaries between technology and management by introducing new digital tools and concepts that are dramatically altering how firms face new managerial challenges, innovate, develop relationships, and conduct business [51].

To remain competitive in the new digital environment, firms must use digital technologies and platforms for data collection, integration, and utilization in order to adapt to the platform economy [52]. Atluri et al. [53] confirmed that digital transformation and the resultant BM opportunities are still in nascent stage.

Both business model innovation and digital transformation are the ways for mature organizations in renewing their competitive benefit as per the concept of [26–34, 42]. Both activities are in the motive of helping the companies to grow in this dynamic world. A big variation relies in that kind of digital transformation, which is focused on the establishment of new technology into the trade model, irrespective of its make, that is, whether on operational level or strategic level. The intersection amid digital transformation and business model innovation, the tool to manage digitalization can be asserted to enclose: the strategic realignment of business activities to develop a new trade model with bigger value compared with the previous stuff, which is made certainly through the establishment of new digital technology as noted as follows. **Figure 2** shows the intersection between digital transformation and the business model innovation.

### 2.5 Advanced digital business models

Opportunities are provided to all the organizations in the field on two crucial dimensions: understanding and knowledge of business design and end customer, that is, breadth of provisions of goods and services. These sorts of dimensions integrate to create four trade models for value creation (seen in **Figure 3**): Multichannel Businesses, Ecosystem Drivers, Modular Producers, and Suppliers.

Suppliers have a direct understanding and knowledge about the priorities of end consumers, perhaps or certainly have a direct association with one another. These organizations tend to sell their goods and services to the distributors side in terms of value chain. Because of the ease in digital search, they act vulnerable toward commoditization and pricing pressures since consumers are in the hunt for less costly alternatives.

If individuals are unaware of end customers and not intended to resolve their issues, organizations will be in the need of finding other possible ways of preventing commoditization.

Multichannel businesses possess in-depth knowledge and understanding about their customers as they get to experience direct association with one another.

Extensive understanding about the life-event requirements of consumers is quite important for developing the integrated experience, which will significantly retain the present customers and grab the new customers as well.

Further, the rivalry or competition is too powerful in case of Suppliers, it's essential for the offerings to remain well priced as well as creative.

Ecosystem Drivers possess the best of broad supply base as well as deep end-customer knowledge. They tend to leverage these sorts of dimensions to offer seamless experience to the customers that sell not proprietary goods and services alone but as even from offerers all throughout the whole ecosystem. Hence they develop value while obtaining rent from one another. Since the study of Weil and Woerner exhibits the prospect for value creation, which is significant and predominant for the organizations that take part in ecosystems instead of value chains, thus Ecosystem Drivers contain biggest capability of creating value.

All the four paths are noted of being viable routes to promote success, if you remain precise about your generic plan and what is needed to execute the strategy. Even if you tend to lose consumers or having a gradual growth or development compared with your industry, it's important to consider migrating toward various quadrant, either through extending your understanding of the end customers or through turning more of ecosystem.

### 2.6 Foundations of DBMI attributes

In the reviewed literature, five broad qualities surfaced besides being commonly in use by DBMI academics: intentional, nontrivial, vibrant, transition in crucial areas of business operations, and digitalization. These characteristics are the foundation of novel description and will be debated further below.

### 2.7 DBMI is purposeful and deliberate

The review of the literature shows a discussion as to whether DBMI is intentional and meaningful or occurs on an ad hoc and unexpected basis [21, 54]. As per Kotarba [55], adjustments in a company's digital business model can either be optional, where the company took an assertive influence in forming its future digital business model, or reactionary, where unexpected and unforeseen adjustments have a negative impact on the business model and necessitate restructuring or emergency operations. The majority of scholars were motivated by a strategic decision made by an entrepreneur or manager [16, 56–58].

Considering (digital) business model innovation to be intentional or meaningful is consistent with a large community of strategic planning academics who regard business models (and their advancement) as distinguishable occurrences connected to strategy [59].

Cavalcante [54] wants to introduce a pre-stage to DBMI that is defined by conducting experiments and knowledge construction and can lead to real DBMI. Even when the method is more experimental, DBMIs do not appear out of nowhere; thereby, the characteristic of intentional could be used to introduce the meaning.

## 2.8 DBMI is novel and nontrivial

Various propositions have been constructed to measure novelty while the most established one is to distinguish new to the world and new to the firm. In literature, it is mentioned that DBMI should be new to the world so that it can be considered as novel strategy [60, 61]. Others, on the other hand, take a more nuanced approach to DBMI's novelty [62]. Several make the argument, for example, that the new digital business model must be difficult to replicate [47], that a significant portion of the business must be converted to digital [63], or that digital refers to companies that rely heavily on the Internet [20].

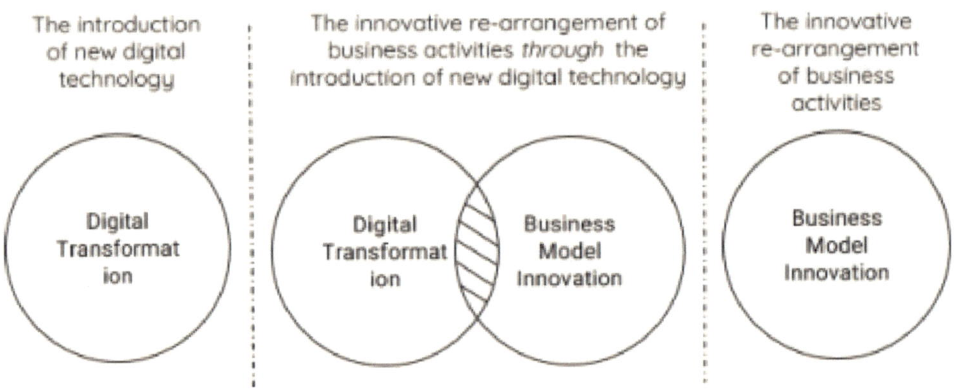


**Figure 2.**
*The intersection between digital transformation and business model innovation.*

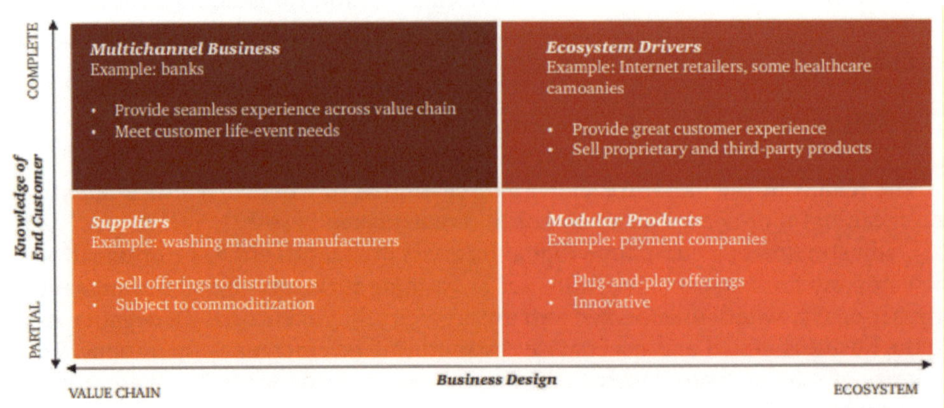


**Figure 3**
*Advanced digital business models.*

Further evidence for this nuanced viewpoint comes from Warner and Wäger [12], who argue that the creation of truly new digital business models is unlikely for most incumbents. Indeed, Li [16] extensively discusses the question of what a new business model entails, concluding that truly novel (digital) business model innovations are difficult to come by, as precedents almost always exist. As a result, the authors of our reviewed literature frequently identify various levels of digitalization in terms of business model innovation [1, 63, 64]. Li [16] described a continuum of how firms can enhance, extend, transform, or redefine their value propositions through digitalization.

### 2.9 DBMI is dynamic

The advent of digitalization has resulted in a strong changing situation. Firms are frequently faced with security flaws and possibilities as a result of the pervasive explosion of smart technologies, customer adaptation to the digital culture, and competitive intensity in online markets due to reduced barriers of entry [5, 22, 65]. This dynamic environment has been dubbed VUCA (volatile, uncertain, complex, and ambiguous) [12, 38].

As a result, it is not surprising that many scholars have addressed the dynamics of DBMI [66]. According to researchers, digital business models evolve over time [16, 62, 67–69] and that developing a successful DBMI is a journey [65]. Being constantly on the move is especially important in digital business models because they are often transparent to all [65].

König et al. [69] concluded that digital ventures, as relative to specific ventures, advance their business models to achieve the required proper. Kohtamäki et al. [64] sometimes encourage supervisors to discover (digital) business model innovation on a constant basis because it is vital to living. As a result of these findings, DBMIs are highly dynamic, and this dynamic is a key characteristic of the notion.

### 2.10 DBMI requires changes in the key elements of the business model

According to the reviewed literature, a business model describes a firm's overall logic, including the three key components of value proposition, value creation, and value capture. Changes in one or more of these components constitute business model innovation [47, 62, 70], for example, emphasize the importance of business model alignment by arguing that firms must evaluate and understand their shortcomings in each of these key components, and that any changes made to one of them must always take the other components into account.

As a result, DBMI scholars rely heavily on traditional business model thinking when it comes to changes in business model components. One reason for this is that there is currently no agreement on the essential components of digital business models.

### 2.11 DBMI entails transformation from analog to digital format

The involvement of digital technologies in facilitating DBMI is widely discussed in latest DBMI literary works [16, 60, 71, 72]. According to Aagaard [15], the use of digital technologies is central to DBMI. Firms can make such a transition using a variety of digital technologies. There it seems to be a starting to emerge agreement in the literature based on the classification of digital technologies, such as automated processes (e.g., robotic systems, additive manufacturing, artificial intelligence), interplay (e.g., wearable tech, internet Technology, apps, social media), facilitation (e.g., distributed ledgers, cryptocurrency), data (e.g., big data, predictive analysis, predictive algorithms), and interconnection (e.g., broadband, cloud computing, sensors).

However, this variety of options for digital technologies is at the heart of criticism about the operational definitions value of the definition of digital technologies for the DBMI construct [39]. Parida et al. [4], for instance, argue that the concept is difficult to apply due to the variety of technologies and their applications. To avoid this conceptual stumbling block in the definition of DBMI and to broaden the debate, we will refer to digitization in a very broad sense. Several academics in their sample agree that digitization is the transformation of processes, content, or objects that were previously mainly (or wholly) physical or analogue to primarily (or entirely) digital [3, 7, 17, 73]. Even though some make the argument that this perception of digital understates the construct's far-reaching ramifications [55, 74], it is presumed that at this early stage in DBMI research, this broad understanding means allowing for even more inclusive, exploratory research, which is required to advance the field.

### 2.12 Future of DBMI

The workplace is expected to change dramatically over the next 10 years. First, digital technology can help and/or restrict the formation and seize of correct value. Firms can use mechanization, interplay, facilitation, data, or interconnection technologies to boost disruptive DBMI on the enablement side [45, 75]. Businesses can select from a stream of unparalleled technological advances and apply them to the realization of their DBMI. As a result, the empowering role provides an online asset bundle from which companies can choose, utilize, and/or develop.

Nevertheless, on the limiting side, the limited availability from certain mobile technology (e.g., a 5G network) and connecting directly to complementary technologies (e.g., advanced sensory technologies) may make such digital technologies less helpful for interruptive DBMI (e.g., technological barriers to making driverless vehicles), whereas the rapid speed of technology technological development may make a firm's investing in digital technologies dangerous or more efficient [76]. Second, digital technologies can be direct enablers and/or constraints for DBMI while also generating a triggering context in which DBMI's purpose-making may arise. The dual role of technologies will shape a new opportunity landscape for starting new businesses, this line of questioning will also be important for future entrepreneurship [77].

To summarize, the literature review shows that there is currently no agreement on the critical parts that characterize digital business models. Even so, in the particular instance of DBMI, the logical implication that changes in the critical parts of a business strategy is a key characteristic.

## 3. Research approach

The present article collects the multiple reviews through various secondary databases including EBSCO, Google scholar, OpenDOAR, etc. Specifically, the literature search was completely carried out by utilizing electronic databases include ACM Digital Library (https://dl.acm.org/); Science IEEE Xplore Digital Library (https://ieeexplore.ieee.org/Xplore/home.jsp); and direct (https://www.sciencedirect.com/). Only peer-reviewed English-language publications that discussed the concept of DBMI were considered. The importance of review articles in management science is well established [78, 79]. Wolfswinkel et al. [80] propose a five-stage approach to rigorously reviewing the literature, which includes (1) defining the scope of the review, (2) searching the literature, (3) selecting the final sample, (4) analyzing the corpus, and (5) presenting the findings. The collected articles were restricted to 2009–2021. This review did not include keynotes, opinion pieces, conference papers, or workshop notes. The Braun and Clarke [81] iterative approach to thematic analysis motivated the article analysis, which includes a few stages such as familiarizing oneself with the information, trying to generate coding categories, naming themes, and evaluating and trying to define themes. In the first step, the researcher carefully reads all of the chosen studies [82] before selecting the relevant articles.

## 4. Findings and discussion

The majority of the studies in this review were published within the last 5 years (from 2016 to 2020). This is encouraging because it shows a strong and growing interest in the field. However, it also encourages researchers to improve the clarity of the concept so that research efforts do not diverge in unrelated directions. But the articles included the papers from 2010 to give more clarity to the research. When considering the quantity and diversity of existing definitions, it is clear that the paper contribution is relevant and timely. Throughout the analysis, it was discovered that only a few studies in the sample explicitly provided information about the current DBMI trend, albeit with varying degrees of clarity and detail [16, 60, 71, 72].

The number of articles evaluated have a good base in typical business model research, either expressly discussing the concept or reliance on well-established discussion (e.g., [26, 29]). To elevate the consumer's empathy, companies are using various tools, which are generally associated with the design thinking [30]. These kinds of tools involve the journey maps [31] and empathy maps [32] was noted. This showed the performance of organization in designing business model innovation.

It is further noted that the digitalization has impact the businesses, as a result, business firms adopt DBMI concept [4]. However, digital transformation is a management issue rather than a technical one [37]. Firms should layout, create, and be equipped to address business model innovation to benefit from digital technologies and remain competitive in this complex digital business context [38]. Furthermore, recent research indicates that firms use external venturing modes to develop dynamic capabilities (e.g., start-up programs and accelerator [83, 84]). As a result, digitalization is viewed as an entrepreneurial process [85, 86], in which firms pursuing digital transformation render formerly successful BMs obsolete [87, 88] through business model innovation (BMI), which is revolutionizing many industries. Firms adopting digital technologies, for example, regard data streams as critical and assign them a central role in supporting their digital transformation strategies [89], in contrast to traditional BM frameworks [90].

This is an important finding because it demonstrates that the impact of digital on business model innovation remains hazy [1] and that a digital conundrum prevails in the literature where key concepts lack construct clarity [17]. However, such a lack of focus on digital is problematic because simply adding a few digital features when discussing innovative business models leads to the horseless carriage fallacy [11]. In other words, the digital era offers a radically different context that is incomparable to previous environments where generic business model innovation has been studied

[2, 40]. However, most researchers working at the intersection of digital and business model innovation fail to clearly define the DBMI concept.

## 5. Conclusion

This chapter has clearly showed the growth of digital business model innovation in recent years especially in COVID-19 period. During this period, majority of the businesses adopted digitalization as a result, their business models also innovative and digitalized. This scenario would not be changed in future because of increasing digital impact on several businesses. Therefore, it is recommended for all types of businesses to adopt digital business model innovation to attain competitive advantage.

## Author details

Abdulrahman Ahmad N. Alkenani
University of Jeddah, Saudi Arabia

*Address all correspondence to: alkenani24@gmail.com

## References

[1] Rachinger M et al. Digitalization and its influence on business model innovation. Journal of Manufacturing Technology Management. 2019;**30**(8): 1143-1160. DOI: 10.1108/JMTM-01-2018-0020

[2] Volberda HW et al. Strategizing in a digital world: Overcoming cognitive barriers, reconfiguring routines and introducing new organizational forms. Long Range Planning. 2021;**54**(5): 102110. DOI: 10.1016/j.lrp.2021.102110

[3] Fichman RG, Dos Santos BL, Zheng Z (E). Digital innovation as a fundamental and powerful concept in the information systems curriculum. MIS Quarterly. 2014;**38**(2):329-343. DOI: 10.25300/MISQ/2014/38.2.01

[4] Parida V, Sjödin D, Reim W. Reviewing literature on digitalization, business model innovation, and sustainable industry: Past achievements and future promises. Sustainability. 2019;**11**(2):391. DOI: 10.3390/su11020391

[5] Venkatesh R, Mathew L, Singhal TK. Imperatives of business models and digital transformation for digital services providers. International Journal of Business Data Communications and Networking. 2019;**15**(1):105-124. DOI: 10.4018/IJBDCN.2019010107

[6] Ehret M, Wirtz J. Unlocking value from machines: Business models and the industrial internet of things. Journal of Marketing Management. 2017;**33**(1–2): 111-130. DOI: 10.1080/0267257X.2016.1248041

[7] Loebbecke C, Picot A. Reflections on societal and business model transformation arising from digitization and big data analytics: A research agenda. The Journal of Strategic Information Systems. 2015;**24**(3):149-157. DOI: 10.1016/j.jsis.2015.08.002

[8] Teece DJ, Linden G. Business models, value capture, and the digital enterprise. Journal of Organization Design. 2017;**6** (1):8. DOI: 10.1186/s41469-017-0018-x

[9] Hanelt A et al. A systematic review of the literature on digital transformation: Insights and implications for strategy and organizational change. Journal of Management Studies. 2021;**58**(5):1159-1197. DOI: 10.1111/joms.12639

[10] Matt C, Hess T, Benlian A. Digital transformation strategies. Business & Information Systems Engineering. 2015; **57**(5):339-343. DOI: 10.1007/s12599-015-0401-5

[11] El Sawy OA, Pereira F. Business Modelling in the Dynamic Digital Space. Berlin, Heidelberg: Springer Berlin Heidelberg (SpringerBriefs in Digital Spaces); 2013. DOI: 10.1007/978-3-642-31765-1

[12] Warner KSR, Wäger M. Building dynamic capabilities for digital transformation: An ongoing process of strategic renewal. Long Range Planning. 2019;**52**(3):326-349. DOI: 10.1016/j.lrp.2018.12.001

[13] Linde L et al. Evaluation of digital business model opportunities. Research-Technology Management. 2021;**64**(1): 43-53. DOI: 10.1080/08956308.2021.1842664

[14] Vial G. Understanding digital transformation: A review and a research agenda. The Journal of Strategic Information Systems. 2019;**28**(2):118-144. DOI: 10.1016/j.jsis.2019.01.003

[15] Aagaard A, editor. Digital Business Models. Cham: Springer International Publishing; 2019. DOI: 10.1007/978-3-319-96902-2

[16] Li F. The digital transformation of business models in the creative industries: A holistic framework and emerging trends. Technovation. 2020; **92–93**:102012. DOI: 10.1016/j.technovation.2017.12.004

[17] Bican PM, Brem A. Digital business model, digital transformation, digital entrepreneurship: Is there a sustainable "digital"? Sustainability. 2020;**12**(13): 5239. DOI: 10.3390/su12135239

[18] Schallmo DRA, Williams CA. Digital transformation of business models. In: Digital Transformation Now! New York City, New York, United States: Springer; 2018. pp. 9-13. DOI: 10.1007/978-3-319-72844-5_3

[19] Blaschke M et al. Designing business models for the digital economy. In: Shaping the Digital Enterprise. Cham, Switzerland: Springer International Publishing; 2017. pp. 121-136. DOI: 10.1007/978-3-319-40967-2_6

[20] Standing C, Mattsson J. "Fake it until you make it": Business model conceptualization in digital entrepreneurship. Journal of Strategic Marketing. 2018;**26**(5):385-399. DOI: 10.1080/0965254X.2016.1240218

[21] Kohli R, Melville NP. Digital innovation: Areview and synthesis. Information Systems Journal. 2019;**29** (1):200-223. DOI: 10.1111/isj.12193

[22] Veit D et al. Business models. Business & Information Systems Engineering. 2014;**6**(1):45-53. DOI: 10.1007/s12599-013-0308-y

[23] Foss NJ, Saebi T. Business models and business model innovation: Between wicked and paradigmatic problems. Long Range Planning. 2018;**51**(1):9-21. DOI: 10.1016/j.lrp.2017.07.006

[24] Gong C, Ribiere V. Developing a unified definition of digital transformation. Technovation. 2021;**102**: 102217. DOI: 10.1016/j.technovation.2020.102217

[25] Trischler MFG, Li-Ying J. Digital business model innovation: Toward construct clarity and future research directions. Review of Managerial Science [Preprint]. 2022. Available from: https://link.springer.com/content/pdf/10.1007/s11846-021-00508-2.pdf. DOI: 10.1007/s11846-021-00508-2

[26] Sund KJ et al. Managing tensions between new and existing business models. MIT Sloan Management Review. 2016;**57**(4): 8-10

[27] García-Gutiérrez I, Martínez-Borreguero FJ. The innovation pivot framework: Fostering business model innovation in startups. Research-Technology Management. 2016;**59**(5): 48-56. DOI: 10.1080/08956308.2016.1208043

[28] Eksell A, Härenstam A. Business Model Innovation for a Digital Future. Chalmers University of Technology; 2017. Accessed at https://publications.lib.chalmers.se/records/fulltext/250572/250572.pdf

[29] Amit RH, Zott C. Business model innovation: Creating value in times of change. 2010. Working Paper WP-870. 2010. DOI: 10.2139/ssrn.1701660 Available from: https://media.iese.edu/research/pdfs/DI-0870-E.pdf

[30] Carlgren L, Rauth I, Elmquist M. Framing design thinking: The concept in idea and enactment. Creativity and

Innovation Management. 2016;**25**(1):38-57. DOI: 10.1111/caim.12153

[31] Rosenbaum MS, Otalora ML, Ramírez GC. How to create a realistic customer journey map. Business Horizons. 2017;**60**(1):143-150. DOI: 10.1016/j.bushor.2016.09.010

[32] Gibbons S. Empathy Mapping: The First Step in Design Thinking. Nielsen Norman Group; 2018. Accessed at https://www.nngroup.com/articles/empathy-mapping/

[33] Collin J et al. IT Leadership in Transition: The Impact of Digitalization on Finnish Organizations. Finland: Espoo; 2015

[34] Jansson J, Andervin M. Leading Digital Transformation. Flexband, Sweden: Adlibris; 2016

[35] Dufva T, Dufva M. Grasping the future of the digital society. Futures. 2019;**107**:17-28. DOI: 10.1016/j.futures.2018.11.001

[36] Organisation for Economic Co-operation and Development. Key Issues for Digital Transformation in the G20. Berlin, Germany; 2017

[37] Li L et al. Digital transformation by SME entrepreneurs: A capability perspective. Information Systems Journal. 2018;**28**(6):1129-1157. DOI: 10.1111/isj.12153

[38] Schoemaker PJH, Heaton S, Teece D. Innovation, dynamic capabilities, and leadership. California Management Review. 2018;**61**(1):15-42. DOI: 10.1177/0008125618790246

[39] Lanzolla G et al. Digital transformation: What is new if anything? Emerging patterns and management research. Academy of Management Discoveries. 2020;**6**(3):341-350. DOI: 10.5465/amd.2020.0144

[40] Nambisan S. Digital entrepreneurship: Toward a digital technology perspective of entrepreneurship. Entrepreneurship Theory and Practice. 2017;**41**(6):1029-1055. DOI: 10.1111/etap.12254

[41] Diebner R, Silliman E, Ungerman K, Vancauwenberghe M. Adapting customer experience in the time of coronavirus. 2020. Accessed at https://www.mckinsey.com/capabilities/growth-marketing-and-sales/our-insights/adapting-customer-experience-in-the-time-of-coronavirus

[42] Fitzgerald M et al. Embracing digital technology: A new strategic imperative. MIT Sloan Management Review. 2014;**55**(2):1-12

[43] Kane GC et al. Strategy, Not Technology, Drives Digital Transformation: Becoming a Digitally Mature Enterprise. Cambridge: Massachusetts, United States; 2015

[44] Liu D, Chen S, Chou T. Resource fit in digital transformation. Management Decision. 2011;**49**(10):1728-1742. DOI: 10.1108/00251741111183852

[45] Sebastian IM et al. How big old companies navigate digital transformation. MIS Quarterly Executive. 2017;**16**(3):197-213

[46] Bharadwaj A et al. Digital business strategy: Toward a next generation of insights. MIS Quarterly. 2013;**37**(2):471-482. DOI: 10.25300/MISQ/2013/37:2.3

[47] Ghezzi A, Cavallo A. Agile business model innovation in digital entrepreneurship: Lean startup approaches. Journal of Business

Research. 2020;**110**:519-537. DOI: 10.1016/j.jbusres.2018.06.013

[48] Dal Mas F et al. Strategy innovation, intellectual capital management, and the future of healthcare: The case of kiron by nucleode. In: Knowledge, People, and Digital Transformation. New York City, New York, United States: Springer; 2020. pp. 119-131. DOI: 10.1007/978-3-030-40390-4_9

[49] Lasi H et al. Industry 4.0. Business & Information Systems Engineering. 2014; **6**(4):239-242. DOI: 10.1007/s12599-014-0334-4

[50] Yoo Y, Henfridsson O, Lyytinen K. Research commentary —The new organizing logic of digital innovation: An agenda for information systems research. Information Systems Research. 2010;**21**(4):724-735. DOI: 10.1287/isre.1100.0322

[51] Bresciani S, Ferraris A, Del Giudice M. The management of organizational ambidexterity through alliances in a new context of analysis: Internet of Things (IoT) smart city projects. Technological Forecasting and Social Change. 2018;**136**: 331-338. DOI: 10.1016/j.techfore.2017.03.002

[52] Petrakaki D, Hilberg E, Waring J. Between empowerment and self-discipline: Governing patients' conduct through technological self-care. Social Science & Medicine. 2018;**213**:146-153. DOI: 10.1016/j.socscimed.2018.07.043

[53] Atluri V, Sahni S, Rao S. The Trillion-Dollar Opportunity for the Industrial Sector: How to Extract Full Value from Technology. London: United Kingdom; 2018

[54] Cavalcante SA. Preparing for business model change: The "pre-stage" finding. Journal of Management & Governance. 2014;**18**(2):449-469. DOI: 10.1007/s10997-012-9232-7

[55] Kotarba M. Digital transformation of business models. Foundations of Management. 2018;**10**(1):123-142. DOI: 10.2478/fman-2018-0011

[56] Aversa P et al. Customer complementarity in the digital space: Exploring Amazon's business model diversification. Long Range Planning. 2021;**54**(5):101985. DOI: 10.1016/j.lrp.2020.101985

[57] Bouwman H, Nikou S, de Reuver M. Digitalization, business models, and SMEs: How do business model innovation practices improve performance of digitalizing SMEs? Telecommunications Policy. 2019;**43**(9): 101828. DOI: 10.1016/j.telpol.2019.101828

[58] Priyono A, Moin A, Putri VNAO. Identifying digital transformation paths in the business model of SMEs during the COVID-19 pandemic. Journal of Open Innovation: Technology, Market, and Complexity. 2020;**6**(4):104. DOI: 10.3390/joitmc6040104

[59] Teece DJ. Business models, business strategy and innovation. Long Range Planning. 2010;**43**(2–3):172-194. DOI: 10.1016/j.lrp.2009.07.003

[60] Sahut J, Dana L, Laroche M. Digital innovations, impacts on marketing, value chain and business models: An introduction. Canadian Journal of Administrative Sciences/Revue Canadienne des Sciences de l'Administration. 2020;**37**(1):61-67. DOI: 10.1002/cjas.1558

[61] Zott C, Amit R. Business model innovation: How to create value in a digital world. NIM Marketing

Intelligence Review. 2017;**9**(1):18-23. DOI: 10.1515/gfkmir-2017-0003

[62] Bouncken RB, Kraus S, Roig-Tierno N. Knowledge- and innovation-based business models for future growth: Digitalized business models and portfolio considerations. Review of Managerial Science. 2021;**15**(1):1-14. DOI: 10.1007/s11846-019-00366-z

[63] Kraus S et al. Digital entrepreneurship. International Journal of Entrepreneurial Behavior & Research. 2019;**25**(2):353-375. DOI: 10.1108/IJEBR-06-2018-0425

[64] Kohtamäki M et al. Digital servitization business models in ecosystems: A theory of the firm. Journal of Business Research. 2019;**104**:380-392. DOI: 10.1016/j.jbusres.2019.06.027

[65] Weill P, Woerner S. Optimizing your digital business model. IEEE Engineering Management Review. 2015;**43**(1):123-131. DOI: 10.1109/EMR.2015.7059380

[66] Hoßbach N, Wiener M, Saunders CS. The unfolding of value sources during online business model transformation. Journal of Business Models. 2016;**4**(2):22-41. DOI: 10.5278/ojs.jbm.v4i2.1623

[67] Gauthier C, Bastianutti J, Haggège M. Managerial capabilities to address digital business models: The case of digital health. Strategic Change. 2018;**27**(2):173-180. DOI: 10.1002/jsc.2192

[68] Katsamakas E, Pavlov OV. AI and business model innovation: Leveraging the AI feedback loop. SSRN Electronic Journal. 2020;**8**(2):21-30. DOI: 10.2139/ssrn.3554286

[69] König M et al. Different patterns in the evolution of digital and non-digital ventures' business models. Technological Forecasting and Social Change. 2019;**146**:844-852. DOI: 10.1016/j.techfore.2018.05.006

[70] Paiola M, Gebauer H. Internet of things technologies, digital servitization and business model innovation in BtoB manufacturing firms. Industrial Marketing Management. 2020;**89**:245-264. DOI: 10.1016/j.indmarman.2020.03.009

[71] Dellermann D, Fliaster A, Kolloch M. Innovation risk in digital business models: The German energy sector. Journal of Business Strategy. 2017;**38**(5):35-43. DOI: 10.1108/JBS-07-2016-0078

[72] Mihardjo LWW et al. Digital leadership role in developing business model innovation and customer experience orientation in industry 4.0. Management Science Letters. 2019;(9):1749-1762. DOI: 10.5267/j.msl.2019.6.015

[73] Bleicher J, Stanley H. Digitization as a catalyst for business model innovation a three-step approach to facilitating economic success. Journal of Business Management. 2019;**5**(2):62-71

[74] Laudien SM, Pesch R. Understanding the influence of digitalization on service firm business model design: A qualitative-empirical analysis. Review of Managerial Science. 2019;**13**(3):575-587. DOI: 10.1007/s11846-018-0320-1

[75] Karimi J, Walter Z. The role of dynamic capabilities in responding to digital disruption: A factor-based study of the newspaper industry. Journal of Management Information Systems. 2015;**32**(1):39-81. DOI: 10.1080/07421222.2015.1029380

[76] Kuk G, Janssen M. Assembling infrastructures and business models for service design and innovation.

Information Systems Journal. 2013;**23**(5):445-469. DOI: 10.1111/j.1365-2575.2012.00418.x

[77] Kraus S, Roig-Tierno N, Bouncken RB. Digital innovation and venturing: An introduction into the digitalization of entrepreneurship. Review of Managerial Science. 2019;**13**(3):519-528. DOI: 10.1007/s11846-019-00333-8

[78] Breslin D, Gatrell C, Bailey K. Developing insights through reviews: Reflecting on the 20th anniversary of the international journal of management reviews. International Journal of Management Reviews. 2020;**22**(1):3-9. DOI: 10.1111/ijmr.12219

[79] Kraus S, Breier M, Dasí-Rodríguez S. The art of crafting a systematic literature review in entrepreneurship research. International Entrepreneurship and Management Journal. 2020;**16**(3):1023-1042. DOI: 10.1007/s11365-020-00635-4

[80] Wolfswinkel JF, Furtmueller E, Wilderom CPM. Using grounded theory as a method for rigorously reviewing literature. European Journal of Information Systems. 2013;**22**(1):45-55. DOI: 10.1057/ejis.2011.51

[81] Braun V, Clarke V. Using thematic analysis in psychology. Qualitative Research in Psychology. 2006;**3**(2):77-101. DOI: 10.1191/1478088706qp063oa

[82] Patton MQ. Qualitative Research & Evaluation Methods: Integrating Theory and Practice. 4th ed. Thousand Oaks, California, United States: SAGE Publications; 2015

[83] Bagnoli C et al. Business models for accelerators: A structured literature review. Journal of Business Models. 2020;**8**(2):1-21. DOI: 10.5278/ojs.jbm.v8i2.3032

[84] Enkel E, Sagmeister V. External corporate venturing modes as new way to develop dynamic capabilities. Technovation. 2020;**96–97**:102128. DOI: 10.1016/j.technovation.2020.102128

[85] Autio E et al. Digital affordances, spatial affordances, and the genesis of entrepreneurial ecosystems. Strategic Entrepreneurship Journal. 2018;**12**(1):72-95. DOI: 10.1002/sej.1266

[86] Henfridsson O, Yoo Y. The liminality of trajectory shifts in institutional entrepreneurship. Organization Science. 2014;**25**(3):932-950. DOI: 10.1287/orsc.2013.0883

[87] Kiel D, Arnold C, Voigt K-I. The influence of the Industrial Internet of Things on business models of established manufacturing companies—A business level perspective. Technovation. 2017;**68**:4-19. DOI: 10.1016/j.technovation.2017.09.003

[88] Tongur S, Engwall M. The business model dilemma of technology shifts. Technovation. 2014;**34**(9):525-535. DOI: 10.1016/j.technovation.2014.02.006

[89] Zott C, Amit R, Massa L. The business model: Recent developments and future research. Journal of Management. 2011;**37**(4):1019-1042. DOI: 10.1177/0149206311406265

[90] Pigni F, Piccoli G, Watson R. Digital data streams: Creating value from the real-time flow of big data. California Management Review. 2016;**58**(3):5-25. DOI: 10.1525/cmr.2016.58.3.5

Chapter 4

# Rural Consumers' Willingness to Pay for Online Grocery Delivery Services during COVID-19 Pandemic: Preliminary Evidence from South Africa

*Mapula Hildah Lefophane*

## Abstract

This study examines the willingness of rural consumers to pay (WTP) for online grocery delivery services during COVID-19, as well as the factors affecting their WTP. To achieve this, the contingent valuation method was used to examine WTP, as it measures consumers' WTP for services without having directly used or paid for the service. Given the ordinal ranking of the WTP variable, the ordered probit model was used to examine factors affecting WTP. The descriptive findings showed that most of the rural consumers were aware of online grocery delivery services and WTP for online grocery delivery services during COVID-19. However, there were mismatches between what rural consumers prefer and the services that are offered by the food retailers. The empirical results showed younger consumers, and those with higher levels of education, higher levels of income, and larger household size are more likely to be WTP amounts higher than the premium amount. This implies that the food retailers should target high-income earning young consumers with higher levels of education and larger household sizes. Overall, the findings provide information on consumers' awareness, preferences, and WTP, which would assist the retailers in developing marketing, pricing, payment, and delivery strategies that are appropriate for the rural consumers.

**Keywords:** willingness to pay, online grocery delivery services, rural consumers, South Africa, COVID-19

## 1. Introduction

The lockdown restrictions, which were implemented in various forms across the globe to contain the spread of COVID-19, resulted in a surge in e-service innovation because of the high demand for online grocery services. Some of the notable restrictions that were imposed in the food retail sector include social distancing and a limit on the number of customers inside stores and at checkout points [1, 2]. These restrictions, together with consumers' concerns about their health, triggered consumers to shift away from in-store shopping to online grocery shopping, which resulted in an explosion in demand for online grocery delivery services [2–4].

This propelled food retailers to develop their own online shopping services [5] or to expand their existing services to meet the demand. Thus, COVID-19 and associated restrictions have led to an upswing in online grocery shopping across the world [2, 6]. In South Africa, the major food retail stores have restructured their business model by introducing online grocery delivery services, which they had not previously offered [7], leading to a surge in online sale of grocery. Although the COVID-19 pandemic has led to an upswing in online grocery shopping, online grocery services have not been expanded to rural consumers due to long distances between despatch and delivery points, lack of technical skills, and limited access to internet and digital payment solutions [3, 8–10]. Rural consumers are defined herein, in line with Sanchez-Diaz et al. [9], as being marginalized consumers—consumers who were not considered by food retailers when designing online grocery delivery services and who do not have access to such services because of one or more of these factors.

However, this does not negate the fact that there are several benefits that could accrued to both the rural consumers and food retailers, if online grocery delivery services were to be extended to rural areas. From a consumer's perspective, online grocery delivery services would be beneficial if the consumer could order a variety of food items at a lower price and for a lower delivery cost [11–15]. Thus, rural consumers would prefer online grocery shopping over in-store shopping if they could purchase the food items they want online, provided that the costs of doing so (delivery costs) are lower than the costs involved in purchasing in-store (traveling costs) are.

From the perspective of the retailers, e-service innovation is driven by profit maximization. In other words, retailers strive to increase sales by offering online grocery delivery services to maximize profit. This implies that, if retailers cannot deliver groceries or find a third-party (logistics) service provider that could deliver the groceries at profitable cost, they will not expand their services to rural consumers [9]. It is on this basis that the online grocery delivery services, as well as studies on online grocery delivery services, have been confined to urban areas rather than rural areas [4, 8, 16, 17].

This study departs from the aforementioned studies in that it focuses on whether rural consumers are willing to pay for online grocery delivery services and factors influencing their willingness to pay (WTP). Since online grocery delivery services are confined to urban areas, a contingent valuation method (CVM) is used to examine WTP, as it measures consumers' WTP for services, without having directly used or paid for the services. As such, it is assumed that, while there are no available online grocery delivery services in rural areas, the rural consumers would prefer online grocery shopping, if the costs of doing so (delivery costs) are lower than the costs of traveling to physical stores are. Thus, there is a need to examine rural consumers' WTP for online grocery delivery services.

After determining consumers' WTP, the factors influencing their WTP are examined. These include socioeconomic and other factors (awareness, preference, and COVID-19-related factors). By so doing, this study provides food retailers with a better understanding of which class of rural consumers to target, should they expand their services to rural areas. Moreover, by focusing on awareness, this study informs retailers on whether rural consumers are aware of their online grocery delivery services and thus assists them to raise awareness about their services in rural areas. By focusing on preference, this study informs retailers on what rural consumers like, and thus, assists them to adjust, remodel, and expand their services to accommodate rural consumers. Lastly, by focusing on COVID-19, this study informs service providers on whether rural consumers' WTP would remain after the subsiding of COVID-19—when lockdown restrictions are lifted, vaccines have been rolled out, and consumers are free from fears of COVID-19.

## 2. Aim and objectives

The aim of this study is to examine rural consumers' willingness to pay for online grocery delivery services. The objectives are as follows:

1. to determine the willingness of rural consumers to pay for online grocery delivery services during COVID-19; and

2. to examine the factors influencing rural consumers to pay for online grocery delivery services during COVID-19.

The remainder of the sections in this study are arranged as follows. Section 3 provides an overview of the South African food retail stores and their associated grocery delivery services, together with a review of related literature. Section 4 focuses on the case study, which includes an overview of the study area, data collection, and sampling procedures. Section 5 discusses the findings, as derived from both the descriptive and empirical analyses. Section 6 provides key findings from this study and the implications thereof, as well as descriptions of the limitations of the study and of recommendations for future research.

## 3. Literature review

As this study encompasses online grocery delivery services, the review of literature focuses on an overview of grocery delivery services provided in South Africa. Thereafter, a review of previous studies on online grocery delivery services is conducted. Finally, a key summary of the review is presented in order to highlight a gap in the literature that this study is intending to fill.

### 3.1 An overview of the South African food retail stores and their associated grocery delivery services

South African e-commerce is booming because of a growing trend for using online shopping. For instance, e-commerce in South Africa grew by 66% in 2020 (during the start of the COVID-19 pandemic), relative to 2019 (pre-COVID-19). This growth is attributed to high mobile cellphone penetration, secure payment options, and a shift from shopping in brick and mortar stores to shopping online during the COVID-19 pandemic. However, prior to COVID-19, much of the growth was driven by online shopping for nonfood items such as electronics, clothing, and apparel. Moreover, while there is a notable growth, e-commerce in South Africa is still in the infancy stage, as compared with European markets [18].

According to a Deloitte's study, more than 70% of South Africans are shopping online at least once a month [19]. The top five online stores in South Africa, in terms of net sales, are Takealot.com (US$602m), Superbalist.com (US$85m), Woolworths.co.za (US$57m), mrp.com (US$33m), and amazon.com (US$27m) [20]. It is noted that these online stores, except Woolworths.com, which specializes in food, homeware, fashion, and beauty, are not food retail stores. This suggests that while South Africa has experienced an upswing in grocery shopping during COVID-19, groceries are not among the most-purchased items by online shoppers. This point is in line with Deloitte Africa's 2020 Digital Commerce Survey, which ascertained that the most popular items among online shoppers in South Africa, in line with global online shopping preferences, were household appliances, electronics, health products, clothing, and footwear [21]. The report further revealed that the major reasons for online shopping among the respondents were convenience, COVID-19 concerns, and saving time [19]. The key point derived from this survey, in the context of this study, is that lockdown restrictions and fears over COVID-19 have triggered South Africans into shopping online, resulting in growth in online shopping.

A general growth was experienced in the food sector, overall, as a result of the growth in consumers' demand for online grocery delivery services from online suppliers. In particular, some businesses have restructured their models to allow for the delivery of goods and services, which they had not previously offered. As a case in point, a gifting and floral distributor called NetFlorist restructured its business model during the early stages of COVID-19 to include the delivery of essential goods such as food items. Another case is Quench (an alcohol delivery app), which remodeled its business strategy by integrating the delivery of food items uplifted from Woolworths stores to customers. In the same way, Bottles, an alcoholic delivery app, has partnered with Pick n Pay to deliver groceries to Pick n Pay online shoppers [7]. Other prominent grocery delivery apps developed in the early stages of the COVID-19 pandemic in South Africa are as follows [7]:

- Sixty60, Checkers' exclusive, 1-hour grocery delivery app;
- Bottles for the delivery of groceries to Pick n Pay online shoppers;
- Quench for Woolworths online shoppers;
- Zulzi for the delivery of groceries from various retail stores including Pick n Pay and Woolworths;
- OneCart for the delivery of groceries from Specials, Pick n Pay, Food Lover's Market, and Woolworths;
- Mr D Food for the delivery of fast foods from various restaurants to customers; and
- Bolt Food (formerly Taxify) for the delivery of food from those retailers that do not have delivery partners.

It is noted that, as the pandemic advanced, some food retail stores restructured their business models, rebranded, and partnered with third-party delivery companies for the delivery of goods and services. For instance, Pick n Pay rebranded by relaunching its "Bottles" service, its on-demand grocery delivery app, as Pick n Pay Asap! in 2021. The retailer also partnered with Mr D, an online delivery platform, for delivery of groceries in 2022. Another case is Makro, which partnered with OneCart for the same-day delivery of groceries and liquor (when permitted) to customers.

These e-service innovations have resulted in a surge in online food sales and the growth of the grocery retail market in South Africa. The top three retailers that are at the forefront of this surge are Checkers, Pick n Pay, and Woolworths. The online grocery delivery services (APPs) offered by these retailers, as well as delivery details, are presented in **Table 1**.

Of these stores, Checkers' Sixty60 is the largest online grocery delivery service, with 75% of online sales in the last quarter of 2021, followed by Pick n Pay Asap! at 13%, and Woolworth's Woolies Dash at 12%. Moreover, Checkers' Sixty60 has the highest presence, with 158 stores across the country that offer online grocery delivery services. Thus, Checkers has pioneered the online grocery delivery space in South Africa, having offered services prior to the advent of COVID-19, thus gaining the largest market share of the online grocery retail market.

Other prominent players in the online grocery market are Makro (wholesaler) and Takealot (e-commerce). Makro offers the same-day delivery of groceries and liquor, in partnership with OneCart. Through OneCart, customers can order more than 13,000 grocery and liquor products at a delivery fee of less than R100. On the other hand, Takealot, the largest e-commerce business in South Africa, charges R60 for delivery and offers free delivery for orders over R450, and there is no standard

| | **Checkers (Sixty60 App)** | **Woolworths (Woolies Dash App)** | **Pick n Pay (Pick n Pay Asap!)** |
|---|---|---|---|
| Number of stores offering service | 158 in all provinces | 31 stores in 3 provinces | 392 stores in 7 Provinces |
| Delivery fee | R35 | R35 | R35 |
| Delivery distance | Subject to location | Within 5km of store | Subject to location |
| Delivery time | Same day, 60 minutes | Subject to time slot | Same day, 60 minutes |
| Delivery slot | As selected on checkout, depending on store | Every day, 10:00–20:00 | Mon to Fri: 09:00–19:00 Saturday: 09:00–17:00 |
| Minimum items (value) | R100 | None | R50 |
| Item limit | 35 | 30 | 35 |
| Order tracking | Live tracking, WhatsApp updates | Personal shopper | Real-time tracking |
| Refund and substitution | Yes | Yes | Yes |
| Delivery times | 1-hour slot during operating hours | 1-hour slot during operating hours | 1-hour slot during operating hours |
| Customer rewards integration | Yes | No | Yes |

*Source: Adapted from Staff Writer [22].*

**Table 1.**
*Selected online grocery delivery services by retailers.*

delivery time. Depending on the item and vendor, some items can take 3 days or more to source and then deliver.

In summation, the food retailers in South Africa have restructured their business models, rebranded, and partnered with third parties for the delivery of groceries to customers. Of the retailers, Checkers has the largest market share of the online grocery retail market in South Africa because of its strong presence across South Africa. However, as in other countries, online grocery shopping in South Africa is confined to urban consumers. As such, the next section focuses on a review of related studies, with a focus on urban consumers.

### 3.2 Review of related literature

Previous studies on online grocery shopping can be summarized into four groups of studies, as follows. The first group of studies encompasses studies on grocery shopping behavior [2, 4, 8, 23]. The main findings from these studies are that, with the advent of COVID-19, there was a shift in consumer shopping behavior (panic buying) [4], a strong upswing in online grocery shopping [8], a surge in online sales [2, 23], and a shift from in-store shopping to online shopping [24].

The second group of studies are those that used theories of adoption to identify factors that influenced the adoption of online grocery shopping. These studies identified perceived ease of use, time pressure, attitudes, social norms, relative advantage, and perceived risks as potential factors that influenced the adoption and usage of online grocery shopping in various countries [17, 18, 25–29].

The third group of studies include studies on factors that influenced the adoption of online grocery delivery services, specifically during COVID-19 [4, 8, 30]. These studies found that fear of COVID-19 and concern over ones' health, fear of being infected, age, income, and gender were more likely to influence the adoption of online grocery delivery services.

The fourth group of studies involve those that predicted the future of online grocery delivery services. In these studies, it is predicted that online grocery shopping will continue after COVID-19 [4], as grocery shopping is a recurring and habitual process, which cannot be changed easily [31]. Moreover, a hybrid-shopping channel, involving both online and in-store shopping, could emerge post-COVID-19, rather than a split in choice between online shopping or in-store shopping [4].

The fifth group of studies are studies on consumers' WTP for online grocery delivery services [32, 33]. This includes a study, which found that "perceived inconvenience of shopping groceries in stores" had a positive influence on consumers' WTP for home delivery and use of home delivery of groceries in Europe [32]. Another study conducted before COVID-19 found that French consumers' WTP for e-grocery was low, though they would adopt e-grocery if home delivery services were to be provided [33]. The results further showed that majority of the consumers reported that they will not pay more for the delivery of grocery items. This is because the negative factors associated with in-store shopping did not increase consumers' acceptance of delivery fees (i.e. driving distance to stores, the time it takes to shop in-stores, and bad feeling associated with in-store shopping). Overall, the findings from these studies suggest that the willingness of consumers to pay for online grocery delivery services was low (before COVID-19 pandemic).

In contrast, studies conducted during COVID-19 showed that consumers were WTP for online grocery delivery services. This includes a study which examined consumers' WTP for e-grocery in Milan and Rome during COVID-19 [34]. The results showed that those adopters of e-grocery (i.e. those who have already purchased grocery online more than once) in Milan were WTP for e-grocery more than others. In terms of knowledge about e-grocery, the study found that there was no difference in WTP between consumers with and without knowledge about e-grocery in both Rome and Milan. In terms of frequency of buying, it was found that the lowest frequent buyers in Rome would pay more for e-grocery than the others would.

Concerning gender, the study found that females in Rome were more willing to pay for both the enlargement of the product range and the reduction of the lead time, while those in Milan were WTP less. It was further found that, in both Milan and Rome, full-time workers were WTP two times more than the unemployed for a wider product range, while high-income earners would spend three times more on a wider product range than the low-income earners. The study further found that in both cities, middle-aged consumers were WTP two times more than the over sixties for the preparation of orders [34].

Another study which was conducted during COVID-19 found that consumers in China had higher WTP for vegetables and meat [35]. Various factors, such as anticipated duration of COVID-19, direct exposure to those infected with COVID-19, online shopping shares, income, and gender, had a positive influence on their WTP higher prices for food. The results further attributed the higher WTP to panic about the future and concerns over the increased cost of the food supply. Moreover, higher-income consumers were WTP more than their counterparts.

Overall, studies conducted before COVID-19 suggest that the willingness of consumers to pay for online grocery delivery services was low. In contrast, those conducted during COVID-19 showed that consumers were WTP for food and online grocery delivery services. The main gap in literature, derived from the reviewed studies, is that there are no empirical studies on rural consumers' WTP for online grocery delivery services and factors influencing their WTP, hence, this study. In particular, based on the reviewed studies, there are no studies that used a contingent valuation method to examine rural consumers' WTP for online grocery services, without having directly used or paid for the services.

However, while some studies focused on WTP for online grocery delivery services, they were conducted before COVID-19. As such, the findings of these studies cannot provide an insight into the influence of COVID-19-related factors on consumer's WTP for online grocery delivery services. In addition, while a study by Yue et al. [35] used CVM to examine WTP during COVID-19, it focused on WTP for higher food prices rather than WTP for online grocery delivery services. Accordingly, the findings of their study cannot provide information on rural consumers' WTP for online grocery delivery services and factors affecting their WTP, hence, this study.

## 4. Research methods

### 4.1 Study area

A preliminary study on rural consumers' willingness to pay was conducted in Ga-Mothapo village for several reasons, as follows. Ga-Mothapo village is located in the jurisdiction of Polokwane Local Municipality, 35, 7km east of Polokwane (the capital city of Limpopo Province). The stores that are offering online grocery delivery services in Polokwane (i.e. the Mall of the North), at the time of conducting this study, are Checkers, Woolworths and Pick n Pay. These services are confined to consumers in the urban area of Polokwane, meaning they are not delivered to rural consumers in Ga-Mothapo village. This study focuses on the WTP for online grocery delivery services of those consumers who have not previously directly used or paid for such services; hence, Ga-Mothapo village was chosen as the case study area.

### 4.2 Data collection

The study was based on the collection of primary data, which were collected through face-to-face interviews in 2021, that is, during the COVID-19 pandemic. Face-to-face interviews were conducted to maximize the quality of data collected and to minimize the nonresponse rate. A simple random sampling procedure was used to select a sample size from the overall household population. Household numbers were written on slips of paper that were placed inside a box, from which 120 households were randomly selected and surveyed. The respondents were individuals responsible for grocery-purchasing decisions, as well as the cooking, preparing, and serving of food.

The questionnaire had three separate sections. The first section covered the socioeconomic characteristics of the respondents, while the second section covered online grocery shopping and delivery services. Details of other information related to awareness and preferences were embedded in the second section. The third section covered willingness to pay. The questionnaire was pretested, according to the guidelines published by GAO [36], to improve the reliability and validity of the data collected. In line with ethical standards, the respondents were asked for consent and given assurance that the information collected will be used only for the purpose of the research and will be treated with confidentiality.

## 5. Descriptive and empirical results

This section provides the results for the socioeconomic characteristics of rural consumers and other factors such as awareness, preference, and COVID-19-related factors. The descriptive results for the willingness of rural consumers to pay for online grocery delivery services are also embedded in this section. This is followed by the empirical findings for factors influencing rural consumers to pay for online grocery delivery services.

### 5.1 Descriptive results

#### *5.1.1 Socioeconomic characteristics of rural consumers*

Descriptive analyses were conducted to describe the socioeconomic and other characteristics of rural consumers. Accordingly, the first set of questions covered their socioeconomic characteristics. The descriptive results for the socioeconomic characteristics of rural consumers are presented in **Table 2**.

The findings for gender showed that 52.5% of the respondents were female, while 47.5% were male, which signifies that most of the rural households in the case study were headed by females. In terms of age, the majority of the respondents were between the ages of 22 and 30 years (65%), while none of the respondents was above the age of 40 years. This signifies that most of the households in the case study were headed by young people. Concerning education levels, the majority of the respondents

| Variable | Outcome | | Percentage (100%) | |
|---|---|---|---|---|
| | Categorical variables | | | |
| Gender | Male | | 47.5 | |
| | Female | | 52.5 | |
| Age | Below 21 years | | 5 | |
| | Between 22 and 30 years | | 65 | |
| | Between 31 and 40 years | | 30 | |
| | Above 40 years | | 0 | |
| Educational level | No formal education | | 0 | |
| | Primary education | | 10 | |
| | Secondary education | | 50 | |
| | Tertiary education | | 40 | |
| Employment status | Employed | | 17.5 | |
| | Unemployed | | 57.5 | |
| | Self-employed | | 25 | |
| Income level | Less than R5 000 | | 52.2 | |
| | Between R5 000 and R9 999 | | 37.5 | |
| | Between R10 000 and R14 999 | | 7.5 | |
| | Between R15 000 and R19 999 | | 2.8 | |
| | Above R20 000 | | 0 | |
| Source of income | Wages/salaries | | 23.7 | |
| | Self-employment | | 31.3 | |
| | Investment | | 8.8 | |
| | Grants | | 36.2 | |
| | Pension | | 0 | |
| | Continuous variables | | | |
| | Min | Max | Mean | Standard deviation |
| Household size | 1 | 10 | 2 | 0.952 |
| No. of employed people in a household | 1 | 3 | 1 | 0.844 |

**Table 2.**
*Socioeconomic characteristics of rural consumers.*

had attained the secondary education level (50%), while fewer respondents had attained only the primary education level (10%).

The findings regarding employment status indicated that most of the respondents were unemployed (57.5%), while fewer were employed (17.5%). The results are in line with the country's unemployment rate of 34.9% experienced in the third quarter of 2021 [37]. In terms of the levels of income, most household heads in the case study earned an income of less than R5000 (52.2%), while none of them earned an income of above R20 000.

With regard to sources of income, grants comprised the main source of income for most of the household heads (36.2%), while investment was the least in terms of source of income (8.8%). This finding is substantiated by the fact that social grants comprise the main source of income for most of South African consumers. The statistics for household size show that the average household size was 2, with a minimum of 1 person in a household and a maximum of 10 people. The average number of employed people in a household was 1, with a maximum of 3 and a minimum of 1.

### *5.1.2 Rural consumers' awareness and preference*

The second set of questions, following those on socioeconomic characteristics, was on online grocery shopping and delivery services. The aim was to find out about the awareness of the rural consumers regarding online grocery delivery services, as well as about their preferences. Given that the rural consumers in the case study had not used or paid for such services, their preferences were measured hypothetically—what would they prefer, if they were able to use and pay for the services. The descriptive results for awareness and preferences are described in **Table 3**.

Since this study focuses on consumers' willingness to pay for services, in a case where they have never used or paid for those services, the respondents were first asked if they were aware of online grocery delivery services. The findings are that the majority of the rural consumers were aware of online grocery delivery services, while fewer were not aware. This finding is attributable to the fact that most of the respondents were young people (65%), with access to online information. Those who stated that they were aware were asked to state their source of information about online grocery delivery services. Most of them stated that social media was their source of information about online grocery delivery services (42.5%). These results are attributed to the strong media presence by stores that offer online grocery delivery services (i.e. Checkers, Woolworths and Pick n Pay).

After determining awareness, respondents were asked about their preferences, without having used or paid for the services. In terms of preferred method of ordering, the majority of the rural consumers stated that they would prefer to order through phone apps (60%), suggesting that phone apps are the most-preferred method of ordering among rural consumers. This finding is contradictory to the observation that online grocery services have not expanded to rural consumers because of their limited access to internet, among other things [8]. Concerning the frequency of ordering, most of them stated that they would order once a month, suggesting that the frequency of ordering by rural consumers would be low.

Consumers were further asked about the food items that they would order. Most of them stated that they would order frozen foods (37.5%), confirming the preference of most rural consumers for ordering frozen foods. In terms of the period of ordering (based on the popular paydays), most of the consumers indicated that they would prefer to order on the 22$^{nd}$ (27.5%) or 25$^{th}$ (27.5%). This signifies that most of the rural consumers would order once in a month, and on the 22$^{nd}$ or 25$^{th}$ of every month. In terms of the method of payment, most of the respondents stated that they would prefer to use cash to pay for online grocery delivery services (i.e. 60%), although this method is not used by stores for the payment of online grocery delivery services. This signifies that rural consumers in the study area have not yet embraced digital payment solutions. In other words, there appears to be a mismatch between what rural consumers prefer regarding the method of payment and the services that are offered by

| Variable | Outcome | Percentage (100%) |
|---|---|---|
| Aware | Yes | 70 |
| | No | 30 |
| Source of information | TV | 35 |
| | Radio | 7.5 |
| | Newspaper | 0 |
| | Friends/family | 15 |
| | Social media | 42.5 |
| Method of ordering | Web browser | 35 |
| | Phone app | 60 |
| | Phone call | 5 |
| | Other | 0 |
| Frequency of ordering | Not often | 15 |
| | Once a month | 60 |
| | Two or more than two times a month | 25 |
| | Once a week | 0 |
| | Two or more than two times a week | 0 |
| | When I have money | 0 |
| Food items to order | Staple food | 7.5 |
| | Fruits and vegetables | 17.5 |
| | Canned foods | 0 |
| | Frozen foods | 37.5 |
| | Dairy | 27.5 |
| | Pasta | 2.5 |
| | Boxed foods | 5 |
| | Other | 2.5 |
| Time period to order | Beginning of the month | 17.5 |
| | Only 15$^{th}$ | 15 |
| | Only 22$^{nd}$ | 27.5 |
| | Only 25$^{th}$ | 27.5 |
| | Month-end | 12.5 |
| Method of payment | Cash | 60 |
| | Debit card | 10 |
| | Credit card | 30 |
| | Electronic funds transfer (EFT) | 0 |
| | Mobile payment | 0 |
| | Direct deposit | 0 |
| | Others | 0 |

| Variable | Outcome | Percentage (100%) |
|---|---|---|
| Main reason for ordering | COVID-19 | 30 |
| | Affordability | 12.5 |
| | Busy schedule | 17.5 |
| | Time-saving | 22.5 |
| | Distance | 10.5 |
| | Long queues | 2.5 |
| | Other reasons | 5.0 |
| Concern over COVID-19 and associated regulations | "Afraid to get infected" | 46 |
| | "Tired of long queues" | 21 |
| | "Tired of wearing masks" | 21 |
| | "Afraid to die due to COVID-19" | 12 |

**Table 3.**
*Descriptive statistics for awareness and preference.*

the retail stores. However, as of the date of writing this study, cash payment is only offered by Takealot, an e-commerce business, and not by the food retail stores (Checkers, Pick n Pay and Woolworths) or by Makro, a wholesaler.

Consumers were also asked about the main reason why they would order groceries online for delivery. Most of them stated "COVID-19" as being the main reason they would order groceries online for delivery, signifying that most rural households would order groceries online due to concerns over or fears of COVID-19. These findings are in line with those of previous studies [4, 23]. Respondents were further asked regarding what it is about COVID-19 that would compel them to order groceries online. The results entail that most would order groceries online for fear of being infected with COVID-19 (46.6%). This finding raises a question of whether rural consumers would still order groceries online after COVID-19 has subsided—when lockdown restrictions are lifted and consumers are vaccinated and free from fear of COVID-19.

### *5.1.3 Rural consumers' preferred grocery stores and online delivery services*

The third set of questions involved questions on the preferred grocery stores and delivery services to underline the store that rural consumers would like to order from and the delivery service they would like to use. The results are described in **Table 4**.

Six delivery services were placed before respondents with an option to specify their preferred delivery service. This entailed prominent services by the food retail stores, wholesalers, distributors, and e-commerce. It is important to note that Checkers' Sixty60 is the only online grocery delivery service by a food retail store that the consumers prefer (i.e. only 7.2% of the respondents). This is because, while the services by food retail stores are confined to urban areas rather than rural areas, Checkers' Sixty60 is the most prominent and more established service among the stores' online grocery delivery services. Hence, Checkers has the largest market share of online grocery retail market in South Africa [24]. The striking results are that majority of the rural consumers have identified Takealot, an e-commerce, as their most preferred delivery service (57.1%). This is alluded to the fact that Takealot is the

| Delivery service | Outcome | Percentage (100%) |
|---|---|---|
| Preferred delivery service | Takealot | 57.1 |
| | Bolt Food | 35.7 |
| | Bottles, NKA Pick n Pay Asap! | 0 |
| | Zulzi | 0 |
| | Woolies Dash | 0 |
| | Sixty60 | 7.2 |
| | Others | 0 |
| Preferred store | Shoprite | 39.3 |
| | Woolworths | 22.4 |
| | Pick n Pay | 21.4 |
| | Makro | 10.6 |
| | Spar | 6.3 |
| | Others | 0 |
| Preferred store's online grocery delivery service | Bottles, NKA Pick n Pay Asap! | 26.8 |
| | Woolworths' Woolies Dash | 23.2 |
| | Checker's Sixty60 | 50 |

**Table 4.**
*Preferred grocery delivery services.*

most popular e-commerce that is offering delivery services across all provinces of South Africa, including rural areas.

Given this, food retail stores, those offering and not offering online delivery services (excluding Checkers), were placed before respondents for them to choose a store they would prefer to order from, if that store were to provide online grocery delivery services. The store that most of the rural consumers would order from is Shoprite (39.3%), a store that is not offering grocery delivery services, as of this writing. This finding is attributable to the fact that Shoprite is more accessible to rural households, as it has more stores around the country [38].

In light of this, the respondents were further asked, which of the food retail stores offering online grocery delivery services they would order from. Most of the consumers stated that they would order from Checkers (50%), followed by Pick n Pay (26.8%) and Woolworths (23.2%). This finding is in line with the earlier observation that, out of the services offered by the food retail stores, Checker's Sixty60 is the online grocery delivery service that rural consumers prefer.

### *5.1.4 Rural consumers' WTP for online grocery delivery services*

After establishing preference, consumers were asked about their WTP for online grocery delivery services. Thus, the fourth set of questions covered rural consumers' willingness to pay for online grocery delivery services. The results are presented in **Table 5**.

The respondents were asked about their theoretical WTP for online grocery delivery services, although they had never used or paid for those services. The results are

| Variable | Outcome | | Percentage | |
|---|---|---|---|---|
| WTP | Yes | | 95 | |
| | No | | 5 | |
| | Min | Max | Mean | Standard deviation |
| WTP amount | 10 | 50 | 24.5 | 10.11 |

**Table 5.**
*Willingness to pay for online grocery delivery services.*

that the majority of the rural consumers (95%) are WTP for online grocery delivery services. However, the average amount that they are WTP (R24.50) is lower than the delivery fees charged by stores for the delivery of groceries (R35.00). This suggests that there is a mismatch between the amount that rural consumers are WTP for online grocery delivery services and the amount charged by stores.

The contingent valuation method (CMV) was used to determine the willingness of rural consumers to pay for online grocery delivery services (Objective 1). This method was used because it measures consumers' WTP for services, without them having directly used or paid for the service in the past. In applying CMV, a payment card was used to present possible levels of WTP. To determine the levels of willingness, respondents were asked, "suppose your favorite grocery store has a delivery service that has a price premium, will you pay more for the delivery service?" The levels of WTP vary from those of previous studies in that they account for consumers who are not WTP for online grocery delivery services. Moreover, they account for whether consumers would be WTP amounts higher than the premium amount. The rationale is to validate whether online shopping induce consumers to pay more for the cost of food delivery services during COVID-19, as observed in China by Yue et al. [35]. The amount that retailers are charging for delivery was used as a premium amount. The results for the levels of WTP are set out in **Table 6**.

In terms of the classes of WTP, most of the rural consumers (55%) are WTP exactly the same amount that the stores are charging in the urban areas for the delivery services (R35). Further to this, none of the consumers is WTP more than 20% of the amount charged by stores for delivery services. These results are in line with those of Nicholson and Snyder [39], who found that consumers are willing to pay lower prices. However, the results are contradictory to those of Yue et al. [35], who found that online shopping induced Chinese consumers to pay more for the cost of food delivery services during COVID-19.

### 5.2 Empirical results

Given the four classes of WTP and their ordinal ranking, the ordered probit model was used to examine factors influencing rural consumers to pay for online grocery delivery services (Objective 2). However, three classes of WTP were used in the analysis, as the fourth class of WTP had very low observations. The ordered probit model was chosen because it has been widely used to evaluate WTP [40–42]. The model is set up around a latent regression that begins with the following equation [42]:

$$Y* = X^{'}\beta + \varepsilon \tag{1}$$

| Question | Outcome | Percentage |
|---|---|---|
| Suppose your favorite store has a delivery service, how much would you be willing to pay? | Not willing to pay | 0 |
| | Willing to pay exactly R35 | 55 |
| | Willing to pay extra 9% of R35 | 17.5 |
| | Willing to pay extra 10–14% of R35 | 17.5 |
| | Willing to pay extra 15–20% of R35 | 10 |
| | Willing to pay more than 20% of R35 | 0 |

**Table 6.**
*Classes of WTP.*

where Y* = WTP, X' is a vector of predictor variables, β represents a vector of coefficients, and ε is the error term. Y* is unobserved, and what can be observed is as follows:

$$y = 0 \text{ if } y* \leq \mu_1; y = 1 \text{ if } 0 \leq y* < \mu_2; y = 2 \text{ if } \mu 1 \leq y* \leq \mu_3; \ldots; y = j, \\ \text{if } \mu_{j-1} < y* < \mu_j, \text{and } \mu_0 = -\infty, \\ \mu_m = \infty \tag{2}$$

In Eq (2), the μ's are unknown parameters to be calculated with β. The following probabilities are derived, after normalizing the mean and variance to 0 and 1.

$$\begin{aligned} Prob\ (y = 0|X) &= F\ (X'\beta) \\ Prob\ (y = 1|X) &= F\ (\mu_3 – X'\beta) - f\ (X'\beta) \\ Prob\ (y = 2|X) &= F\ (\mu_2 – X'\beta) - f(\mu_3 – X'\beta) \\ \ldots Prob\ (y = j|x) &= 1 - F\left(\mu_{j-1} – X'\beta\right) \end{aligned} \tag{3}$$

All the probabilities must be positive, and then the following condition will be established:

$$0 < \mu_3 < \mu_2 < \mu_1 < \ldots\ldots < \mu_{j-1}$$

This model estimation aims to identify the relevant factors that explain consumers' WTP for online grocery delivery services. The final model is specified as follows:

$$WTP^* = \beta_0 + \beta_1 X_1 + \beta_2 X_2 + \beta_3 X_3 + \beta_4 X_4 + \ldots\ldots + \beta_{20} X_{20} + \varepsilon \tag{4}$$

where: WTP* = WTP for online grocery delivery services; $\beta_0, \beta_1, \beta_2, \beta_3, \beta_3, \ldots, \beta_{20}$ = parameters to be estimated; $X_1, X_2, X_3, \ldots, X_{20}$ = predictor variables (i.e. socio-economic variables, awareness and preference variables); and ε = Disturbance term.

### *5.2.1 Model robustness*

The empirical analyses were conducted using the Statistical Packaging for the Social Sciences (SPSS). The (-2) log-likelihood of the estimated model is 223.101, which implies that the model can be relied upon to predict WTP. A Nagelkerke pseudo-$R^2$ of 0.67 was obtained, which signifies that the predictor variables account for 67% of the variation in WTP. Ten variables of the 20 predictor variables were found to be significant. The results are presented in **Table** 7.

*5.2.2 Interpretation and discussion of the results*

The ordered probit model was also used to derive the predicted probabilities and marginal effects for each level of WTP. The results for the estimated coefficients and marginal effects are discussed concurrently. The results for the predicted probabilities, as well as the marginal effects, are presented in **Table 8**. As per default, the values for the predicted probabilities for the levels of WTP sum to 1, while the values for the marginal effects for the three levels of WTP are equal to 0.

The age of the consumer ($X_2$) had a negative influence on the WTP for online grocery delivery services. This suggests that older consumers are less likely to be willing to pay for online grocery delivery services, relative to younger consumers. The marginal effects for age were positive for the first level of WTP (WTP to pay exactly R35), but negative for the rest of the levels (i.e. willing to pay extra 9% of R35 and willing to pay extra 10–14% of R35). The implication is that older consumers are less likely to be willing to pay an amount greater than the premium amount, compared with younger consumers. These results are similar to those of Eriksson and Stenius [4], who found that older consumers are less likely to be adopters of online grocery shopping.

The level of education of the consumer ($X_3$) had a positive influence over the WTP for online grocery delivery service, meaning that the higher the level of education achieved is, the more likely the consumer would be WTP for online grocery delivery services. The marginal effects for the level of education were negative for the first level of WTP, but positive for the other two levels. This implies that rural consumers with higher levels of education are more likely to be willing to pay amounts higher the premium amount, relative to those with lower level of education. These findings are in line with those of a previous study, which found that higher education level increases the likelihood of doing online grocery shopping [5].

The level of income of the consumer ($X_4$) had a positive influence over the WTP for online grocery delivery services. This suggests that rural consumers who earn higher incomes are more likely to be willing to pay for online grocery delivery services than those earning lower incomes would be. The marginal effects for the level of income were negative for the first level of WTP, with positive effects for the remaining two levels. This signifies that rural consumers with higher levels of income are more likely to be willing to pay amounts higher than the premium amount, relative to those with lower levels of income. These results are in line with those of Eriksson and Stenius [4], who found that the adoption of online grocery shopping was influenced by income.

Household size ($X_8$) had a positive influence over the willingness of rural consumers to pay for online grocery delivery services. This signifies that the larger the size of the household is, the more likely it would be that a consumer in that household would be willing to pay for online grocery delivery services. The marginal effects for household size were negative for the first level of WTP, but positive for the other two levels. The implication is that rural consumers with larger households are more likely to be willing to pay amounts higher than the premium amount, relative to those with smaller households. These finding are in line with those of Eriksson and Stenius [4],

| Variable | Coefficient | Standard error | T-statistics |
|---|---|---|---|
| Socio-economic characteristics | | | |
| $X_1$ | 0.554 | 1.315 | 0.421 |
| $X_2$ | −0.662 | 0.495 | 1.783* |
| $X_3$ | 0.930 | 0.481 | 2.035** |
| $X_4$ | 0.928 | 0.354 | 2.621*** |
| $X_5$ | −0.100 | 0.324 | 0.308 |
| $X_6$ | −0.547 | 0.638 | 0.857 |
| $X_7$ | −0.394 | 0.340 | 1.158 |
| $X_8$ | 0.576 | 0.2430 | 2.370** |
| Awareness variables | | | |
| $X_9$ | 0.719 | 0.367 | 1.959* |
| $X_{10}$ | 0.063 | 0.205 | 0.307 |
| Preference variables | | | |
| $X_{11}$ | −1.870 | 0.484 | 3.863*** |
| $X_{12}$ | 0.813 | 0.299 | 2.719*** |
| $X_{13}$ | 0.186 | 0.2498 | 0.746 |
| $X_{14}$ | −0.251 | 0.598 | 0.419 |
| $X_{15}$ | 0.286 | 0.534 | 0.535 |
| Preferred store and grocery delivery services | | | |
| $X_{16}$ | 0.520 | 0.238 | 2.184** |
| $X_{17}$ | 0.777 | 0.404 | 1.923* |
| $X_{18}$ | −0.835 | 0.589 | 1.417 |
| Reasons for ordering | | | |
| $X_{19}$ | 0.189 | 0.410 | 0.460 |
| $X_{20}$ | 0.385 | 0.318 | 1.210 |
| Model summary | | | |
| (−2) Log-likelihood | | 223.101 | |
| Pseudo R-square | | | |
| Cox and Snell R-square | | 0.64 | |
| Nagelkerke R-square | | 0.67 | |

*Source: Research Data (2021).*
*$^{*}p < 0.1$. $^{**}p < 0.05$. $^{***}p < 0.01$.*

**Table 7.**
*Ordered probit model results.*

who found that the higher the household size is, the more likely the adoption of online grocery shopping would be.

The variable, awareness about online delivery services ($X_9$), had a positive influence on rural consumers' WTP for online grocery delivery services. This denotes that rural consumers who are aware about online grocery delivery services are more likely

| WTP levels | WTP = 1 | WTP = 2 | WTP = 3 |
|---|---|---|---|
| Predicted probabilities | 0.40 | 0.30 | 0.30 |
| Variables | | Marginal effects | |
| Age of the consumer ($X_2$) | 0.472 | −0.264 | −0.208 |
| Level of education ($X_3$) | −0.091 | 0.047 | 0.044 |
| Level of income of the consumers ($X_4$) | −0.076 | 0.042 | 0.030 |
| Household size ($X_8$) | −0.054 | 0.032 | 0.022 |
| Awareness ($X_9$) | −0.018 | 0.008 | 0.010 |
| Method of ordering ($X_{11}$) | 0.082 | −0.044 | −0.038 |
| Frequency of ordering ($X_{12}$) | −0.087 | 0.046 | 0.041 |
| Method of payment ($X_{15}$) | −0.0013 | 0.009 | 0.004 |
| Preferred delivery service ($X_{16}$) | −0.001 | −0.002 | 0.003 |
| Preferred store variable ($X_{17}$) | −0.001 | −0.002 | 0.003 |

**Table 8.**
*Results for predicted probabilities and marginal effects.*

to be willing to pay for online grocery delivery services. The marginal effects for awareness were negative for the first level of WTP and positive for the remaining levels. This implies that rural consumers who are aware of online grocery delivery services are more likely to be willing to pay amounts higher than the premium amount, relative to those who are unaware. This is contradictory to findings of a previous study, which showed that there was no difference in WTP between consumers who were aware and unaware of e-grocery in Rome and Milan [34].

The variable for the method of ordering ($X_{11}$) that a consumer would prefer to use had a negative influence on rural consumers' WTP for online grocery delivery services. This means that rural consumers who prefer to order groceries via phone apps are less likely to be willing to pay for online grocery delivery services. The marginal effects for method of ordering were positive for the first level of WTP and negative for the last two levels. The implication is that rural consumers who prefer to order via phone apps are less likely to be willing to pay amounts higher than the premium amount, relative to those who prefer other methods (phone calls and the web). This finding asserts the observation that rural consumers have not yet embraced digital innovation [3, 8–10]. Hence, those preferring to order grocery via phone apps are less likely to be willing to pay for online grocery delivery services.

The variable for frequency of ordering ($X_{12}$) had a positive influence on a rural consumer's WTP for online grocery delivery services, suggesting that the higher the frequency of ordering is, the more likely it is that the consumer would be WTP for online grocery delivery services. The marginal effects for the frequency of ordering were negative for the first level, but positive for the other two levels of WTP. This implies that rural consumers who would order grocery more frequently are more likely to be willing to pay amounts higher than the premium amount, relative to those who would order less frequently. This is contradictory to the finding that the lowest frequent buyers in Rome would pay more for e-grocery than the others would [34].

The variable for method of payment ($X_{15}$) had a positive influence on rural consumers' WTP for online grocery delivery services. This means that rural consumers who would pay for online grocery delivery services in cash are more likely to be willing to pay for online grocery delivery services. The marginal effects for the method of payment were negative for the first level of WTP and positive for the other two levels. The implication is that rural consumers who would pay using cash are more likely to be willing to pay amounts higher than the premium amount, relative to those who would use other payment methods (debit and credit cards). These findings are attributed to the earlier observation that rural households have not yet embraced digital payment solutions.

The variable for preferred delivery service ($X_{16}$) had a positive influence on the willingness of rural consumers to pay for online grocery delivery services. In other words, rural consumers who prefer to use Takealot are more likely to be willing to pay for online grocery delivery services, as compared with those who prefer to use other delivery services. The marginal effects for the preferred delivery service were negative for the first level, but positive for the other levels of WTP. Thus, rural consumers who prefer Takealot are more likely to be willing to pay amounts higher than the premium amount, relative to those who prefer other online grocery delivery services (Bolt Food, Sixty60, Woolies Dash, Pick n Pay Asap! and others). These results are in line with the observation that many consumers in the United States (US) purchased groceries through an online platforms such as Walmart, the second largest e-commerce retailer in the US, during COVID-19 pandemic [43].

The preferred store variable ($X_{17}$) had a positive influence on rural consumers' WTP for online grocery delivery services. This suggests that rural consumers who would like to order from Shoprite, a store that does not offer online grocery delivery services, are more likely to be willing to pay for online grocery delivery services. The marginal effects for the preferred store were negative for the first level and positive for the other two levels of WTP. The implication is that rural consumers who prefer Shoprite are more likely to be willing to pay amounts higher than the premium amount, relative to those who prefer other stores (Shoprite, Woolworths, Pick n Pay, Makro, Spar, and others). This finding is attributable to the fact that Shoprite is more accessible to rural households, through its strong presence in rural towns [38].

Surprisingly, the variables regarding COVID-19 had no significant influence on rural consumers' WTP for online grocery delivery services. This casts a doubt on whether rural consumers would be willing to order groceries online after COVID-19 has subsided – when lockdown restrictions are lifted, and consumers are vaccinated and free from fears of COVID-19. These results are contrary to the predictions that online grocery shopping would continue after COVID-19 [4], as grocery shopping is a recurring and habitual process, which cannot be changed easily [31].

## 6. Conclusion

COVID-19 restrictions have compelled certain food retail stores in South Africa to rebrand and restructure their business models and to partner with third parties for providing online grocery delivery services. However, as in other countries, online grocery delivery services are confined to urban consumers. As such, this study examined the willingness to pay (WTP) of rural consumers for online grocery delivery services and the factors affecting their WTP. To achieve this, the contingent valuation method was used to examine WTP, as it measures rural consumers' WTP for services, without them ever having directly used or paid for those services. The findings provide information on rural consumers' awareness, preferences, and WTP, which would assist the retailers in developing marketing, pricing, payment, and delivery strategies that are appropriate for the rural population.

In terms of awareness, the majority of the rural consumers were aware of online grocery delivery services (70%). Therefore, the food retailers who are intending to expand their services to rural areas should further raise awareness about their services in order to reach those rural consumers who are unaware of their online delivery services.

Concerning preference, there were mismatches between what rural consumers prefer and the services that retailers are providing. For instance, most rural consumers have identified Takealot, an e-commerce business, as their most preferred delivery service (57.1%), rather than retailers' online delivery services, due to the popularity of Takealot in South Africa, including in rural areas. Moreover, most of the rural consumers stated that their preferred method of payment is cash, which is one of the payment methods accepted by Takealot, and not by the food retail stores (Checkers, Pick n Pay and Woolworths), or by the wholesaler, Makro. Therefore, the food retail stores should consider partnering with Takealot for the delivery of groceries to rural consumers and accepting cash payment.

It is acknowledged that the retailers would expand their services to rural consumers if it were profitable for them to do so. The findings showed that rural consumers who prefer Takealot are more likely to be willing to pay amounts higher than the premium amounts (i.e. more than the R35.00 that the retailers are charging for delivery). This shows that it would be economically viable for retailers to expand their services to rural consumers through partnership with Takealot.

Another notable mismatch relates to the store that most consumers would like to order from—the majority would like to order from Shoprite, although it does not offer grocery delivery services, as of this writing. Given this, the Shoprite Group should consider remodeling its business model by extending its sister company's delivery services (i.e. Checkers' Sixty60) to rural consumers. It would be viable to do so, as the empirical results showed that rural consumers who would like to order from Shoprite are more likely to be WTP amounts higher than the premium amount (i.e. more than R35.00 that the retailers are charging for delivery).

Another mismatch is in terms of WTP. In particular, while most of the rural consumers were WTP for online grocery delivery services (95%), the average amount that they were WTP (R24.50) was less than the amount charged by retailers (R35.00). Thus, the food retailers who are intending to expand their services to rural areas should consider reviewing their pricing strategies to suit rural consumers.

After determining the rural consumers' WTP, the factors influencing their WTP were examined. The results provide food retailers with a better understanding of which class of rural consumers to target, should they expand their services to the rural areas. More specifically, the retailers should target high-income earning young consumers, with higher level of education and larger household sizes.

It is worth noting that the COVID-19-related variables had no significant influence on WTP. This casts a doubt on whether rural consumers would order groceries online after COVID-19 has subsided—when lockdown restrictions are lifted and consumers are vaccinated and free from fears of COVID-19.

The study was conducted with certain delimitations, which are explained in terms of the four areas for future research. The first area involves extending the research to other rural areas across South Africa as to enable a generalization of the results. The second area requires the inclusion of other online grocery delivery services, which were unaccounted for in this study. The third area involves examining WTP according to the individual lockdown levels experienced (i.e. Alert Level 5 through to Alert Level 1), as WTP could have changed as the lockdown restrictions were relaxed, as we moved down through to the lower levels of lockdown. The fourth area requires the use of valuation methods, which capture consumers' actual behavior rather than the CVM, which captures hypothetical behavior [44]. In other words, methods that captures actual WTP instead of what consumers would pay, if they were to use or pay for the services.

## Author details

Mapula Hildah Lefophane
University of Limpopo, Polokwane, South Africa

*Address all correspondence to: hildajie@gmail.com

## References

[1] Perlman Y, Yechiali U. Reducing risk of infection–The COVID-19 queueing game. Safety Science. 2020;**132**:104987

[2] Tyrväinen O, Karjaluoto H. Online grocery shopping before and during the COVID-19 pandemic: A meta-analytical review. Telematics and Informatics. 2022;**101839**

[3] Nielsen. COVID-19 has flipped the value proposition of omnichannel shopping for constrained consumers [Internet]. 2020. Available from: https://nielseniq.com/global/en/insights/analysis/2020/covid-19-has-flipped-the-value-proposition-of-omnichannel-shopping-for-constrained-consumers/. [Accessed March 4, 2022]

[4] Eriksson N, Stenius M. Changing behavioral patterns in grocery shopping in the initial phase of the COVID-19 crisis—A qualitative study of news articles. Open Journal of Business and Management. 2020;**8**:1946-1961

[5] Shen H, Namdarpour F, Lin J. Investigation of online grocery shopping and delivery preference before, during, and after COVID-19. Transportation Research Interdisciplinary Perspectives. 2022;**14**:100580

[6] McKinsey. How European shoppers will buy groceries in the next normal [Internet]. 2020. Available from: https://www.mckinsey.com/industries/retail/our-insights/how-european-shoppers-will-buy-groceries-in-the-next-normal. [Accessed: April 2, 2022]

[7] Lefophane MH. COVID-19 and South Africa's food industry: Challenges, trends and the path ahead [Internet]. 2020. Available from: https://www.mzansiagritalk.com/archives/4240. [Accessed: May 24, 2021]

[8] Dannenberg P, Fuchs M, Riedler T, Wiedemann C. Digital transition by COVID-19 pandemic? The German food online retail. Tijdschrift voor Economische en Sociale Geografie. 2020;**111**(3):543-560

[9] Sanchez-Diaz I, Vural CA, Halldórsson Á. Assessing the inequalities in access to online delivery services and the way COVID-19 pandemic affects marginalization. Transport Policy. 2021;**109**:24-36

[10] Borenstein S, Saloner G. Economics and electronic commerce. The Journal of Economic Perspectives. 2001;**15**(1):3-12

[11] Rust RT, Lemon KN. E-service and the consumer. International Journal of Electronic Commerce. 2001;**5**(3):85-101

[12] Brynjolfsson E, Hu Y, Smith MD. Consumer surplus in the digital economy: Estimating the value of increased product variety at online booksellers. Management Science. 2003;**49**(11):1580-1596

[13] Brown JR, Goolsbee A. Does the Internet make markets more competitive? Evidence from the life insurance industry. Journal of Political Economy. 2002;**110**(3):481-507

[14] Keeling K, Macaulay LA, McGoldrick P. DiTV and e-commerce among disadvantaged community groups. Behaviour & Information Technology. 2007;**26**(6):545-560

[15] Bhatti A, Akram H, Basit HM, Khan AU, Raza SM, Naqvi MB. E-commerce trends during COVID-19 Pandemic. International Journal of Future Generation Communication and Networking. 2020;**13**(2):1449-1452

[16] Driediger F, Bhatiasevi V. Online grocery shopping in Thailand: Consumer acceptance and usage behavior. Journal of Retailing and Consumer Services. 2019;**48**:224-237

[17] Brand C, Schwanen T, Anable J. 'Online Omnivores' or 'Willing but struggling'? Identifying online grocery shopping behavior segments using attitude theory. Journal of Retailing and Consumer Services. 2020;**57**:102195

[18] Pargo. The rise of South African ecommerce [Internet]. 2022. https://pargo.co.za/blog/the-rise-of-south-african-ecommerce/. [Accessed: March 10, 2022]

[19] Kibuacha. E-Commerce in South Africa: The Growth, and the Future [Internet]. 2021. Available from: https://www.geopoll.com/blog/e-commerce-south-africa/. [Accessed: March 10, 2022]

[20] ecommerceDB. Ecommerce market in South Africa [Internet]. 2022. Available from: https://ecommercedb.com/en/markets/za/all#:~:text=South%20Africa%20is%20the%2041st,for%20eCommerce%20continue%20to%20increase. [Accessed: March 15, 2022]

[21] Deloitte Africa. SA Digital Commerce Consumer Report. 2020

[22] Staff Writer. The explosive growth of e-commerce in South Africa [Internet]. 2022. Available from: https://businesstech.co.za/news/business/568272/the-explosive-growth-of-e-commerce-in-south-africa/#. [Accessed: March 10, 2022]

[23] Grashuis J, Skevas T, Segovia MS. Grocery shopping preferences during the COVID-19 pandemic. Sustainability. 2020;**12**(13):5369

[24] Hansen T. Consumer adoption of online grocery buying: A discriminant analysis. International Journal of Retail & Distribution Management. 2005; **33**(2):101-121

[25] Verhoef PC, Langerak F. Possible determinants of consumers' adoption of electronic grocery shopping in the Netherlands. Journal of Retailing and Consumer Services. 2001;**8**(5):275-285

[26] Bauerová R, Klepek M. Technology acceptance as a determinant of online grocery shopping adoption. Acta Universitatis Agriculturae et Silviculturae Mendelianae Brunensis. 2018;**66**(3):737-746

[27] Hansen T. Consumer values, the theory of planned behaviour and online grocery shopping. International Journal of Consumer Studies. 2008;**32**(2): 128-137

[28] Mortimer G et al. Online grocery shopping: The impact of shopping frequency on perceived risk. The International Review of Retail, Distribution and Consumer Research. 2016;**26**(2):202-223

[29] Vinerean S. Understanding consumers' online shopping behavior during the Covid-19 pandemic: Empirical research. The International Review of Retail, Distribution and Consumer Research. 2020;**8**(2):140-150

[30] Chenarides L, Grebitus C, Lusk JL, Printezis I. Food consumption behavior during the COVID-19 pandemic. Agribusiness. 2021;**37**(1):44-81

[31] Hoyer WD, MacInnis DJ, Pieters R. Consumer Behavior. Boston: Cengage Learning; 2016

[32] Teller C, Kotzab H, Grant DB. The consumer direct services revolution in grocery retailing: An exploratory investigation. Managing Service Quality:

An International Journal. 2006;**16**(1):78-96

[33] Goethals F, Leclercq-Vandelannoitte A, Tütüncü Y. French consumers' perceptions of the unattended delivery model for e-grocery retailing. Journal of Retailing and Consumer Services. 2012;**19**(1):133-139

[34] Maltese I, Le Pira M, Marcucci E, Gatta V, Evangelinos C. Grocery or@grocery: A stated preference investigation in Rome and Milan. Research in Transportation Economics. 2021;**87**:101096

[35] Yue W, Liu N, Zheng Q, Wang HH. Does the COVID-19 pandemic change consumers' food consumption and willingness-to-pay? the case of China. Food. 2021;**10**(9):2156

[36] Kingsbury NR. Applied Research and Methods: Assessing Data Reliability [internet]. 2019. Available from: https://www.gao.gov/assets/gao-20-283g.pdf. [Accessed: May 29, 2022]

[37] Statistics South Africa. Quarterly Labour Force Survey (QLFS) [Internet]. 2021. Available from: https://www.statssa.gov.za/?p=14957. [Accessed: March 10, 2022]

[38] Mkasi FN. Households' Food Consumption Behaviour during COVID-19 Pandemic: Evidence from Rural Households in South Africa. Polokwane: University of Limpopo; 2021

[39] Nicholson W, Snyder CM. Microeconomic Theory: Basic Principles and Extensions. Boston: Cengage Learning; 2012

[40] Boccaletti S, Moro D. Consumer willingness-to-pay for GM food products in Italy. AgBioforum. 2000;**3**(4):259-267

[41] Cranfield JA, Magnusson E. Canadian consumer's willingness-to-pay for pesticide free food products: An ordered prohibit analysis. International Food and Agribusiness Management Review. 2003;**6**(4):1-18

[42] Senyolo GM, Wale E, Ortmann GF. Consumers' Willingness-To-Pay for underutilized vegetable crops: The case of African leafy vegetables in South Africa. Journal of Human Ecology. 2014;**47**(3):219-227

[43] Wang Y, Xu R, Schwartz M, Ghosh D, Chen X. COVID-19 and retail grocery management: Insights from a broad-based consumer survey. IEEE Engineering Management Review. 2020;**48**(3):202-211

[44] King DM, Mazzotta MJ. Ecosystem valuation: Methods; section 6; Contingent valuation method [internet]. 2000. Available from: http://www.ecosystemvaluation.org/contingent_valuation.htm. [Accessed: July 18, 2022]

Section 2

# Digital Transformation of Education

Chapter 5

# Perspective Chapter: Building an Online Ecosystem for English Teaching and Learning in the Times of Covid-19 Pandemic and Beyond

*Nguyen Quoc Hung Luu*


## Abstract

Online education is a revolutionary trend of educational technology today, particularly, since the Covid-19 pandemic, online classes have become the cornerstone of modern education. The rapid growth of online learning is challenging the relevance of traditional higher education systems. Although many efforts from educational institutions to promote online teaching and learning have rapidly increased, progress is far from sufficient, especially when a model of an online learning system needs further examination in practice after the pandemic. This chapter reports a case study at the center of foreign languages in Vietnam, addressing the need to develop an online learning ecosystem during the pandemic crisis and beyond. Characteristics of an online learning ecosystem are presented and basic steps of developing an online ecosystem for English teaching and learning are discussed in detail. The suggested ecosystem should cover the five key components including teaching environment, relationships between teachers and learners and between learners and learners, teaching methods, teaching content and resources, and teaching evaluation. Several recommendations for strengthening an online learning ecosystem are also presented.


**Keywords:** Covid-19, characteristics, learning ecosystem, online learning, pedagogy

## 1. Introduction

The pandemic's impact over the past 2 years has required adaptation in almost every area of teaching and learning and prompted most educational institutions to rapidly adapt to online learning. Most of the classes are currently conducted using various web conferencing tools for synchronous applications like Zoom, Google Meet, or MS Teams. Various kinds of Learning Management Systems like Moodle or Google Classroom are being used to deliver online courses, and even most examinations are being managed online, using various technology applications. The constraints of the pandemic provided an opportunity for educators to consider building a strong learning ecosystem during and after the pandemic times. The term "ecosystem" is usually associated with the scientific community; however, when it comes to the context of online education, it helps to view an online learning ecosystem as a socio-technical system consisting of species (tools, resources, curricular, policy), populations and communities (learners, teachers, experts, management) in a mutually interacting environment [1]. This metaphor will help educational leaders to establish and conduct strategic plans to create specific learning ecosystems to withstand, sustain and develop during the crisis and beyond.

As reflected in the definition of ecosystem, the idea of ecosystem can be applied to any learning, and an online learning ecosystem for teaching and learning English is worth considering in greater detail. For many educational institutions like the case study examined in the following chapter, sustaining continued learning has become an urgent development when the global pandemic has expanded. A strong online learning ecosystem can help institutions survive and grow during the crisis. More importantly, a strategic online learning ecosystem is necessary to help institutions to keep up with their fast-changing learning needs by creating opportunities for development and enhancing continuous learning of all types. Being ready to adapt ecosystem-based changes for sustained learning in the pandemic and in the new normal requires educators to understand what it means to become a learning ecosystem, what they need, and how they proceed to develop the system.

## 2. Online learning ecosystem and its characteristics

Ecology, which was first proposed by German biologists in the mid-nineteenth century, has developed into a comprehensive discipline in the present century [2]. In a general context, a natural ecosystem is a biological community of interacting organisms with their physical environment. Every organism has a role to fulfill and for an ecosystem to flourish and evolve, all aspects of the ecosystem should have a harmonious balance. In a specific context, each ecosystem may comprise different elements. A business ecosystem, for example, is a network of buyers, suppliers, and markets of related products or services in their socio-economic environment. An educational institution can be conceptualized as a gradually evolving and responsive learning ecosystem, which constantly adapts and self-regulates itself according to internal and external changing needs [3]. In the context of online education, online learning ecosystem is the term used to describe all the components required to implement an online solution. In many respects, an online learning ecosystem is very similar to a biological ecosystem, where organisms interact with one another and with their physical environment.

In the process of English teaching, the concept of ecosystem can be applicable as the English teaching environment is similar to the natural environment in the category of ecological theory, and the relationship between teachers and learners is similar to the relationship between the producers and consumers in the business context.

In existing literature on online learning in regard to English teaching [4], there are four typical characteristics of an online learning ecosystem which include openness, harmonious symbiosis, flexible interactions, and individual differences.

### 2.1 Openness

Openness generally refers to the connection among the elements inside and outside the system. In an online learning setting, all the elements of teachers, students, and online learning environment form a whole ecosystem, and they are open to each other. Teachers and learners, and learners in one class can communicate together, with other classes, with other schools, and with the external environment, to learn from each other and to promote their own development. The characteristic of openness in an online learning ecosystem also refers to open educational resources that allow learners to use, adapt, and share learning resources. In this information age, this type of openness is critical for learners to create and share experiences and knowledge. Openness of learning environments allows the learning process to be more visible and inviting to critique and new ideas. Innovative ideas and dynamic interactions can only occur in open learning ecosystems [5].

### 2.2 Harmonious symbiosis

This relationship mainly focuses on the positive relationship between teachers and learners, teachers and colleagues, and among learners. A specific English ecological online class will be successful when it can promote the continuous growth of the teacher and learners in which teachers are full of positive energy and enthusiasm, and learners are full of learning and exploring passion, and most importantly, teachers and learners can inspire each other. Harmonious relationships have a positive influence on learners' experience and generally promote their continuous efforts with online learning [6].

### 2.3 Flexible interaction

An online learning ecosystem should have the feature of flexible interactions thanks to which all participants in the system can effectively interact with one another and with their physical environment. In a specific English ecological class, the interactions can be categorized into three types: teacher-learner, learner-learner, and learner-content. The first type of teacher and learner interaction is widely considered vital for an effective online classroom in Vietnam as for many past decades, both teachers and learners have been accustomed to traditional teaching method known as the teacher-centered approach. To enhance the teacher and learner interaction, teachers should play their roles as facilitators, stimulating learners' interest and motivation, and guiding each learner through online learning experiences. The second type of interaction, learner-learner occurs as learners share information with their peers and receive feedback. Virtual environments are often collaborative, and learners can interact in a variety of ways. Online discussion boards can even be more useful than face-to-face discussions in a traditional classroom because learners can take time to reflect on their responses [7]. Generally, learners can interact to collaborate with one another, instruct each other, encourage one another or befriend each other. The third type of interaction, learner-content interaction, is especially vital because it provides learners with the necessary knowledge in language competence and contributes to the success of online learning. Interaction, in all forms, can be perceived as an effective way to promote distance education. It is a fact that in the medium of distance education, activities, dimensions, functions, and the other components of online learning including the concept of interaction must be used distinctively from traditional face-to-face education [8].

### 2.4 Individual differences

Learning is generally more effective when individual differences can be recognized and valued. Family background, academic ability, motivation for learning, and personality traits are some main differences between learners that should be considered for developing an online learning ecosystem. Individual differences are much emphasized in an ecological class because the core of ecological class teaching is people-oriented, respecting individual differences such as physical characteristics, intelligence, perception, gender, ability, and learning styles. An effective and productive learning and teaching process can be designed and undertaken by carefully considering these individual differences of the learners [9].

## 3. Importance of an online learning ecosystem in the times of Covid-19 pandemic and beyond

For the past many decades, most academic institutions have relied exclusively on traditional learning, but the sudden outbreak of Covid-19 pandemic shook all educational systems by forcing a shift to online teaching and learning. During times of the pandemic crisis for the past 2 years, every educational institution should strive to maintain or enhance its competitive advantage, which is primarily achieved by its people. To provide continuous learning frameworks for learners during the crisis and beyond, educators should build their online learning ecosystems. Online learning ecosystems are necessary to help educational institutions withstand crises and generate long-term benefits [10].

An online learning ecosystem may offer a range of benefits, including creating a good learning environment, enhancing the overall quality of relationships between teachers and learners, promoting the rationality of teaching language, and increasing the diversification of teaching methods [11]. Creating a good learning environment is beneficial. The main purpose and function of an online learning ecosystem are to enable dynamic relationships and interactions between teachers and learners with online content. Learners and teachers and their interactions are important features of the virtual learning ecosystem. Today's learners generally prefer a learning environment that is not as obsolete as traditional classrooms but that is specifically engineered to support thinking. In an online ecological class, learners may have a new learning experience, so a sense of belonging is important for a meaningful learning process. Teachers need to create a supportive online learning environment where learners feel more comfortable and engaged.

Enhancing the overall quality of the relationship between teachers and learners has important, positive, and long-lasting implications for both teachers and learners in an English ecological class. Teachers should take a more learner-empowering approach to classroom management for building learners' self-awareness and enhancing their self-regulation. Teachers should be responsible for following each learner's progress through the course. Teachers should continually be assessing learners' learning, diagnosing learning needs, and prescribing solutions. At the same time, in a healthy classroom ecosystem, learners are the primary producers of education, who build the classroom environment and keep it alive [12].

Promoting the rationality of teaching language is also very important. Rationality, or rational thinking, generally helps to develop problem-solving skills, the ability to memorize the content, and writing skills which are particularly useful in foreign language teaching and learning [13]. In the process of English teaching, the complexity of teaching generally requires teachers to question their practices for their own professional development in order to improve and increase learner performance [14].

Increasing the diversification of teaching methods is another advantage of an online ecological class. Similar to the natural ecological system, the ecological system of English teaching also contains many elements, and there are also interrelated and contradictory relations among the elements. Teaching is not one size, that can fit all approaches. Teaching is eclectic and dynamic [15]. Diverse teaching methodologies can meet different learners' learning styles and help to engage more learners through various teaching strategies. Teachers should take notice of the innovation of teaching content, and then support the development of an ecological education system in the direction of diversification. Diversification of teaching methods will enable online teachers to reach more learners since this diversity fits better the learners' learning styles [16].

## 4. Basic components of an online learning ecosystem

Creating a learning ecosystem generally requires a focus on the people, content, technology, data, and governance in the organization. In the context of English teaching, an online ecological English class should focus on an effective learning environment, relationships between teachers and learners, learning content, learning methods, and learning evaluation [17].

The ecological online learning environment is particularly important, which is the most basic condition of the process of online teaching and learning. An effective learning environment should emphasize active roles of both teachers and learners. Teachers will often act as facilitators, organizing activities that engage learners directly rather than relying too heavily on lectures and memorization. Successful online learners have to be self-directed, stay motivated, and stay on top of their workload independently [18]. Collaboration is a key indicator of effectiveness in an online ecological English class. Small group assignments and forum discussions can give opportunities for learners to engage more effectively.

Ecological relationship between teachers and learners is of great importance. Online environment facilitates and strengthens a new teacher-learner relationship which is characterized by teacher-led and learner-centered characteristics. The traditional classroom is teacher-centered, in which the teacher is the authority of knowledge, but the ecological class should emphasize the symbiosis between supportive teachers and engaged learners. A supportive teacher is one who efficiently creates a positive environment in the classroom. Teachers should have to shift traditional teaching methods and should apply strategies, focusing on practical activities and cooperative learning. Teachers should promote effective learning and interaction with learners and engaged learners should be involved practically in learning. Learners should be given practical activities regarding their practical life so that they can learn to practice in reality [19].

Teaching content is the foundation and center of an online ecological class. The content may be further categorized into two primary elements: class content and website content. Class content can include any document file, presentation file, audio file, or video file that may be used to deliver online classes. The content is mainly distributed through the electronic channels by employing the internet, satellite TV, radio, and storage devices like compact discs, hard discs, pen-drives, etc. Website content with its multimedia elements, interactive features, and a higher level of accessibility is an effective tool for online learners. Learners generally expect information, services, academic content, interactive tools, and user-friendliness from the websites of their institutions [20]. In different teaching and learning contexts, website content can be modified and applied in four main different methods, which can be web-supported in a face-to-face course, web-enhanced in a face-to-face course with internet resources, web-enabled in a face-to-face course with online learning activities, or web-delivered in a fully online course [21].

In regard to teaching methods, online learning is catalyzing a pedagogical shift in how people teach and learn. There is a shift away from top-down lecturing and passive learners to a more interactive, collaborative approach in which learners and teachers should work together to create an effective learning environment. The teacher's role is changing from the "sage on the stage" to "the guide on the side" [22]. In the new development of English ecological class, teaching methods should be based on a learner-centered approach. In this approach, learners can learn at their own pace and take full responsibility for learning. Teachers can use various kinds of teaching methods, such as the communicative language teaching method, task-based language teaching method, total physical response method, audio-visual method, and group cooperation method. Only the teaching ways are ecological, can students' learning be ecological [23].

Teaching evaluation is a means to test the teaching situation, and it reflects the effect of classroom teaching. The ecological teaching evaluation is critical as the core of ecological class is the sustainable development of teaching. The traditional teaching evaluation is unilateral, that is, teachers mainly evaluate their learners. The evaluation of ecological class can be diverse; that is, the learners themselves, classmates, teachers, and parents all should be involved in the evaluation with the aim of enhancing the teaching and learning process.

## 5. Research approach

In the current study, the research method used is qualitative with a case study approach with data collection through documentation review and case observation. Data analysis techniques consist of data reduction, data presentation, and drawing conclusions. Case study has proven particularly useful for studying institutional innovation and development, and the results can provide institutional leaders with a detailed description of a specific situation for their policy decision-making process [24].

## 6. The Center of Foreign Languages (CFL) and its current practices of developing an online learning ecosystem

### 6.1 CFL and its online programs

The Center of Foreign Languages, Can Tho University, Vietnam (hereafter referred to as "the Center" or CFL) has provided fee-paid language courses in English, French, Chinese, Japanese, and Korean to the local community. Currently, there are approximately 2000 of learners of both adult learners and young learners. Most of the courses are on-site, and the online program makes up a small part of different programs at the Center before the pandemic crisis. During the country's period of social distancing, the Center shifted to emergency online teaching and learning in early May of 2021 and began to offer more online classes. Teachers basically used web conference software such as Zoom or Google Meet as the technical tool of instruction for their synchronous classes. Online class size is relatively small, between 15 and 24 learners. The course duration is between 8 and 10 weeks, and each class has 2 or 3 synchronous sessions per week. With the shift to online teaching, the Center took some immediate actions from adjusting the course content of all its programs, reorganizing the syllabi, providing teachers with online pedagogical approaches, and, most practically, preparing the necessary technological facilities, such as internet connectivity and software service licenses to conduct online classes.

### 6.2 Weaknesses in the current system before the change

At the beginning of the pandemic crisis, the Center was facing the challenge of transferring all levels of physical onsite classes to emergency online teaching and learning. This emergency remote education at the Center was mainly an obligation and was not based on much theoretical and practical knowledge in a systematic manner. Online teaching at the early stage of change was needed for surviving during the pandemic crisis, but it posed challenges for all the stakeholders. Major challenges include lack of appropriate technology, teachers' lack of online teaching skills, and learners' lack of motivation for online learning. One fundamental problem was that the system of online teaching and learning was not fully ready and well-planned by institutional educators, teachers, and learners.

### 6.3 CFL's practices of developing an online learning ecosystem

According to Hodges and his colleagues [25], the typical planning, preparation, and development time for a fully developed online course may take up to 9 months; the Center, therefore, in the very early stage of the pandemic, decided to undertake a holistic plan to establish an online learning ecosystem, not only for conducting emergency online teaching during the crisis but also for designing a sustainable system of online teaching and learning.

There are basic steps of the plan, which include identifying the institutional needs and readiness, constructing the technology infrastructure, providing appropriate training for online pedagogy, developing online content, and evaluating the online learning environment.

Identifying the institutional needs and readiness is the first step in the plan. A need analysis can help the Center assess the institution's readiness for the change and become proactive in approaching potential challenges. These major concerns of adopting an online learning ecosystem were closely examined, including teachers' lack of online teaching experience, technology shortage, learners' distraction, etc. In this early phase, the Center also identified and established specific goals and outlined a roadmap with important activities for developing an online learning ecosystem.

Constructing the technology infrastructure is the next important step in the plan. Requirements of technology can be various in specific online contexts, but in general context, the technology infrastructure consists of a learning management system, content delivery system, and tools. A learning management system (LMS) is a platform that helps teachers manage and organize teaching materials online and conduct online courses. At present, the Center has been using Moodle as the basic LMS for conducting different online courses as the platform offers many advantages to teachers and learners such as control over the content, control over the time spent learning, and thus the process can be adapted according to the learner needs and objectives of learning [26].

A content delivery system (CDS) is online software that allows the teaching content to be delivered over the Internet in two common ways: synchronous and asynchronous. Synchronous content delivery system enables the content to be delivered to learners in real-time, allowing learners to communicate with each other and teachers at the same time; for example, at the Center, the learners can participate in a live Zoom session at a specific time for the learning. This learning environment facilitates a classroom community and increases learners' motivation [27]. According to these authors, asynchronous delivery can be provided and accessed by learners when they choose; for example, the learners can watch a posted recording of a lecture, not in the real-time of the lesson. In asynchronous environments, learners engage with the content at their own pace, allowing for flexible learning.

In online teaching and learning environment, there is a variety of digital tools. Online learning tools refer to any software, apps, or platform that aid online teachers in enhancing learners' engagement [28]. At present, the Center has invested to equip necessary toolkits including programs for creating and presenting online teaching and learning content, software for editing images and videos, apps for creating quizzes and games, and online providers for cloud storage and file-sharing.

It is critical that an online learning ecosystem should be built with the correct and economical technology solution to be feasible and successful. The Center needed to ensure that the new online learning applications can integrate with many of the existing systems.

Providing appropriate training for online pedagogy is necessary. Pedagogical approaches are the various strategies and skills teachers employ to help learners realize their full educational potential and achieve learning outcomes [29]. In modern language classrooms, eclectic approach or eclecticism has become popular, thanks to which teachers can generally select various teaching methods or techniques depending on the aims of lessons and learners' abilities. While traditional approaches such as the communicative approach are still useful for effective language teaching, it is important to explore and implement new teaching strategies such as the use of smartphones or tablets in the new learning environment.

With regard to preparation and support for online teaching, most teachers at the Center began with little or no training or preparation specific to this delivery mode. Online teachers need adequate preparation of adequate strategies for effective teaching. Teachers need support and training in the pedagogy of online instruction, especially they need support with technology [30]. Teachers should be trained in how to use the functions of the online system and should know who to contact for technological help. Due to time constraints and modality of instruction, online teachers can become more isolated from colleagues and therefore miss out on meaningful discussions, constructive feedback, and a sense of collegiality. To help mitigate these potential concerns, forming teachers' communities where teachers can share ideas and assist each other in online teaching can be of great consideration.

Developing online content is of great importance. Generally speaking, online course content should be interactive and engaging. Interactive learning content helps learners to be more active and more attentive with their online learning. When creating content online, teachers are expected to combine the content of text, image, audio, and video relevantly. Interactive learning content can comprise a series of activity-oriented lessons that can enhance learners' understanding of content through practice.

Designing a course for the online learning environment requires significant planning time and effort. The course design should begin with identifying learning outcomes and also determine appropriate assessment methods and teaching and learning activities. In addition, teaching resources and materials, and online learning tools are important considerations. Technology selected should be compatible with varied student needs. Technical support should be available to both teachers and learners [31].

Evaluating the online learning ecosystem is critical. The Center should conduct evaluations of its online learning ecosystem after the construction. The system needed continual attention to adapt to the changing online learning environment. There are different evaluation designs and models of evaluation that can be used to evaluate a program or project. The Context, Input, Process and Product (CIPP) evaluation model can be effectively used for evaluating the quality of education. Context presents the goals, objectives, history, and background of the institution. Inputs refer to material, time, physical and human resources needed for effective working. Process includes all the teaching and learning processes, and product focuses on the quality of teaching-learning and its usefulness for the society [32].

## 7. Recommendations for establishing a strong learning ecosystem

### 7.1 Recommendations for practice

For an online learning ecosystem to be successful, all components in the system should be dynamic and mutually interactive. An important strategy to develop a more effective online learning environment is to continually improve the ecosystem as a whole. Cultivating a strong learning ecosystem involves thinking strategically and planning each component in concert with the others. It also involves making changes when necessary. In practice, as new technologies and online learning systems come to market, new strategies should be accordingly adopted. Listening to learners and evaluating the learning process is also critical to a healthy learning ecosystem.

### 7.2 Recommendations for future research

This study is to continue as a guide for further research on the online learning ecosystem in different disciplines, particularly in the post-pandemic times. In a further research step, the proposed online learning ecosystem for teaching and learning English can be evaluated in terms of motivation and satisfaction of teachers and learners.

Regarding the research methodology, the current case study method was employed appropriately for understanding and describing the current practices of building an online learning ecosystem; however, for better generalizing the results, further research can consider applying mixed methods.

## 8. Conclusion

The online revolution of teaching and learning has transformed almost every aspect of society. Along with modern technology, ecosystem metaphors have changed the approach of educational models. The learning ecosystem in general and the online learning ecosystem in teaching and learning English, in particular, are evolving at a significant rate. This new learning ecosystem represents a significant shift from traditional conceptions of how education is organized and delivered during the pandemic crisis, and in the future, this trend continues to encourage lifelong learning, enhance learners' innovative thinking, and foster the skills necessary for the twenty-first century workplace.

The post-pandemic age is an era of adaptation. Creating an online learning ecosystem for teaching and learning English is vital to success of online courses or programs. In this system, teachers and learners are the main subjects of any activity. A harmonious and pleasant teacher-learner relationship and learner-learner relationship should be focused. Teachers as course facilitators should guide learners to choose their own learning content and learning methods, solve problems independently and regulate the learning process effectively. Learners should be empowered to participate and contribute to maximizing the resources with continuous collaboration to meet the desired learning objectives.

Learning ecosystems are currently evolving at a significant rate. Learning is no longer a standalone learner-teacher-content interaction, but it has now become an enriched complex mechanism that has the potential to truly maximize the learning outcome. Online education in general and online teaching and learning of English are certainly going to play a great role in shaping the learning ecosystem and making it more fruitful, both for individuals and educational institutions in the times of post-pandemic and beyond.

## Acknowledgements

The author acknowledges great thanks to the Center of Foreign Languages, Can Tho University, and all the teachers, especially Ms. Vo Pham Trinh Thu, for their participation in and contributions to this book chapter.

## Conflict of interests

The author declares no conflict of interest.

## Author details

Nguyen Quoc Hung Luu
Can Tho University, Vietnam

*Address all correspondence to: nqhung@ctu.edu.vn

## References

[1] Väljataga T, Poom-Valickis K, Rumma K, Aus K. Transforming higher education learning ecosystem: Teachers' perspective. Interaction Design and Architecture(s) Journal. 2020;**46**:47-69. DOI: 10.55612/s-5002-046-003

[2] Shirvan ME, Rahmani S, Sorayyaee L. On the exploration of the ecology of English language teachers' personal styles in Iran. Asian-Pacific Journal of Second and Foreign Language Education. 2016;**1**:1-17

[3] Kallas EV, Solovjeva TP, Minakova LY. Implementation of ecological education in a higher school. Social and Behavioral Sciences. 2015;**200**:453-459. DOI: 10.1016/j.sbspro.2015.08.095

[4] Zhou Z. The model construction of English ecological class in the high school in China. English Language Teaching. 2017;**10**:227-231

[5] Panda S, Santosh S. Faculty perception of openness and attitude to open sharing at the Indian National Open University. International Review of Research in Open and Distributed Learning. 2017;**18**:89-111

[6] Luo N, Zhang Y, Zhang M. Retaining learners by establishing harmonious relationships in e-learning environment. Interactive Learning Environments. 2019;**27**:118-131. DOI: 10.1080/10494820.2018.1506811

[7] Keaton W, Gilbert A. Successful online learning: What does learner interaction with peers, instructors and parents look like? Journal of Online Learning Research. 2020;**6**:129-154

[8] Abrami PC, Bernard RM, Bures E, Tamim R. Interaction in distance education and online learning: Using evidence and theory to improve practice. Journal of Computing in Higher Education. 2011;**23**:82-103. DOI: 10.1007/s12528-011-9043-x

[9] Moallem M. Accommodating individual differences in the design of online learning environments: A comparative study. Journal of Research on Technology in Education. 2007;**40**:217-245

[10] Dhawan S. Online learning: A panacea in the time of COVID-19 crisis. Journal of Educational Technology Systems. 2020;**49**:5-22. DOI: 10.1177/0047239520934018

[11] Gou J. Research on the ecological model of English teaching. In: Proceedings of the 2nd International Conference on Social Science and Technology Education (ICSSTE 2016); 14-15 May 2016; Guangzhou, China: Atlantis Press; 2016

[12] Huang Q. (2018) Examining teachers' roles in online learning. The EuroCALL Review. 2018;**26**:3-18. DOI: 10.4995/eurocall.2018.9139

[13] Lee O, Porter AC. Bounded rationality in classroom teaching. Educational Psychologist. 1990;**25**:159-171. DOI: 10.1207/s15326985ep2502_4

[14] Floden R, Felman S. Should teachers be taught to be rational? Journal of Education for Teaching. 2006;7:274-283. DOI: 10.1080/0260747810070307

[15] Tremblay-Wragg E, Raby C, Menard L, Plante I. The use of diversified teaching strategies by four university teachers: What contribution to their students' learning motivation? Teaching in Higher Education. 2019;**26**:97-114. DOI: 10.1080/13562517.2019.1636221

[16] Zeid HA, Assadi N, Murad T. The Effect of junior high school teachers' motivation and willingness to change on the diversity of their teaching methods. Theory and Practice in Language Studies. 2017;7:1160-1170. DOI: 10.17507/tpls.0712.02

[17] Wang L. Research on English classroom teaching from the perspective of ecological linguistics. Advances in Social Science, Education and Humanities Research. 2019;**286**:153-156

[18] Lopukhova Y, Makeeva E. Creating virtual learning environment: Shared online learning in university education. International Journal for Cross-Disciplinary Subjects in Education. 2020;**8**:3046-3054

[19] Feroz S, Khan M. Social ecology of teacher student relationship. Nobel Research Journal. 2020;**1**:67-76

[20] Kir E, Kayak S. The evaluation of websites teaching English as a foreign language. Social and Behavioral Sciences. 2013;**106**:2788-2795. DOI: 10.1016/j.sbspro.2013.12.320

[21] Dinc E. Web-based education and accessibility. International Journal of Technology in Education and Science (IJTES). 2017;**1**:29-35

[22] Morrison C. From 'Sage on the stage' to 'Guide on the side': A good start. International Journal for the Scholarship of Teaching and Learning. 2014;**8**:1-15. DOI: 10.20429/ijsotl.2014.080104

[23] Fataar A, Norodien F. Towards an e-learning ecologies approach to pedagogy in a post-COVID world. Journal of Education. 2021;**84**:154-168. DOI: 10.17159/2520-9868/i84a08

[24] Leymun SO, Odabaşı HF, Yurdakul IK. The importance of case study research in educational settings. Journal of Qualitative Research in Education. 2017;**5**:369-385. DOI: 10.14689/issn.2148- 2624.1.5c3s16m

[25] Hodges C, Moore S, Lockee B, Trust T, Bond A. The difference between emergency remote learning and online learning. Education Review. 2020;**27**:1-12

[26] Suresh M, Priya V, Gayathri R. Effect of e-learning on academic performance of undergraduate students. Drug Invention. 2018;**10**:1797-1800

[27] Hrastinski S, Keller C, Carlsson S. Design exemplars for synchronous e-learning: A design theory approach. Computers & Education. 2010;**55**:652-662. DOI: 10.1016/j.compedu.2010.02.025

[28] Bhatia R. Features and effectiveness of E-learning tools. Global Journal of Business Management and Information Technology. 2011;**1**:1-7

[29] Khurshid F. E-pedagogical skills of online instructors: An exploratory study. Bulletin of Education and Research. 2020;**42**:235-250

[30] Gabriel M, Kaufield KJ. Reciprocal mentorship: An effective support for online instructors. Mentoring and Tutoring. 2008;**16**:311-327

[31] Mahyoob M. Challenges of e-Learning during the COVID-19 pandemic experienced by EFL learners. Arab World English Journal. 2020;**11**:351-362. DOI: 10.24093/awej/vol11no4.23

[32] Aziz S, Mahmood M, Rehman Z. Implementation of CIPP model for quality evaluation at school level: A case study. Journal of Education and Educational Development. 2018;**5**:189-206. DOI: 10.1080/13611260802233480

Chapter 6

# Perspective Chapter: Digitization of Traditional Higher Education Touchpoints

*Adam Malešević*


## Abstract

This chapter presents the possibilities of using e-services in the context of higher education. Modern technologies provide an opportunity to create a stronger bond between the higher education institution and its stakeholders, among whom students and employees are the most important and those who have the greatest needs in terms of the number and frequency of use of e-services. The main objective of this chapter is to explore the role of e-services in relationship management in the higher education complex ecosystem. There is a possibility to digitize a lot of traditional higher education touchpoints, such as everyday administration processes, admission, enrollment, relevant information sharing, e-learning, Q&A, and similar. The comprehensive e-services system was developed and implemented in one of the higher educational institutions. The upcoming generations of students are increasingly likely to have prominent previous experience with the major use of digital technologies as a part of their elementary and secondary level education. Higher education institutions should expand the portfolio of their e-services, given that the demands of students are expected to increase in the future.


**Keywords:** e-services in higher education, stakeholder relationship management, student relationship management, information systems in higher education, e-business in higher education

## 1. Introduction

The way of running businesses in the last decade has drastically changed in such a way that it is impossible to imagine doing any business without the application of information communications technology (ICT). This, naturally, is becoming even more important with the outbreak of the COVID-19 pandemic [1]. However, even before this pandemic, ICT applications became an integral part of the everyday business of a large portion of business systems [2]. Over time, ICT has been gaining its importance becoming more and more important in the daily functioning of all business organizations.

Higher educational institutions are regarded as organizations, which according to their business, are considered special companies (justifiably to some extent), and yet many good practices that have been applied in successful business systems, particularly corporations, are not applied in higher educational institutions, neither state nor

 IntechOpen

privately owned ones. However, a pandemic does not make a difference between corporations and higher educational institutions but points out that educational institutions cannot be regarded as separate entities but have to adjust to changed circumstances and different ways of working [1].

Although higher educational institutions organize their business dealings differently when compared with classic companies, certain segments of their work function exactly the same way as in classical companies (they both require human resources management, financial policy, goods or services procurement, work promotion, etc.).

With the development of competition in the higher education market and the emergence of many new higher educational institutions and study programs, some elements that have never been considered before in higher education attract the limelight—approaching students as stakeholders [3], developing and maintaining the relationship with students [4], struggling to attract new students [5], taking care about relationships with students and employees, etc. The complex ecosystem of a higher educational institution is made up of many relations similar to those already mentioned, and which imply a whole series of business processes and activities. In order to satisfy those relations in a proper manner, it takes a thorough and comprehensive approach at the level of higher educational institutions, which should integrate and take care of many intertwined business activities.

How can proper use of technologies affect the quality rating improvement of a higher educational institution in the present competitive market? The Association of Colleges in North Carolina established that a corporate information system aimed at a student as a stakeholder can also provide better chances to attract enrollment and retain new students [6]. Let us take, for example, the situation which has changed the manner in which people behave—the coronavirus pandemic. If there had not existed some use of e-services on behalf of higher educational institutions until the onset of the pandemic, the relationship between universities and students would have been totally disrupted. Never before the application of information technologies in the everyday relationship between teachers and students have become so prominent. It is not just about the educational process itself but also about the comprehensive relationship that an educational institution has with its user—the need to digitalize as many points of contact as possible.

## 2. Students as stakeholders in higher education

Although some find it difficult to accept the idea that students are the same as stakeholders in reality that is what they are. In today's market, more competitive than ever before, institutions offer students study programs, inter-faculty exchanges, practices, and similar activities that enrich a student's life. They are customers who enroll in study programs, aimed at getting their diplomas, and donating as alumni members. The longer the satisfaction gained from the processes on both sides, the more durable their relationship will be thus bringing benefits to both sides. One of the ways in which faculties can affect the duration of this positive relationship with students is something that many corporations have already incorporated—managing relationships with stakeholders by means of contemporary information communications technologies [7]. The objective of an institution is to manage those relationships in an efficient and effective way in order to create firm and long-lasting relations.

*DOI: http://dx.doi.org/10.5772/intechopen.105926*

## 2.1 Application of contemporary ICTs in higher education

Managing relationships involves the development of strategies, processes, and technologies with the purpose of strengthening relations of the company with a customer during their lifetime—from marketing and sale all the way to post-sale support [8, 9]. The concept of relationship management (customer relationship management, CRM) is widely accepted in the world of corporations but it is still a relatively new phenomenon in the sector of higher education [9]. Similar to other business systems, by accepting the CRM concept relationship managers in higher educational institutions aspire to improve business performance, promote better management practices, and advance relationships with current and potential students.

From the point of view of a customer, CRM business strategy enables him the interaction with the higher education institution through just one entity which encompasses all the necessary data of the individual in question. In the case of a student, this can be seen through his/her interaction with the employees who take his/her data for enrollment and registration, through financial matters, student's account, etc. From the educational institution's point of view, CRM provides a clear and comprehensive picture of every individual and the activities connected with him/her [10].

In order to pay attention to students and realize contact with them, and in doing to gain their loyalty and make them satisfied, higher educational institutions can nowadays turn to e-service concepts in their functioning. The application of e-service for the management of relationships with the users has become a part of business strategy and is not considered merely a marketing tool. That strategy supports the management in decision-making by using the existing information within the organization and, more importantly, by using information technologies for marketing programs and activities of the organization. The primary objective of managing the relationships with users is to notice and deliver services adjusted to each user himself/herself.

Bejou [7] proposes the adoption of customer relationship management as a way to establish and maintain a relationship between a student and a higher education institution. Customer care is represented in a certain form in most educational institutions today, so there are departments for providing services to students. However, real customer service must contain more than a department or a few individuals. CRM must include a special, service-oriented environment, and everyone within the organization should be engaged in trying to achieve that goal [11]. The fact is that today a strong relationship with customers is the key to success in any business [12–15].

If we make an analogy with the development of computer applications, it can be said that e-service technology connects the frontend of the departments, that is, the ones protruding toward the user (such as sales, marketing, and customer care), and the backend departments such as management, finance, logistics, and human resources services, with user's touchpoints [16]. "Touchpoints" represent channels through which the company has contact with its customers, and they can be the Internet, e-mail, sales, call centers, advertising, physical points of sale, and the like. These "touchpoints" are often under the control of special information systems [17].

Tapp et al. [18] state that the use of direct and marketing databases generated through the CRM system can greatly enhance the potential of a higher education institution to attract new candidates. Adoption of the CRM strategy leads to gaining insight into various relevant data on students that may be important, that is, on the basis of which a basis can be formed later for providing a service that will correspond with their expectations, build loyalty on behalf of students, and all that taken together will affect their retention within the institution. Potential customers are likely to hear positive experiences about the services provided by other users. In his study, Hill [19] reveals that there is a correlation between students' expectations regarding services and their satisfaction. The same author also claims that higher education institutions should detect the expectations of their future students from the entry point to the institution until the moment of successful completion of the study program [20].

Very often, the choice of one higher education institution over another one with a similar level of quality may depend on the way the institution communicates with its (potential) students. The modern age is such that most students want established, relevant, and complete communication with the staff of the educational institution. The easiest way for higher education institutions to establish harmonious relationships with their stakeholders is by using an e-service system based on the application of modern ICT. Such a system provides valuable insight into information about students, creating a possibility to build a stronger and more personalized connection with former (alumni), current, and future students. In other words, the mentioned system applied in higher educational institutions enables the institution to constantly update information about stakeholders, facilitating and monitoring every interaction that the institution has with them through various platforms, regardless of where they are located. The e-service system can be designed so that it helps employees by simplifying their work process, and ultimately, improves their relationships with students. The result of all this is an increased interest in enrolling in the institution, increased student retention rates, better communication with students, and a happier and more satisfied team [21].

e-Service system can enable sending automated messages that will remind students of the future exam terms. Simple things such as reminders can help students to better organize their time, prepare more efficiently for exam obligations, and can have a positive effect on their welfare and the results to be achieved.

Collecting means and donations through the creation of long-lasting relationships with the Alumni club members is very much present at many universities. Diversification of higher educational institution revenue apart from traditional students' tuition and public financing has become very important for universities. Nowadays many institutions are faced with the reduction of state financing which leads to financial pressure and the request to reduce their expenses. For that very reason, many higher educational institutions in other countries pay great attention to the relationships with former students (alumni). A comprehensive e-service system centralizes information on donors and Alumni club members and uses them to send automated notifications at certain periods during the year in order to inform all interested parties about the success of the program and the students in the particular institution. The incorporated analytical system examines which events and types of communication that year contributed the most.

## 2.2 The student life cycle

The focus of marketing today is not so much on attracting new customers as it is directed at the customer's satisfaction concept by offering users what they want, taking care of the relationship with them—the relationship which is not only commercial, unidirectional, and impersonal. The consumerist concept in higher education should be in the context of relationship marketing and not transactional marketing. Although students can be considered users, the nature of educational services, especially the relationship duration, suggests the development of the relationship rather than the approach of "pay and buy" [22, 23]. Adoption of CRM on behalf of educational institutions implies in itself the use of appropriate instruments which will help in collecting information about students' requirements regarding education, and adjust services to measure their characteristics and requirements, all with the aim to enhance the educational process and to obtain better results which will reduce the number of students who drop out of university or abandon further education [20, 23–26].

One of the features that separates higher educational institutions from business systems in other branches, and which makes the application of contemporary technologies aimed at CRM ideal for higher education, is the dedication and long-term relationship to which students agree when they enroll in the study program [27]. Other industries do not have that "luxury" to affect the life cycle of a client, which lasts several years. On the other hand, it can be good practice for higher educational institutions to consider their students as users since such an approach enables competitive advantage and enhances the ability of an institution to attract, retain, and offer appropriate service to its students/users.

From the relationship management point of view, the concept of a client's life cycle can be transported to a student's life cycle which is made up of the phases through which a student passes while considering and using the services of an educational institution. The phases in the life cycle of a student are as follows:

Possible → potential → candidate → accepted → enrolled → former student (alumni)

- Possible: any student who, according to the Law, can be a candidate for enrollment in the university.
- Potential: a student who is currently in the phase of gathering information and forming an opinion about a higher education institution.
- Candidate: a student who has made a decision to apply for enrollment in an institution.
- Accepted: the student is accepted when the institution has made a decision to accept the student.
- Enrolled: this is the stage when a student officially becomes a student, that is, part of a higher education institution.
- Former student (alumni): a student who has successfully completed the study program, and if he is satisfied with his academic experience, he will develop a long-term loyalty relationship with his institution.

From the point of view of relationship management activities, student enrollment activities related to the conversion of a possible into an accepted student constitute a marketing component. The conversion of accepted into enrolled is a component of sales, while the continuous enrollment and the presence of alumni is a component of customer support and retention. However, the student life cycle involves several complex interactions, especially during the retention phase because the academic program, counseling, and student life play a key role in student retention.

According to the results of a study conducted by Ogunnaike et al. [28], it was found that a student's desire to recommend the institution of which he was a part, or still is, increases if the student life cycle is well managed by the institution. It was also noticed that a strong connection of the educational institution with parents leads to the situation that the student recommends his/her institution to others. Managing a good relationship with the parents of students also increases the desire of students to continue their postgraduate studies at the same institution.

The research conducted by Hilbert et al. [5] expresses a slightly different approach. It states that the student life cycle consists of three phases: entry, presence, and departure. In the entry phase, students are considered as potential clients, the present phase is made up of existing clients, and in the departure phase, they are already lost. However, the departure of students from the university/college does not mean that their communication with the institution is interrupted. At that point, universities strive to keep relationships with their students using some strategic methods [15].

## 3. Comprehensive e-service system

The comprehensive model of the e-service system in the complex business ecosystem of higher education is shown in **Figure 1**. The model takes care of managing relations with a large portion of stakeholders of the higher education institution, among which students and employees are the most demanding in terms of the number and scope of electronic services. In addition to relations with stakeholders, the model represents support for the proper and efficient conduct of business functions: marketing, education, science, human resource management, finance and accounting, and procurement.

The model consists of numerous elements and is based on cloud computing. The central part of the model is the infrastructure as a service (IaaS). A public cloud consisting of several virtual private servers (VPS) was chosen as the appropriate form of cloud computing. Each of the servers has a dedicated purpose and they have been separated with the intention, primarily because of the better optimization, higher security offered by this approach, and other practical reasons.

The comprehensive e-service system is based on open-source technologies. The system was developed by using Python programming language in combination with Django as a web framework. MySQL was chosen as a relational database management system.

As shown in **Figure 1**, the system consists of several modules. Some of the modules are actually specific Django applications, which have been integrated together into the main project. This has been done respecting one of the principles of Django design—DRY (Do not Repeat Yourself). The important part of the e-service system's architecture is web services which are used to improve the performance of the system by utilizing Django's cache framework.

Which are the benefits offered by implementing a comprehensive e-service system in higher education in the field of student relationship management? Using adequate communication channels, potential students can obtain appropriate and timely information that is the focus of their interest. When using the online learning platform, candidates are in a position to attend classes without physical presence and prepare for taking the entrance exam for enrollment in the institution. The process of applying for admission to the faculty can be completed much faster and easier with the help of online tools on the portal of the institution. Processing the results of the entrance exam with ICT support drastically shortens the time required for the formation of preliminary and final ranking lists, which shortens the period of stress exposure for

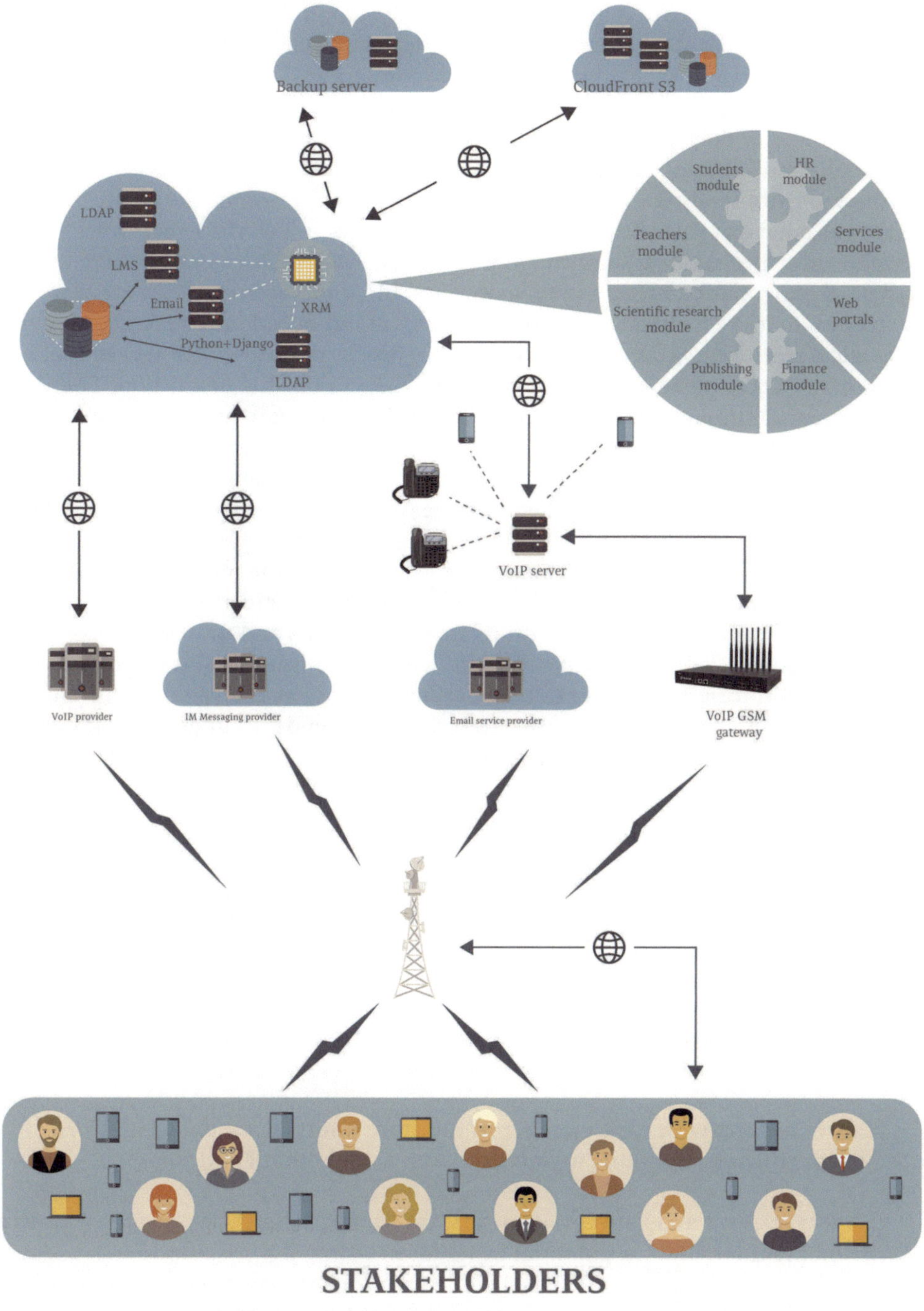


**Figure 1.**
*Infrastructure of the comprehensive e-service system.*

future students. By using the already existing data on candidates in the system, and for the purpose of realizing the enrollment of candidates, there is no data redundancy, and the whole process of enrollment of candidates is accelerated.

Potential students, who decide to enroll in the educational institution, extend their life cycles and become current students of a higher education institution, where their previously existing data are taken over. In this way, a path is established for nurturing the relationship with the student during his entire life cycle from the moment he becomes a potential candidate until the act of graduating. The whole process of studying is then further facilitated for current students in several aspects—by using students' modules they are able to apply for and cancel exams, follow all notifications, monitor all their teaching and pre-examination obligations, and have access to all information from their student file and use the platform for online learning. These students also have at their disposal timely notifications and all the necessary information relevant to their education through web portals, student services, social networks, email marketing platforms, and mobile services. More importantly, they are given the opportunity to leave feedback on various issues, fill out questionnaires regarding the pedagogical work of teachers and associates, the work of professional services and management, and in doing so greatly influence the work of the institution. There are several channels through which one can contact the institution and get answers to their questions in a short time. This way of working increases the retention rate, raises the reputation of the institution to a higher level, and at the same time reduces the costs of attracting new students, which, on the other hand, protects the income of the institution coming from tuition fees.

Upon graduating from the university, the students become members of the Alumni community thus completing their life cycle at the university. It is important for the institution to stay in touch with its former students and to work on maintaining good relations. It is in this field that the Alumni Portal is important, which helps in informing and organizing various types of events, gatherings, and professional training that are necessary for graduates, sends reminders about events, monitors events, and sends accompanying information.

The comprehensive e-service system can help an institution in one of the following ways:

- nurtures the relationship with the student throughout his/her entire life cycle—from the moment he/she becomes a potential candidate to the act of graduation;

- maintains complete student profiles—centralizes all contact information and helps to understand and analyze potential candidates, at every point of contact;

- realizes contact with each member of the community: potential candidates, current students, alumni, employees, parents, and other contacts;

- delivers relevant and appropriate offers, recommendations, advice, and actions at the moment optimal for potential candidates;

- automates communication, freeing up time for other activities;

- increases the retention rate by improving reputation, reduces attraction costs, and protects the income of the institution coming from tuition fees;

- achieves a more efficient workflow, enabling employees to complete their tasks faster and easier. Reduces paper usage and the need to use a variety of storage solutions;

- enables access, addition, and data modification 24/7, either in the office or on the road, with the use of mobile devices;
- provides students with the fastest possible form of information, helps them to manage their responsibilities in a simple and clear manner, improves communication with the staff of the higher education institution, and provides an easy way to update data;
- invites prospective students, current students, and alumni students to events, facilitates the event management process, sends event reminders, monitors events, and sends accompanying notifications;
- measures the return on investment, provides insight into marketing activities, promotion channels, and determines what exactly brings revenue, and how.

The services covered in the work process by applying the comprehensive e-service model are as follows:

- providing service information (notices, news, current events, and other important information on relevant activities);
- management of student files (monitoring and recording of complete student files);
- administration of the study program (support for organizing and conducting classes, organizing and monitoring exam terms);
- monitoring, planning, and keeping records of teaching staff, their engagement, and workload;
- generating the necessary documents, certificates, and other reports for students;
- administration of employees (their personal identification data, contracts, salaries, records of attendance at work);
- online learning environment;
- accounting activities;
- monitoring and recording scientific research work;
- financial statements;
- preparation of various statistical reports on enrollment, student achievement, and other reports necessary for state bodies, the University, or the governing bodies of the college;
- ALUMNI portal for relationships with former graduates;

- different forms and reports necessary for self-evaluation and accreditation of institutions and study programs;
- monitoring, procurement, and records of inventory, materials, and fixed assets.

## 4. e-Services examples overview

This section presents the functionalities of the comprehensive e-services system through the user interface and explanations of the logic behind it. As an integrated system, it can be logically divided into three parts: e-teacher module, e-student module, and supporting departments module.

### 4.1 e-Teacher module

This module enables teaching staff to manage a wide spread of activities:

- informs teaching staff about ongoing exams and details (**Figure 2**);
- gives an overview of students who registered for an exam within the given term (**Figure 3**);

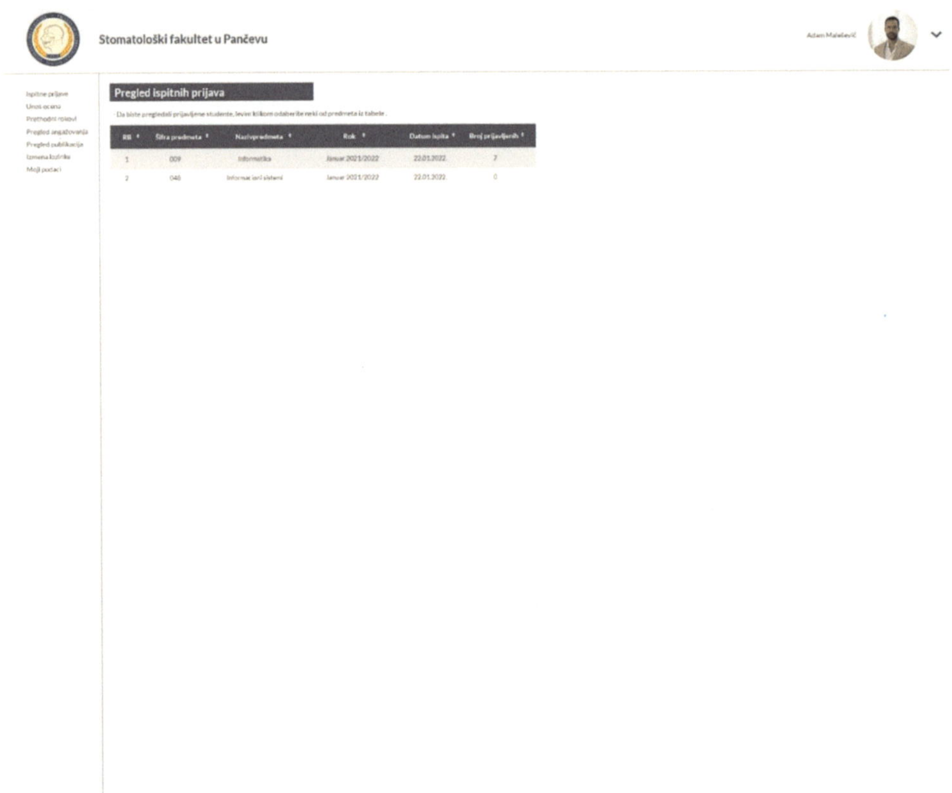


**Figure 2.**
*Overview of ongoing exams.*

**Figure 3.**
*Overview of students who registered for the exam within the given term.*

- gives an overview of subjects for which grades were not supplied (**Figure 4**);
- allows teaching staff to add students' grades for the appropriate exam period and the appropriate subject (**Figure 5**);
- archives previously held exams for the appropriate subjects (**Figure 6**);
- shows the records of those students who have registered for the relevant exam within the appropriate term (**Figure 7**);
- shows an overview of teaching staff engagement across subjects in the study program (**Figure 8**);
- provides an overview of published scientific results for each employee within the teaching staff (**Figure 9**).

### *4.1.1 Ongoing exams*

In the Ongoing exams section, teachers and associates have the opportunity to review registered students, within the given term, for the subjects they are engaged in (**Figure 2**).

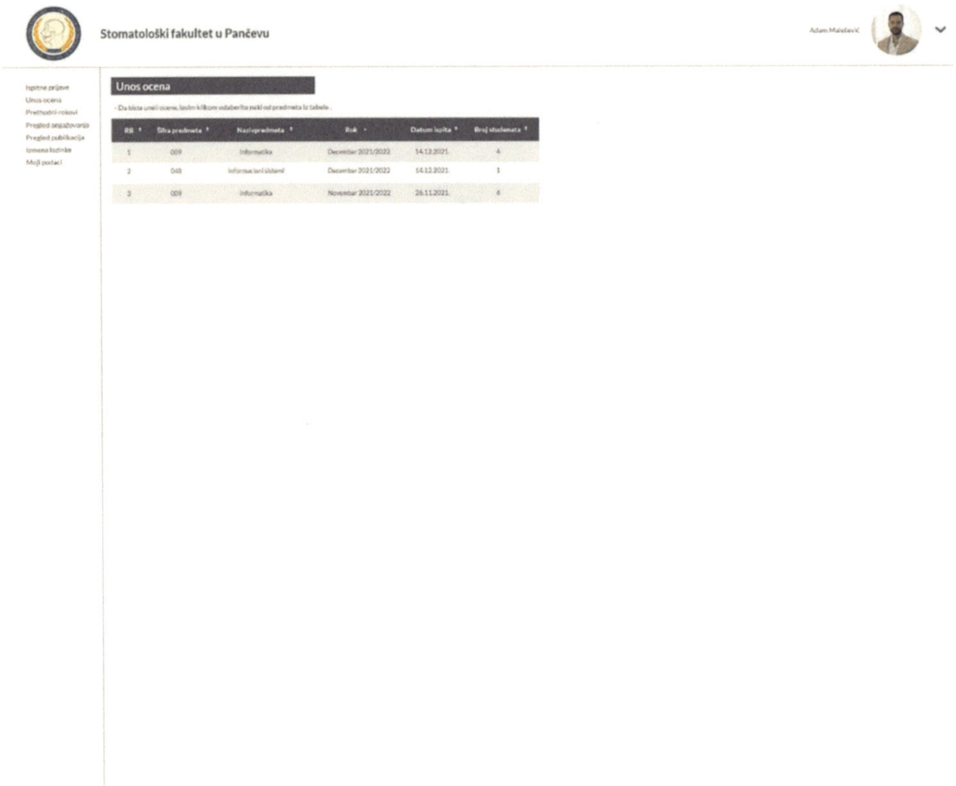


**Figure 4.**
*Overview of subjects for which grades were not provided.*

Students registered for the selected subject can be displayed by selecting one of the subjects from the table (**Figure 3**).

### *4.1.2 Grades entry for previous exams*

In the Grades entry for previous exams section, grades are added by selecting the appropriate subject from the table (**Figure 4**). The list shows all subjects for which grades in previous exam terms have not been added.

If the teaching staff wants to leave the entry for later, the teacher can temporarily save grades that have been added and later continue with the entry and confirmation of those grades, or they can do so immediately by clicking the *Add grades* button (**Figure 5**).

The *Previous exam terms* page lists all exam terms that the teacher or associate is currently engaged in. The teaching staff user is presented with the date of the exam and the number of students who registered for that exam (**Figure 6**).

Clicking on a certain record in the table gives a more detailed presentation of the respective exam term, which includes a list of students who have applied for the exam within the specified term, grades, and the date of the exam (**Figure 7**).

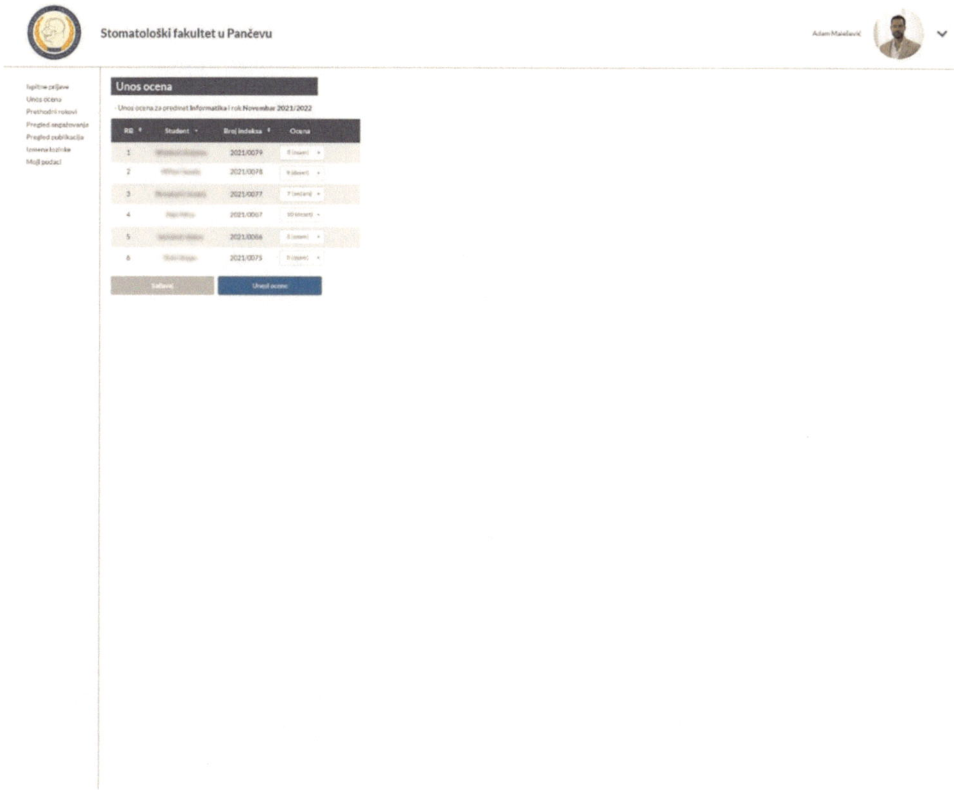


**Figure 5.**
*Adding students' grades for the appropriate subject and exam period.*

### *4.1.3 Subject engagement*

In the *Subject engagement* section, the teacher has the opportunity to see the list of subjects, teaching format per subject (lectures or practices) as well as the number of teaching hours (classes) in which they are engaged (**Figure 8**).

### *4.1.4 Scientific research activities*

The *Scientific research activities* section provides an insight into the scientific publications of the teaching staff, that have been published so far (**Figure 9**).

## **4.2 e-Student module**

This module deals with relevant student data, viewed from two perspectives:

1. Students' data managed by higher education institution.

2. Students' data accessed through students user accounts.

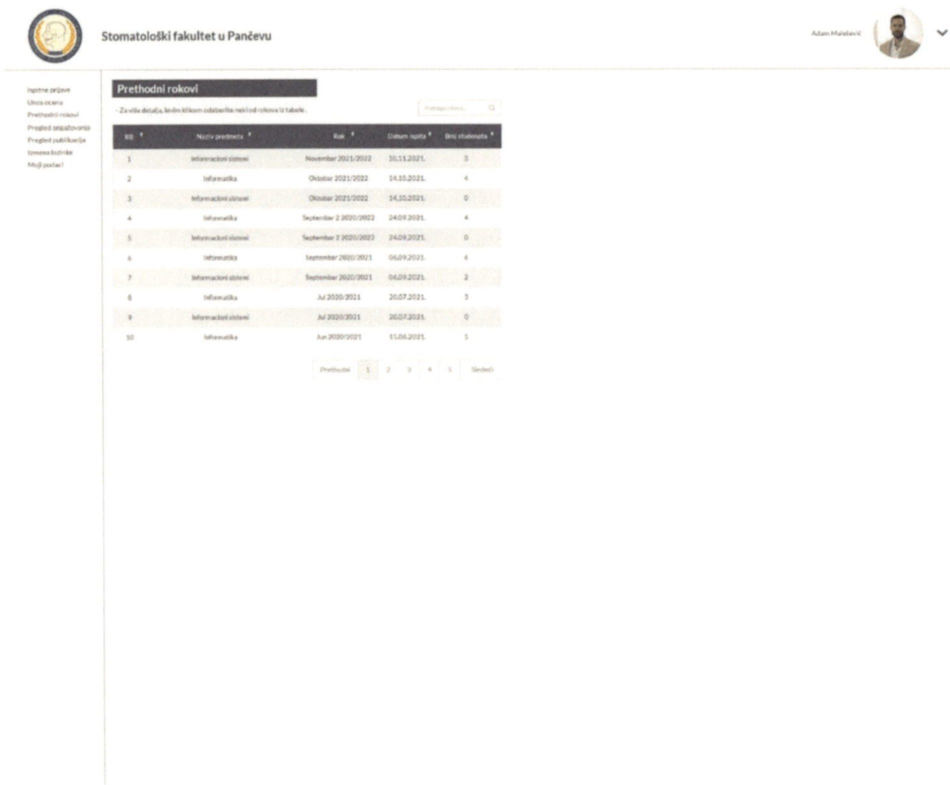


**Figure 6.**
*Archive of the previously held exams for the appropriate subjects.*

### *4.2.1 Students' data search*

Students' data are accessed through the *Student Search* section (**Figure 1**), whereby adding Surnames, Names, or Students' Index Numbers, all students whose data match the ones added are displayed (**Figure 10**).

By selecting one of the students from the table, the Student file and more detailed data are accessed (**Figure 11**).

### *4.2.2 Basic student data*

The section assigned to Students contains personal identification data of students, data on schooling or enrollment in the following years of study in the study program, an overview of all details related to exams taken by students and not passed so far, as well as data on the final paper, diploma supplement, and diploma export opportunities (**Figure 12**).

### *4.2.3 Student's exam lists*

In the section with Exams, all the data on passed and failed exams are shown (**Figure 13**). These data are added on the other page, that is, in the module for teachers, who are obliged to add grades for each of the students after the exam period.

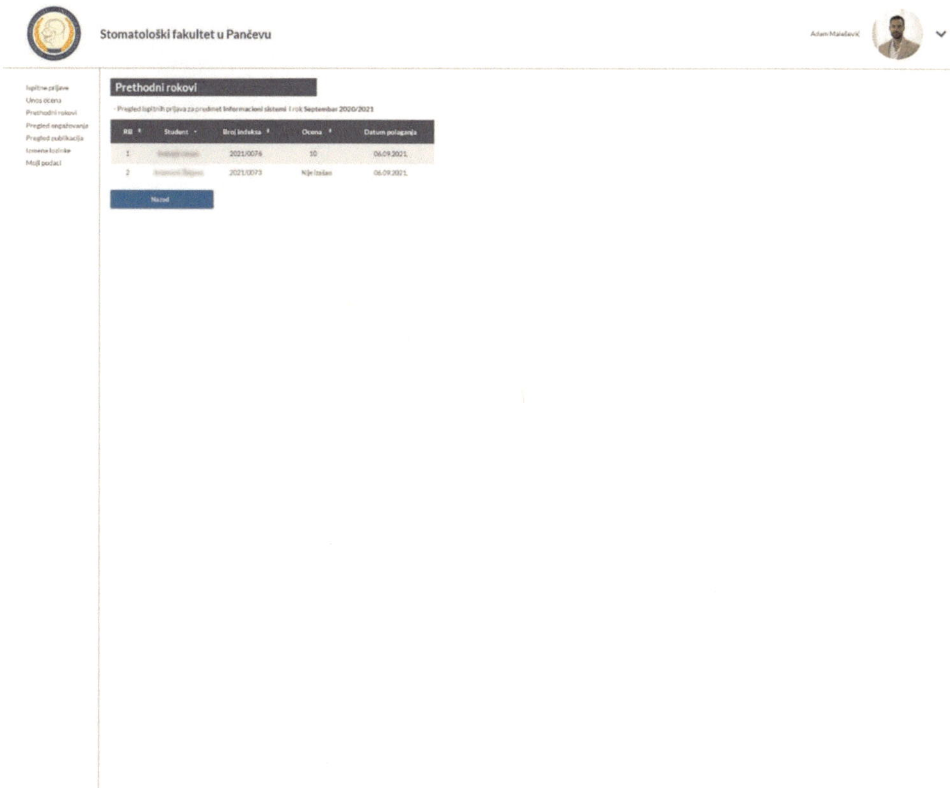


**Figure 7.**
*Students details for those who have registered for the exam within the appropriate term.*

By clicking on the appropriate row in the table, a new page opens in which it is possible to change the data on the held exam.

The second Tab with failed exams shows data on the subjects left for the student to pass in order to complete his/her education (**Figure 14**).

#### *4.2.4 Student's ongoing education*

The section *Ongoing education* shows the movement of students through the study program and years of study with details of the date of enrollment in the following or the same year of study, and the number of ECTS credits earned for each of the school years (**Figure 15**). By clicking on one of the records in the table, it is possible to change the existing or add a new record.

In the section on the Final examination, after the student has successfully defended it, data on the topic of the final paper, the date of the defense, the grade as well as the members of the commission are added (**Figure 16**).

#### *4.2.5 Previous exams terms*

The *Record of exam terms* gives an overview of all exam terms held so far by school years and months with data that include the beginning of the exam application period

**Figure 8.**
*Shows an overview of employee engagement in the relevant study program.*

for students, the end of the exam application period as well as the beginning of the exam term itself and the end of the term (**Figure 17**).

By clicking on one of the entries in the table, it is possible to change the existing or add a new exam term.

### *4.2.6 Students accounts*

Students can access their files using their user accounts, which offer an overview of all relevant data concerning the students. Among the information offered to the students are notices intended for students (**Figure 18**), data on their previous education, a list of passed exams, the ability to apply for and cancel exams, and an overview of their personal identification data.

In the section Study year, students have an insight into their previous student education, that is, enrollment by school years, and the number of ECTS credits earned (**Figure 19**).

In the section *Passed exams*, students have an insight into all previously passed exams, which includes an overview of the grade obtained, the exam term in which the exam was passed, the date of taking it, and the data on the subject teacher with whom the exam was passed (**Figure 20**).

At the same time, the student has an insight into his current average grade and the current number of ECTS credits earned in the given study program.

**Figure 9.**
*An overview of the employee's scientific results published so far.*

In the *Exam application* section (**Figure 21**), students can select the exams for which they want to apply for the given exam term. Similarly, after applying for an exam, if they change their mind, they can cancel it, no later than 24 hours prior to the start of the exam (**Figure 22**).

The *My Data* section provides an insight into the student's basic data, for which the student may request a change through the student service if he/she deems them to be incorrect (**Figure 23**).

### 4.3 Supporting departments module

This module represents the core of the e-services system. *Supporting departments module* is intended for all other business departments, supporting their processes (with the exception of teaching process that is covered with previous modules). It allows employees, administrators, managers, and decision-makers to gather the information they need.

There are several functions provided by this module:

- Human resources data management (employees' contracts, specializations, sick leaves, and similar data management);

- Teaching staff engagement overview;

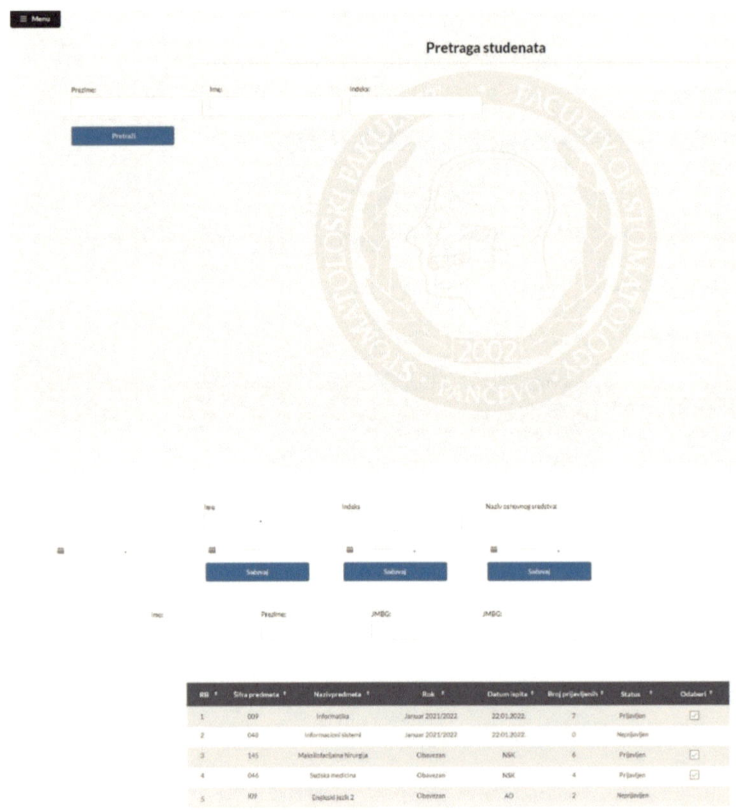


**Figure 10.**
*Search form for students by several different parameters.*

- Financial data and analytics;
- Scientific research results management;
- Institution's publishing activity overview;
- Institution's assets management.

### *4.3.1 Employees master data*

This section shows the records on master data of employees (**Figures 24–26**) and the records of inactive or former employees (**Figure 27**). Records contain data for full-time employees as well as for employees with other types of contracts. The functions available here are:

- search by any of the parameters or employees data,
- data sort for each of the columns,

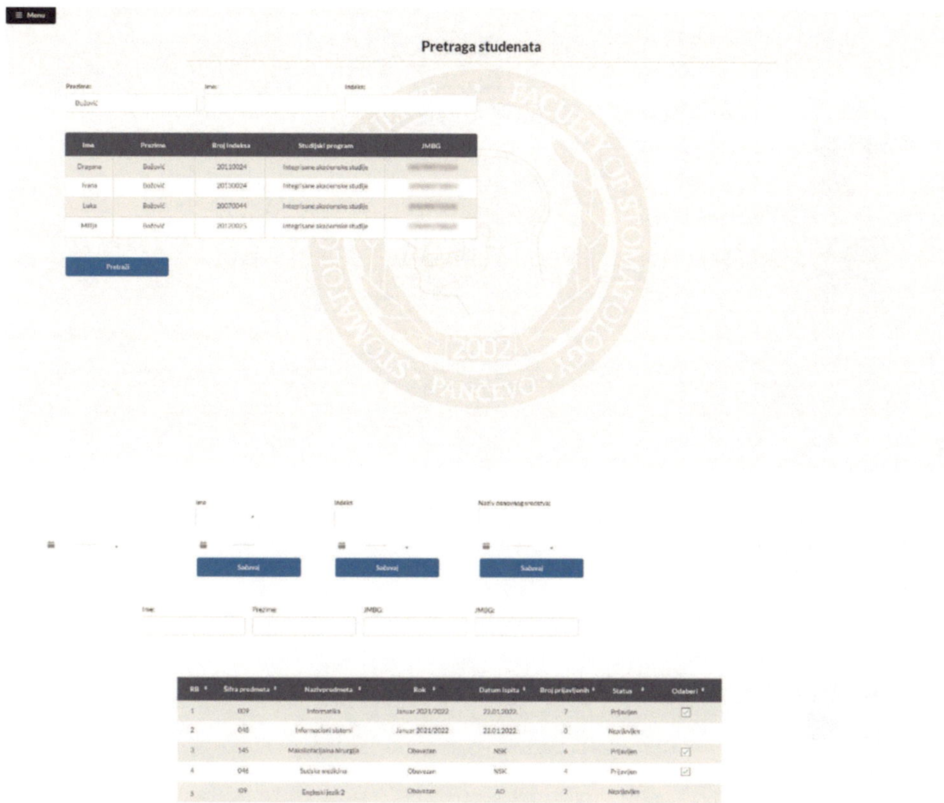


**Figure 11.**
*Student search results.*

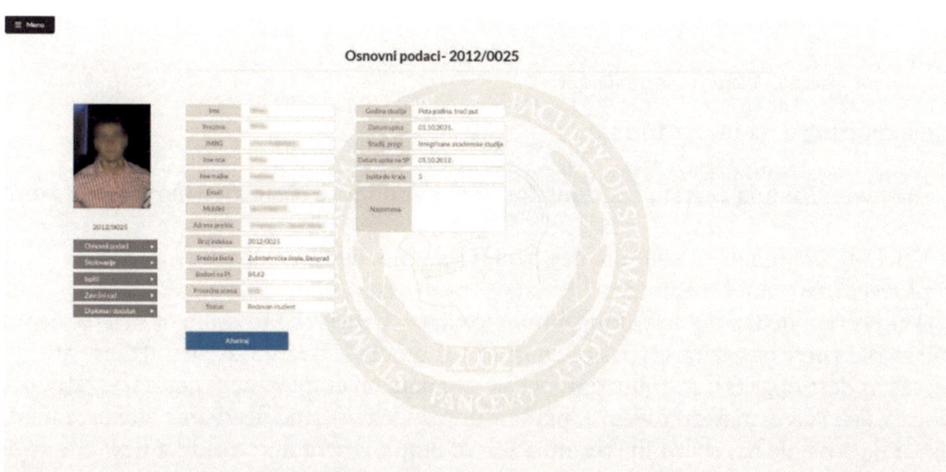


**Figure 12.**
*Page with basic student data and the possibility of updating them.*

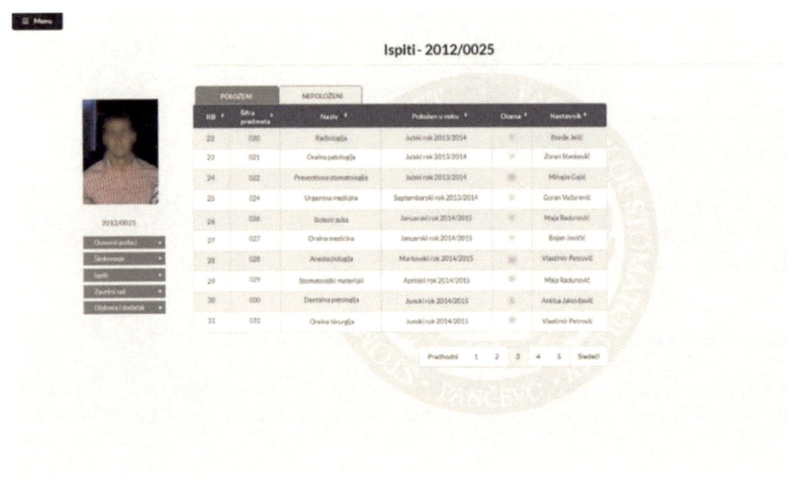


**Figure 13.**
*Report with the list of passed exams.*

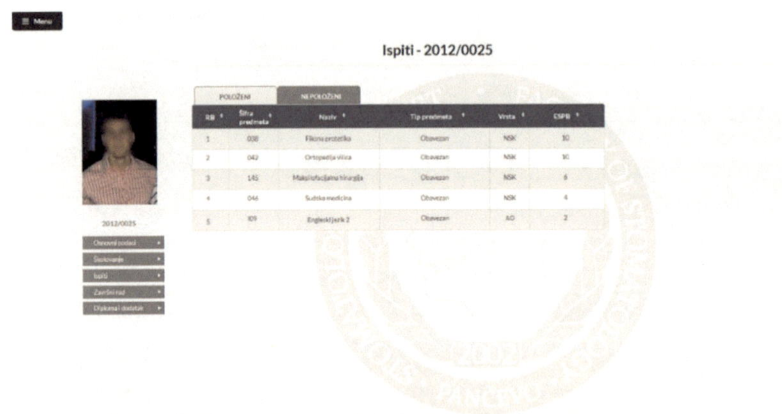


**Figure 14.**
*Report on the second Tab with a list of failed exams.*

- exporting data in .xls format,
- showing/hiding certain columns for easier and more clear viewing if necessary.

Clicking on one of the employees from the table displays a page from which employees' data can be edited.

The section dedicated to editing employee data enables the revision of master data as well as the entry of various types of contracts and details related to them (these are treated as data objects). Administrators can add data on employment contracts, absences (due to sick leave, maternity leave, paid or unpaid leave), and academic advancement. Also, it is possible to record the termination of employment and to add a new employee with relevant data. In that way, the basis for the orderly and accurate keeping of records on teaching and non-teaching staff has been established, which will be further used for planning human resources policy and other services that use the given data.

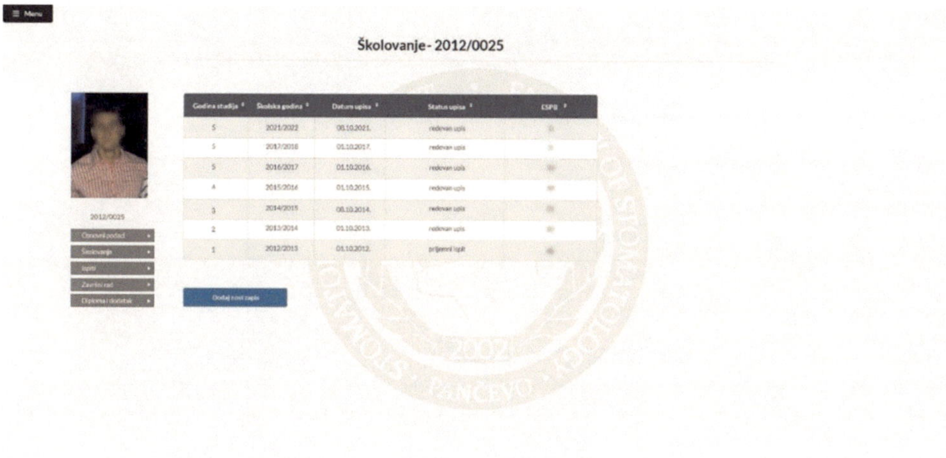


**Figure 15.**
*Overview of the student's education so far - managed by higher education institution.*

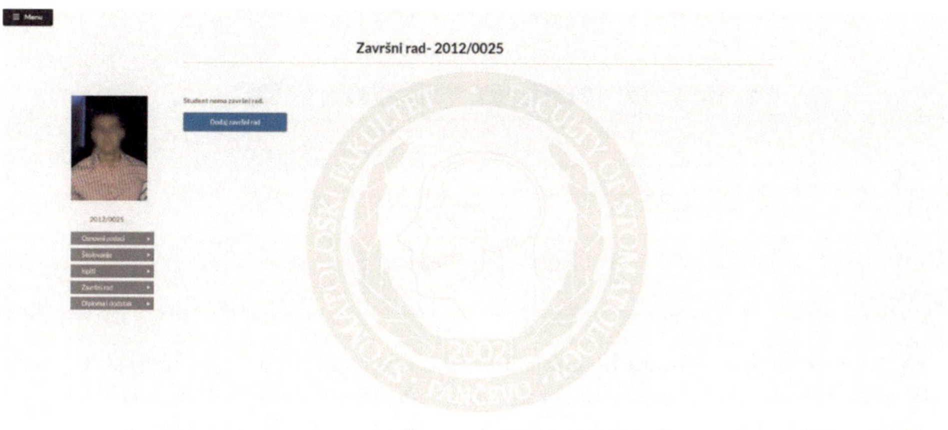


**Figure 16.**
*Page with student's final examination data.*

A *Former employee* section archives data on employees whose employment contract was terminated for a certain reason (retirement, termination of employment, and similar) to systematically store that data on all employees who were part of the institution at some point. In addition, if there is an intention to rehire employees whose contract was terminated earlier, it can be done easily by clicking on the *Activate* button, so that there is no redundancy and reentry of the same data.

### *4.3.2 Teaching staff engagement*

The *Teaching staff engagement* section shows the engagement of teaching staff in study programs, for each of the subjects and for each type of teaching—lectures and practices (**Figure 28**).

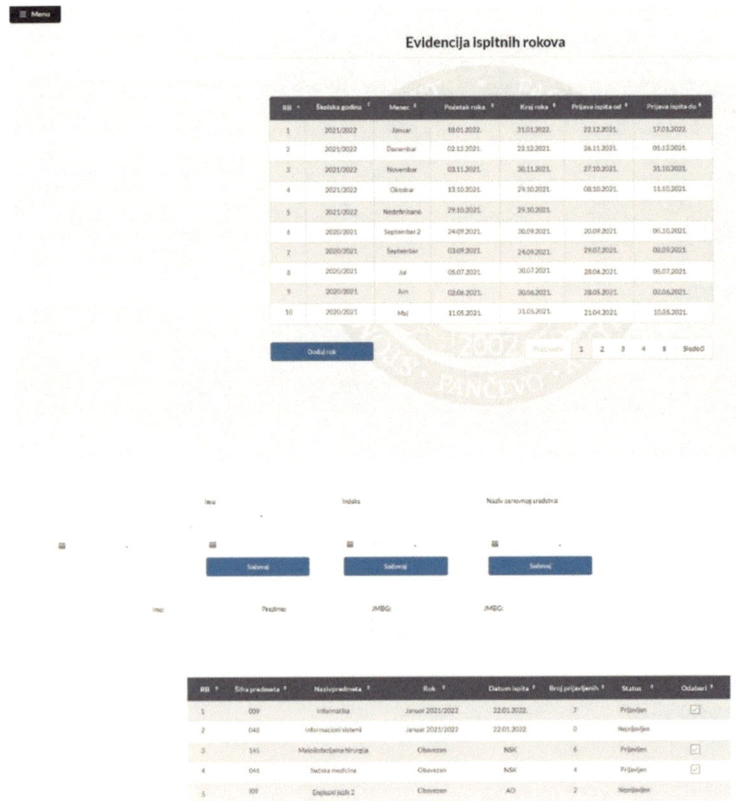


**Figure 17.**
*Archive of previously held exam terms.*

In addition to engagement by subjects and employees, it is possible to summarize engagement in the entire study program, with additional data such as academic promotion dates, period of retirement approaches, and similar (**Figure 29**).

### *4.3.3 Financial data*

The *Financial data* section contains an overview of financial data (**Figure 30**), for instance, changes in the compensation of employees data (**Figure 31**) and records of previous changes in compensations. This module is fully compliant with the accounting norms and relevant legal regulations. This part of the system also has a role in planning and managing the institution's finances.

### *4.3.4 Scientific research results*

The *Scientific research results* part of the system enables administrators to fully manage scientific publications results and prepare data for future use. The results can be easily searched and sorted by various inputs—authors, categories, years, and journals. Published scientific result records are shown in **Figure 32**.

Prior to adding the scientific publication record to the system, it is necessary to ensure that a certain scientific journal or conference against which this record can be

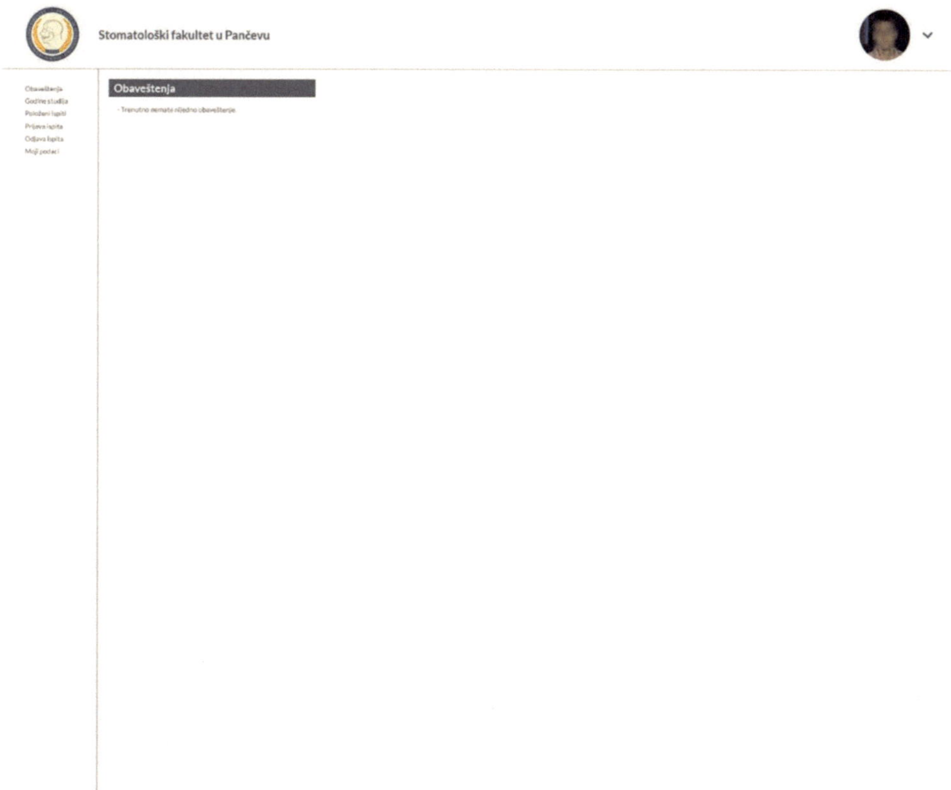


**Figure 18.**
*Notices for students created in the system.*

added is already in the system. To make it easier for users to add scientific publications results, asynchronous JavaScript calls have been implemented (**Figure 33**). By starting data entry, results are obtained in real-time, so users can have an insight into previous entries that may be related to a given record. In this way, feedback is received immediately on whether it is necessary to add publication data only or whether a journal or a conference record must be added previously.

If a given journal does not already exist in the database for a given publication, it must be added first by selecting the *Add new journal* option. A journal can be added easily by filling in the appropriate fields in the pop-up window and clicking the *Add Journal* button. After adding, the user receives a message on the successful (or unsuccessful) database transaction. Analogously, it is possible to add a conference meeting.

The next important feature of this section is the ability to export publication records in .docx format, based on several different parameters (**Figures 34** and **35**). The scientific research activity is an important aspect of higher education institutions' work, and as such serves as a basis for the accreditation of scientific research activity. Given the volume of work on collecting documentation for application in the mentioned process, if the system is kept up to date, this section can be of significant help. It is possible to export all publications for a certain period amd filter publications that originate from doctoral dissertations or those from scientific research projects. Data can be exported in accordance with different needs, so publications can be sorted by authors, by relevant categorization, or by publishing date.

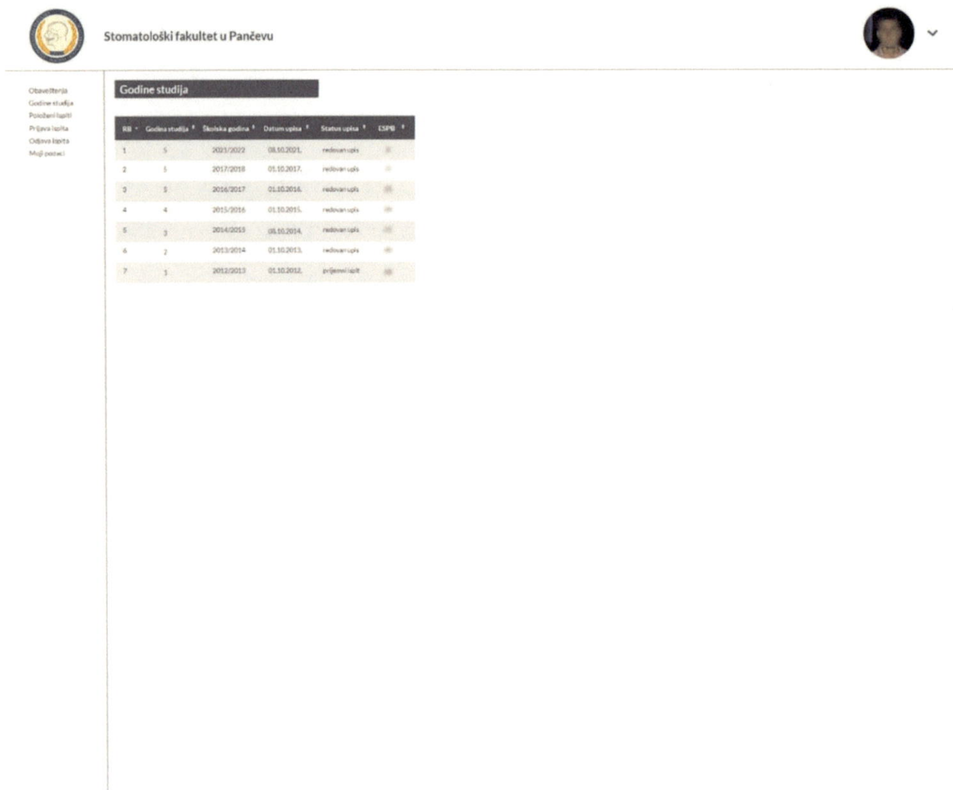


**Figure 19.**
*Overview of the student's education so far - accessed by student.*

The appearance of the obtained data exported in .docx format is shown in **Figure 35**.

### *4.3.5 Publishing activity*

In the *Publishing activity* section, a summary overview of the textbooks can be found, as well as an overview of the status of the selected textbook, and, an option to add a new textbook is also available.

The textbook overview contains basic information about each textbook issued by the institution—its name, code, and value generated by its distribution (**Figure 36**). Selecting one of the entries from the table proceeds to the status display for the corresponding textbook.

### *4.3.6 Institution's services*

The *Institution's services* section contains all the information on services provided to external clients. It enables monitoring of the service activities of the educational institution departments. The following reports can be generated on different levels:

- Service-level overview;
- Department-level overview;

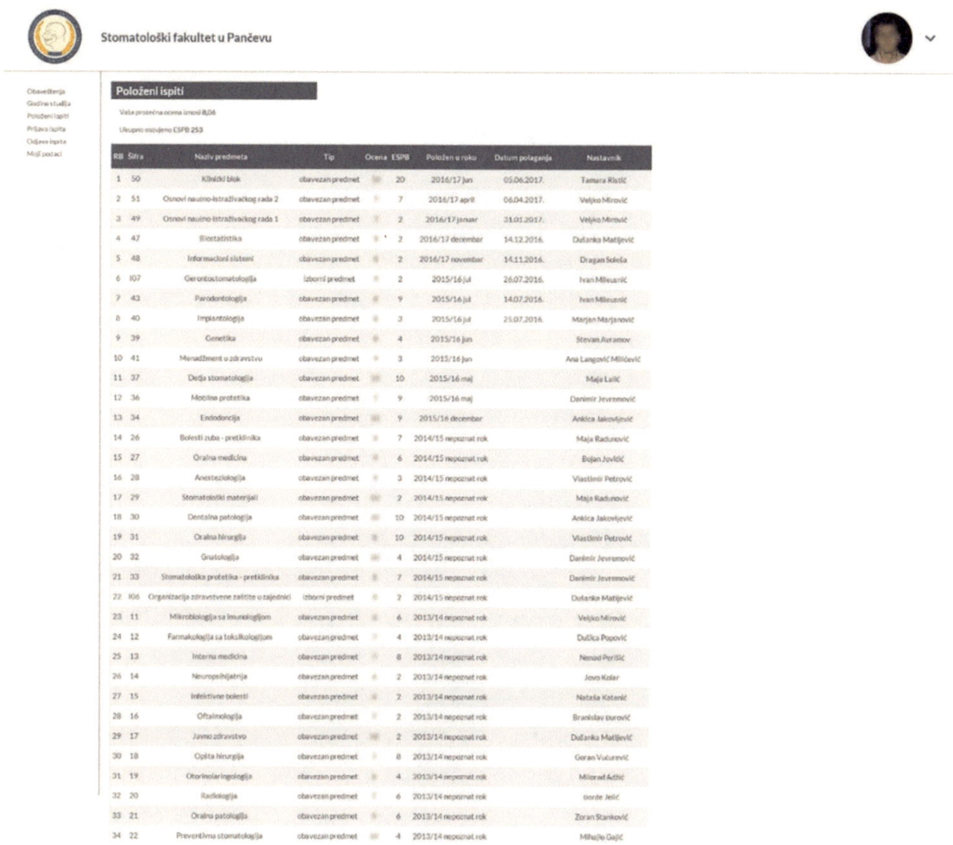


**Figure 20.**
*Overview of the exams passed so far.*

- Institution-level overview, grouped by departments;
- Comprehensive review at the institution-level.

The system records all services provided by the institution (**Figure 37**). By selecting a specific service the system displays detailed information: the number of services performed by months, service revenue, and comparison with the specific period (in terms of frequency and revenue) (**Figure 38**).

Given that each service belongs to one of the institution's department, all of them can thus be grouped and presented in the report on *Services at the department level* (**Figure 38**). By selecting one of the departments, we move on to the next page, which includes services performed at the level of a given department in the current period. This page shows all the services performed in the current period, for the selected department. The data can be compared with the previous period, and there is a review of the scope of work of the department since the recording started.

The last type of report is a summary of the services provided at the level of the institution (**Figure 39**). All services provided since the beginning of monitoring are recorded here, so the overview is very practical for comparing different periods. Also, the numbers of performed services and clients are shown tabularly and graphically, across the time.

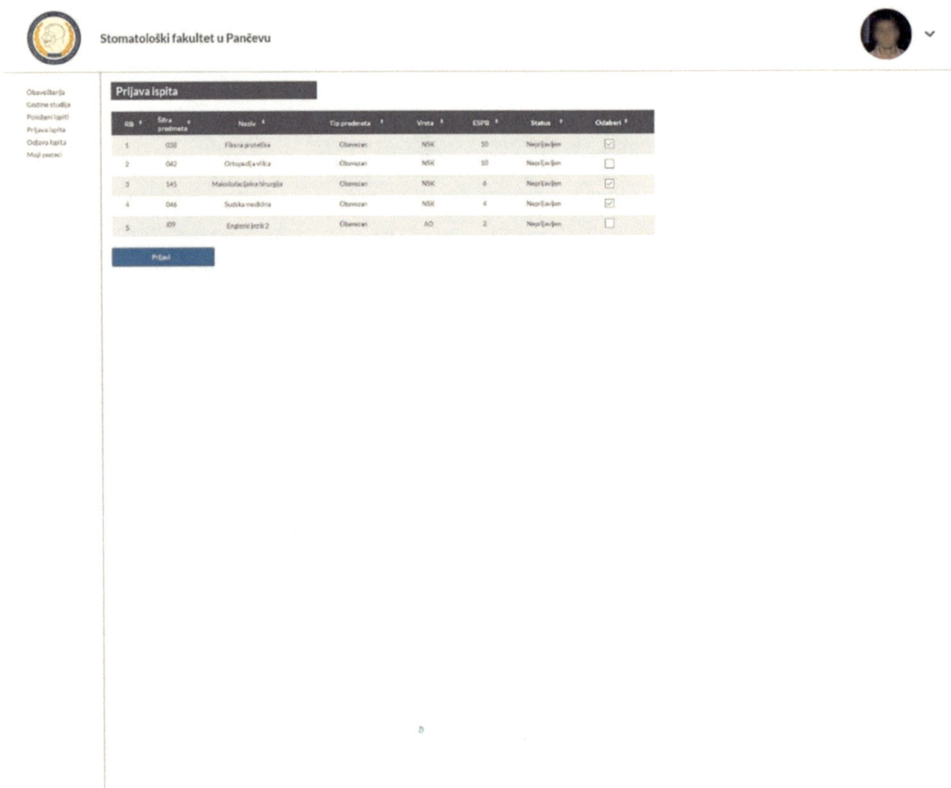


**Figure 21.**
*Exam application section.*

### *4.3.7 Assets management*

Keeping records of the institution's assets and inventory is possible through the provided section in the system that offers data review, entry of new data, and export of lists of assets and inventory (**Figure 40**).

Data on the equipment of the institution can be sorted by columns and quickly filtered through the search. Also, there is an option to export lists of assets and inventory, that is important for classifying assets in an appropriate manner, thus making it easier for those responsible to keep records.

## 4.4 Automated communication system

By integrating a comprehensive e-service model with the REST program interface, one of the instant messaging applications, a system for direct communication with students has been established, which immediately provides the necessary transactional notifications, service information, and reports to the most important stakeholder group of the higher educational institution.

One of the most commonly used instant messaging applications on a global scale today (Rakuten Viber) allows programmers to develop their own bots whose purpose is direct communication 1-1 with users who are subscribed for this type of service.

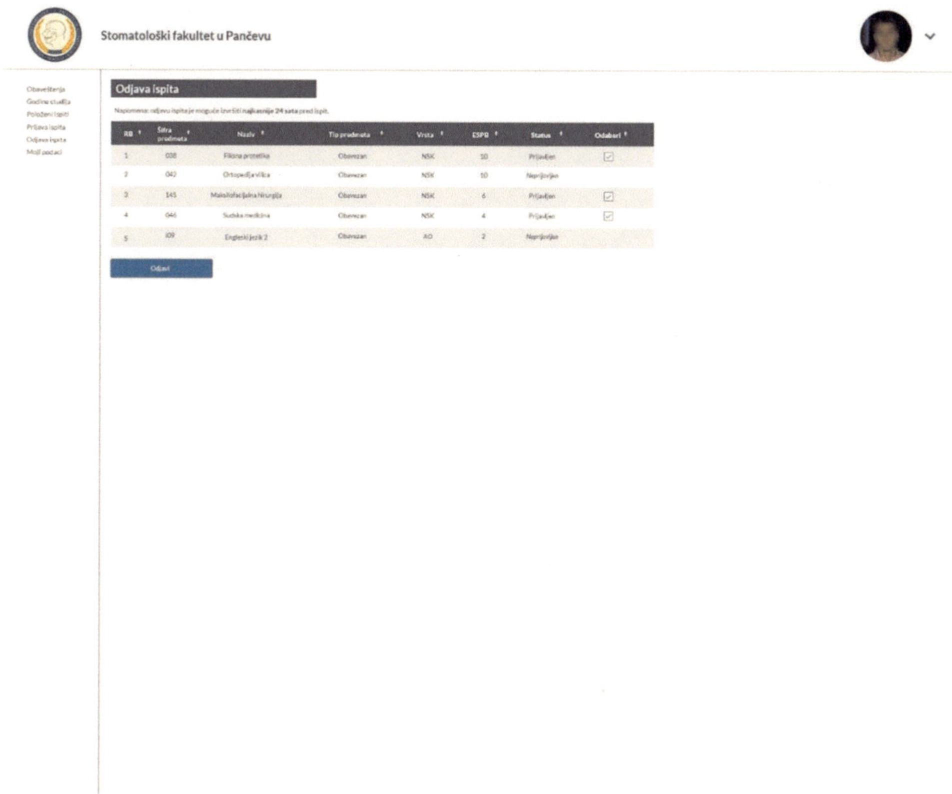


**Figure 22.**
*Section for canceling previously applied exams.*

The following elements are required for the implementation of the Viber REST API [29]:

1. Active account on the platform that supports bots.

2. Active bot that has to be created beforehand.

3. Token for account authentication used for account validation. This token must be included in each individual API request sent to the service.

4. One-time Webhook request during initial setup that defines the types of responses that the bot wants to receive from users.

Viber Chatbots enable free communication with users, but only with those who first contacted the business account, that is, who subscribed to the service. Also, API does not enable downloading information about the user's phone number, but each of the users has its own identification code (User ID).

The flow of message exchange between a Viber business account and regular Viber users is shown in **Figure 41**.

Once all the prerequisites have been met, a one-time Webhook registration for the public account is required. A webhook is a type of application programming interface

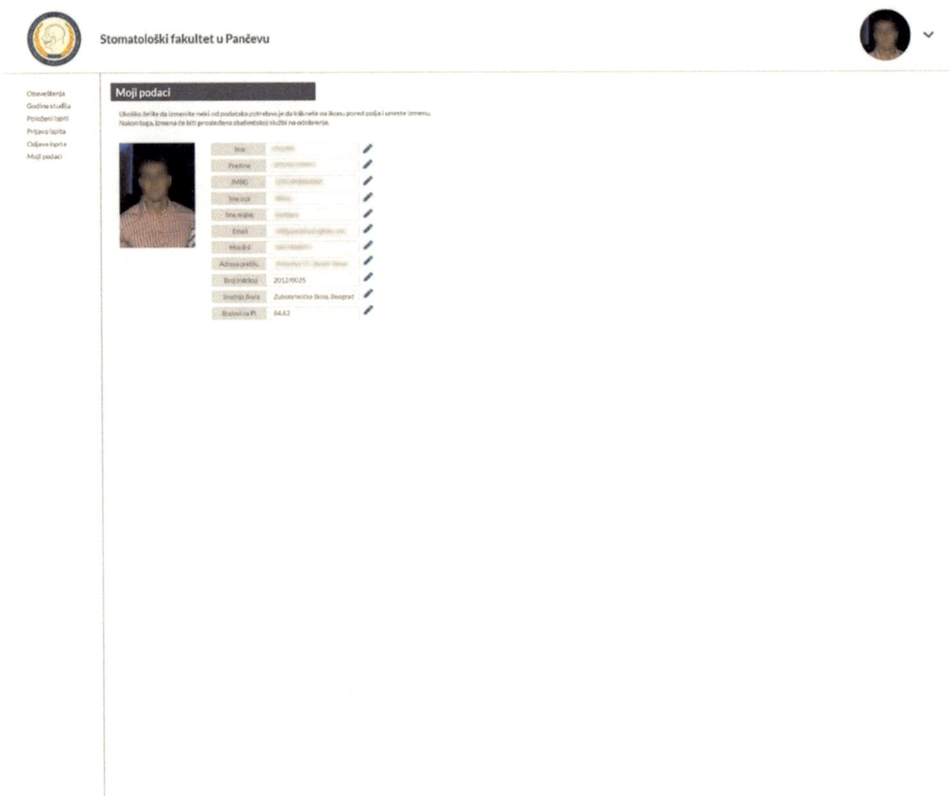


**Figure 23.**
*Overview of general student data.*

**Figure 24.**
*Overview of employee master data.*

which is event-based. It can be defined as a service that enables one application to send data to another when a certain event occurs. Webhook works practically one way, unlike classic APIs whose essence is to a get response based on a previously sent request.

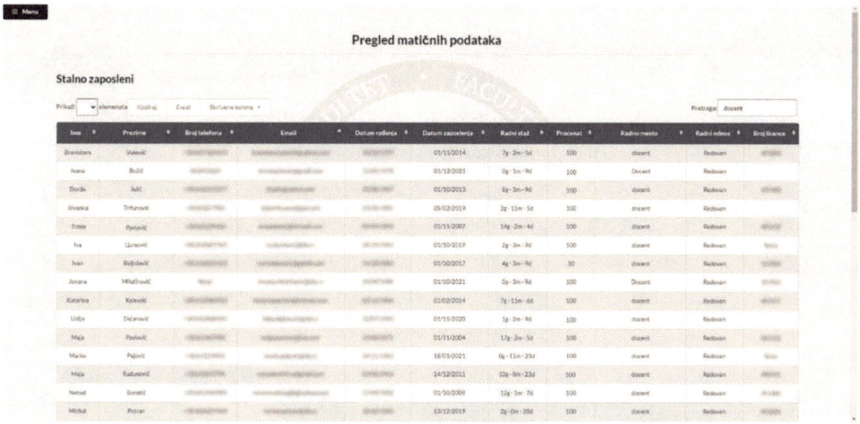


**Figure 25.**
*Overview of master data on employees, filtered data.*

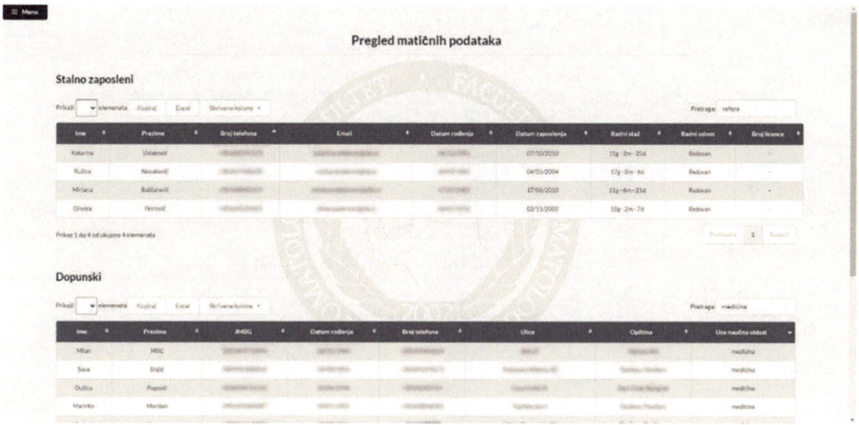


**Figure 26.**
*Overview of master data on employees, hiding certain data columns.*

**Figure 27.**
*Records of employees who are no longer employed at the institution (former employees).*

**Figure 28.**
*Teaching staff engagement overview.*

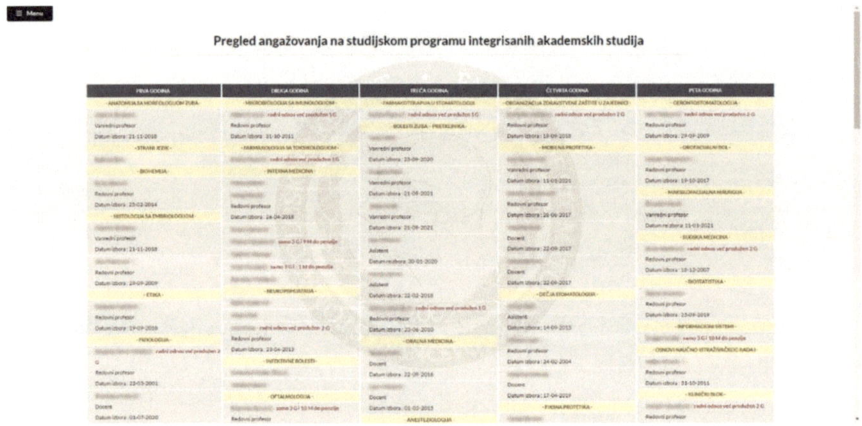


**Figure 29.**
*Summary of the engagement of teachers and associates at the study program level.*

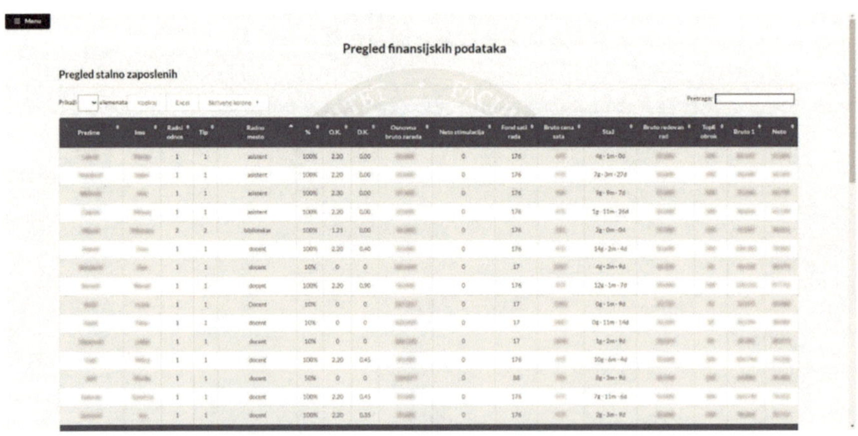


**Figure 30.**
*Financial data for employees overview.*

**Figure 31.**
*Change of financial data for employees.*

**Figure 32.**
*Overview of the scientific research results published by teaching staff.*

Webhook can be configured programmatically or by sending a POST request with the appropriate parameters in the Header and Body, to the URL https://chatapi.viber.com/pa/set-webhook. The parameters required for sending are shown in **Table 1**.

Depending on the type of event that can be registered through the callback function, different types of responses to the user can be defined. The following is an example of the Python code which is in charge of sending a response to a user according to whether the user started a conversation or signed up for the service:

```
from viberbot import Api
from viberbot.api.bot_configuration import BotConfiguration
from viberbot.api.messages.text_message import TextMessage
from viberbot.api.messages.data_types.contact import Contact
from viberbot.api.viber_requests import ViberConversationStartedRequest
```

**Figure 33.**
*Adding a new scientific research publication.*

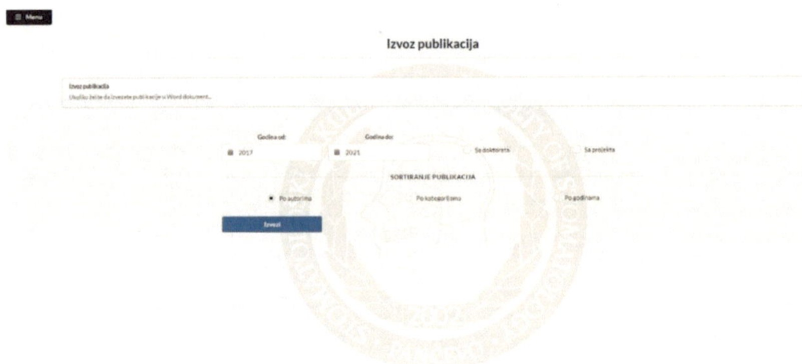


**Figure 34.**
*Exporting scientific publications.*

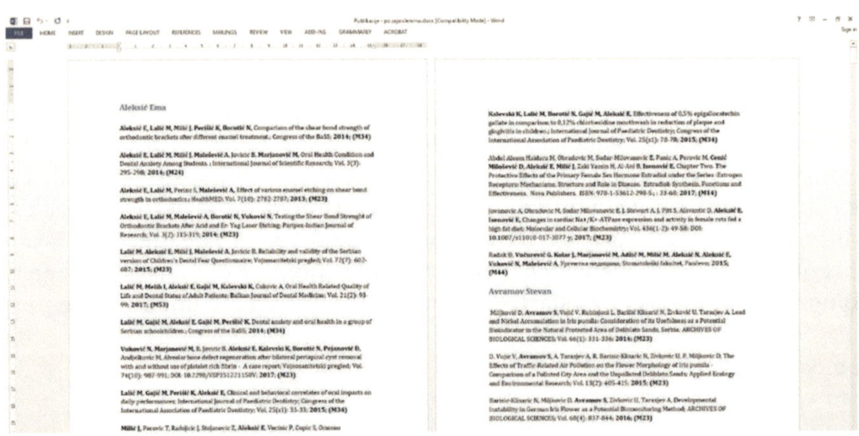


**Figure 35.**
*Data exported in .docx format.*

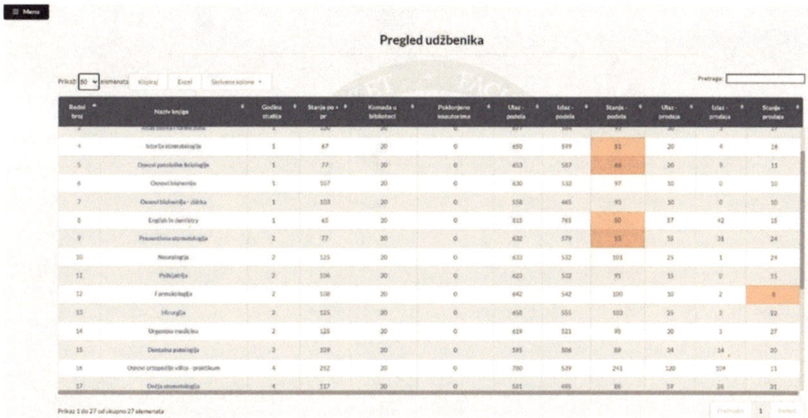


**Figure 36.**
*Summary overview of the textbooks published by the institution.*

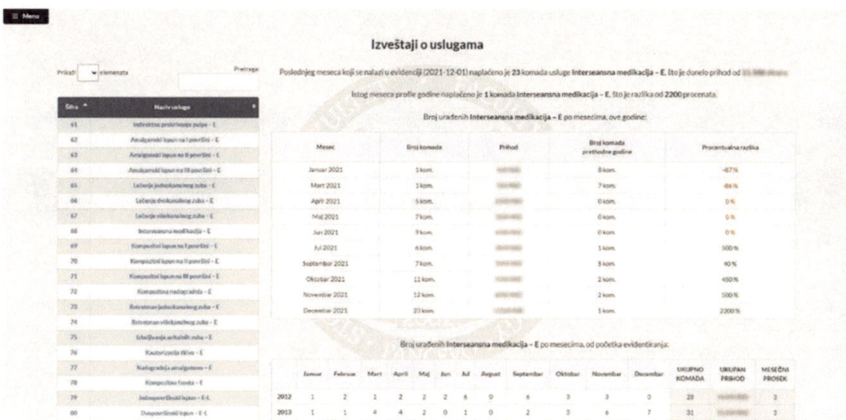


**Figure 37.**
*Reports for the selected service.*

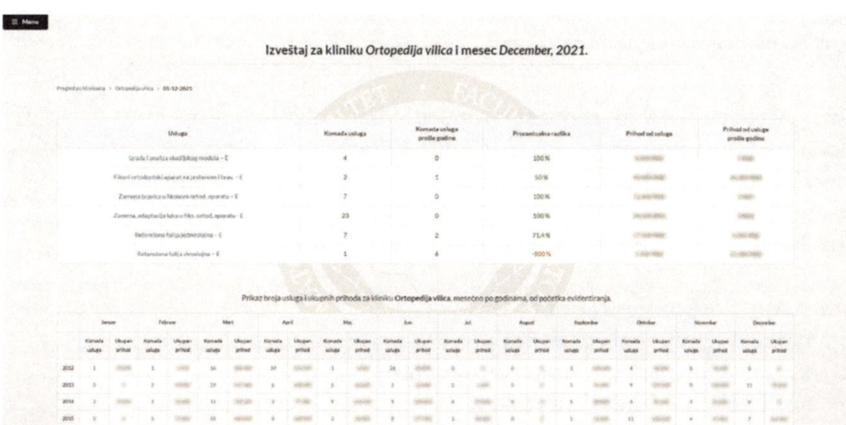


**Figure 38.**
*Reports on services provided for the selected department.*

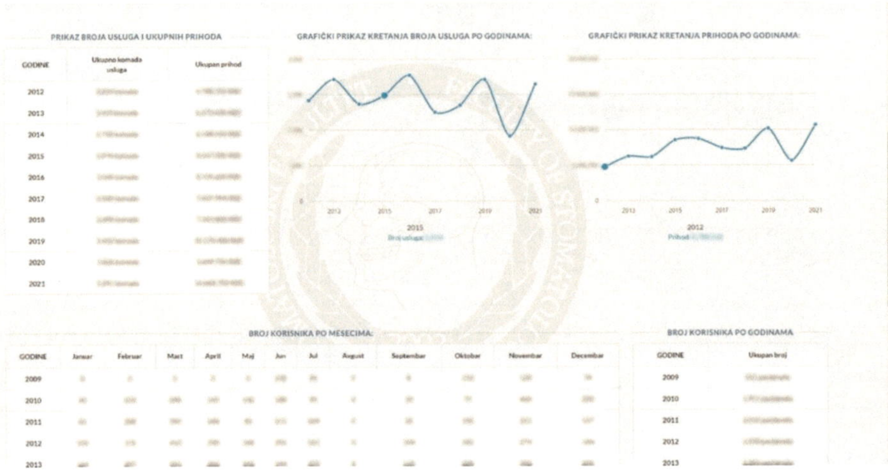

**Figure 39.**
*Summary reports on services provided at the level of the institution.*

**Figure 40.**
*Overview of the institution's assets and inventory.*

```
from viberbot.api.viber_requests import ViberFailedRequest
from viberbot.api.viber_requests import ViberMessageRequest
from viberbot.api.viber_requests import ViberSubscribedRequest
from viberbot.api.viber_requests import ViberUnsubscribedRequest
from django.views.decorators.csrf import csrf_exempt

viber = Api(BotConfiguration(
        name = 'UniversityChatBot',
        avatar = 'https://example.com/avatar.jpg',
        auth_token = 'universitytoken'
))

def hook(request):
```

**Figure 41.**
*Diagram of the flow of messages sent between the user and the public account.*

| Name | Description | Validation |
|---|---|---|
| url | Required. Account webhook URL to receive callbacks and messages from users | Webhook URL must use SSL<br>Note: Viber does not support self signed certificates |
| event_types | Optional. Indicates the types of Viber events that the account owner would like to be notified about. Do not include this parameter in your request to get all events | Possible values: delivered, seen, failed, subscribed, unsubscribed and conversation_started |
| send_name | Optional. Indicates whether or not the bot should receive the user name. Default false | Possible values: true, false |
| send_photo | Optional. Indicates whether or not the bot should receive the user photo. Default false | Possible values: true, false |

**Table 1.**
*Parameters required for sending in order to arrange Webhook requests.*

```
logger.debug("received request. post data: {0}".format(request.get_data()))

viber_request = viber.parse_request(request.get_data())

if isinstance(viber_request, ViberConversationStartedRequest):
        viber.send_messages(viber_request.get_user().get_id(), [
                TextMessage(text = "Welcome!")
        ])
elif isinstance(viber_request, ViberSubscribedRequest):
        viber.send_messages(viber_request.get_user.id, [
                TextMessage(text = "Thank you!")
        ])
return Response(status = 200)
```

This type of communication is used for sending information about the grade students received after successfully passing an exam. The teachers add the grades that the students receive at the exam and the e-service simultaneously sends a notification to the students to their instant messaging accounts through which they previously establish communication with the University bot. In that way, and at the same time, they voluntarily applied for the service. It is possible to establish this type of communication for any needs so that personalized communication 1-1 with each of the university students can be achieved at any time. In addition to information on the grades obtained, it is possible to establish communication for all other types of information and needs, both with students and employees.

## 5. Conclusion

In the uncertain forthcoming days, institutions must be prepared for new technological challenges that may appear. It is of the utmost importance for an institution to investigate what can be done about the creation of high-quality relationships with interested parties in order to not only maintain but also enhance the relationship with them. In such circumstances, proper ICT application can be of inestimable value for the leaders of higher educational institutions, deans, decision-makers, administrators, and others who are to make important strategic decisions.

In addition, there is another very important fact in the future that should not be ignored—as the years go by, new generations of students come with increasing knowledge, higher previous formal education, and, most importantly, the expectation of ICT presence in their "student life." Prospective students will need to be provided with an easier way of learning (including various types of distance learning systems), but also the opportunity to quickly and easily complete all their obligations outside the classroom. They should be provided with all relevant information at their fingertips. From a technological point of view, only the adequate application of modern technologies can provide a basis for meeting these conditions.

Students' expectations regarding the presence of various forms of technology within student activities are today at a much higher level than they were until recently [30]. The availability and proper use of digital technologies in the portfolio of a higher educational institution were especially evident during the coronavirus pandemic, which imposed a completely new way of interaction and communication between students and higher educational institutions [31].

Adoption of the correct use of digital technologies could lead not only to greater student satisfaction but also to the improvement of the technological reputation of the institution. Today, digital technology has become an essential part of students' daily lives and plays a key role in their studying and extracurricular activities. We are living in a new digital reality [32] and educational institutions will have to adapt to it quickly. The proper use of digital technologies could play an important role in the sustainable development of educational institutions in the future [31]. Future generations of higher education students will have more and more prominent previous experience with the significant use of digital technologies in their primary and secondary education [33].

## Conflict of interest

The author declares no conflict of interest.

## Author details

Adam Malešević
Faculty of Stomatology in Pančevo, University Business Academy in Novi Sad, Pančevo, Serbia

*Address all correspondence to: adam@sfp.rs

## References

[1] Jameel AS, Abdalla SN, Karem MA. Behavioural intention to use e-learning from student's perspective during COVID-19 pandemic. In: 2020 2nd Annual International Conference on Information and Sciences (AiCIS). 24-25 November 2020. Fallujah, Iraq: 2020. pp. 165-171

[2] Jameel AS, Abdul-Karem M, Mahmood N. A review of the impact of ICT on business firms. International Journal of Latest Research in Engineering and Management. 2017; **2**(1):15-19

[3] Aguinis H, Ramani RS, Alabduljader N, Bailey JR, Lee J. A pluralist conceptualization of scholarly impact in management education: Students as stakeholders. The Academy of Management Learning and Education. 2019;**18**(1):11-42

[4] Vulić M. Model Upravljanja Odnosima Sa Studentima U Elektronskom Obrazovanju. Belgrade: Faculty of Organizational Sciences; 2013

[5] Hilbert A, Schönbrunn K, Schmode S. Student relationship management in Germany—Foundations and opportunities. Management Review. 2007;**18**(2):204-219

[6] Seeman ED, O'Hara M. Customer relationship management in higher education: Using information systems to improve the student-school relationship. Campus-Wide Information Systems. 2006;**23**(1): 24-34. DOI: 10.1108/10650740610639714

[7] Bejou D. Treating students like customers. 2005. Available from: https://bized.aacsb.edu/articles/2005/march/treating-students-like-customers [Accessed: 21 August 2019]

[8] Winer RS. A framework for customer relationship management. California Management Review. 2001;**43**(4):89-105

[9] Nair C, Chan S, Fang X. A case study of CRM adoption in higher education. In: 2007 Information Resources Managament Association International Conference. 19-23 May 2007. Vancouver, Canada: 2007. Available from: https://pdfs.semanticscholar.org/b312/9b7e7bfa54edb401a9b69644b93a28f297ce.pdf

[10] Grant GB, Anderson G, Katz RN. Web Portals and Higher Education. San Francisco: Jossey-Bass; 2002

[11] Boyd RL. Customer service in higher education: Finding a middle ground. The Mentor: Innovative Scholarship on Academic Advising. 2012;**14**:1-6

[12] Chang TM, Liao LL, Hsiao WF. An empirical study on the e-CRM performance influence model for service sectors in Taiwan. In: 2005 IEEE International Conference on e-Technology, e-Commerce and e-Service. 05-08 July 2005. Kaohsiung, Taiwan: 2005. pp. 240-245

[13] Sin LYM, Tse ACB, Yim FHK. CRM: Conceptualization and scale development. European Journal of Marketing. 2005;**39**(11/12):1264-1290

[14] Greve G, Albers S. Determinants of performance in customer relationship management—Assessing the technology usage—Performance link. In: Proceedings of the 39th Annual Hawaii International Conference on System Sciences (HICSS'06). 04-07 January 2006; Kauai, Hawaii: 2006. p. 111b

[15] Gholami H, Saman MZM, Sharif S, Zakuan N. A CRM strategic leadership towards sustainable development in student relationship management: SD in higher education. Procedia Manufacturing. 2015;**2**:51-60. DOI: 10.1016/j.promfg.2015.07.010

[16] Fickel L. Know your customer: Intimacy, relationships, one-to-one-it's a giant lovefest out there. Available from: https://www2.cio.com.au/article/48612/know_your_customer/ [Accessed: 27 May 2021]

[17] Chen IJ, Popovich K. Understanding customer relationship management (CRM): People, process and technology. Business Process Management Journal. 2003;**9**(5):672-688. DOI: 10.1108/14637150310496758

[18] Tapp A, Hicks K, Stone M. Direct and database marketing and customer relationship management in recruiting students for higher education. International Journal of Nonprofit and Voluntary Sector Marketing. 2004;**9**(4):335-345. DOI: 10.1002/nvsm.258

[19] Hill FM. Managing service quality in higher education: The role of the student as primary consumer. Quality Assurance in Education. 1995;**3**(3):10-21

[20] Wali AF, Wright LT. Customer relationship management and service quality: Influences in higher education. Journal of Customer Behaviour. 2016; **15**(1):67-79. DOI: 10.1362/147539216x14594362873532

[21] Tattersfield K. What do universities use CRM systems for? 2019. pp. 1-6. Available from: https://blog.fullfabric.com/what-do-universities-use-crm-systems-for

[22] Manzuma-Ndaaba NM, Harada Y, Romle AR, Shamsudin AS. Cognitive, affective and conative loyalty in higher education marketing: Proposed model for emerging destinations. International Review of Management and Marketing. 2016;**6**(4S):168-175

[23] Badwan JJ et al. Adopting technology for customer relationship management in higher educational institutions. HAL. 2017;**1**(1):20-28

[24] Rigo G-E, Pedron CD, Caldeira M, de Araújo CCS. CRM adoption in a higher education institution. Journal of Information Systems and Technology Management. 2016;**13**(1):45-60. DOI: 10.4301/s1807-17752016000100003

[25] Nanda Kumari Adikaram C, Ali Khatibi DMAY. The relationship between customer relationship management and customer satisfaction: A study on private higher education institutions in Sri Lanka. International Journal of Arts and Commerce. 2016;**5**(2):69-95. Available from: www.ijac.org.uk

[26] Wahab S, Jusoff K, Al Momani KAM, Noor NAM, Zahari ASM. The influence of usability and enjoyment on electronic customer relationship management performance in Jordan mobile communication services. African Journal of Business Management. 2011; **5**(1):128-134

[27] Sablan B, Hidayanto AN, Budiardjo EK. The critical success factors (CSFs) of social CRM implementation in higher education. In: 2017 International Conference on Research and Innovation in Information Systems (ICRIIS). 16-17 July 2017; Langkawi, Malaysia: 2017. pp. 1-6

[28] Ogunnaike OO, Borishade TT, Jeje OE. Customer relationship management approach and student satisfaction in higher education

marketing. Journal of Competition. 2014;**6**(3):49-62. DOI: 10.7441/joc.2014.03.04

[29] Viber REST API | Viber Developers Hub. Available from: https://developers.viber.com/docs/api/rest-bot-api/. [Accessed: 15 January 2022]

[30] Henderson M, Selwyn N, Finger G, Aston R. Students' everyday engagement with digital technology in university: exploring patterns of use and 'usefulness'. Journal of Higher Education Policy and Management. 2015;**37**(3): 308-319. DOI: 10.1080/1360080X.2015.1034424

[31] Maleševic A, Barac D, Soleša D, Aleksic E, Despotovic-Zrakic M. Adopting xrm in higher education: E-services outside the classroom. Sustainability. 2021;**13**(14):7522. DOI: 10.3390/su13147522

[32] Papouli E, Chatzifotiou S, Tsairidis C. The use of digital technology at home during the COVID-19 outbreak: Views of social work students in Greece. Social Work Education. 2020;**39**(8): 1107-1115. DOI: 10.1080/02615479.2020.1807496

[33] Moorthy K, Yee TT, T'ing LC, Kumaran VV. Habit and hedonic motivation are the strongest influences in mobile learning behaviours among higher education students in Malaysia. Australasian Journal of Educational Technology. 2019;**35**(4):174-191. DOI: 10.14742/ajet.4432

Chapter 7

# Supporting Learning and Teaching with Good Design: Report and Lessons Learned from Learning Experience Design in Higher Education

*Martin Ebner, Sarah Edelsbrunner and Sandra Schön*

## Abstract

Learning experience design (LXD), that is, the conscious design of learning experiences based on the principles and methods of the design discipline, is a term that is increasingly being used in the design of (digital) learning environments. The aim is to make learning a positive, exciting experience for the learner. This article will introduce the understanding of "learning experience design" and describe its application at Graz University of Technology (TU Graz). As creativity is a base for the design discipline, the organizational unit "educational technology" sees LXD as a chance to develop innovative, quality online teaching and learning materials. The article will show the application and results of LXD of several different projects and resources developed for teachers and students by the educational technology team at TU Graz: the student study progress dashboard, the TELucation website relaunch, and the development of a modifiable digital template for lecturer training.

**Keywords:** learning experience design, teaching, university, design, e-learning, instructional design

## 1. Introduction

Learning at higher education institutions in Europe was hardly ever seen as a purely digital or e-service for learners and teachers before the COVID-19 pandemic. During the first weeks and months of closed lecture halls, many Austrian universities tried to continue teaching as well as possible by using video conferencing systems, live streaming, or recordings that were made available to students [1, 2]. Interestingly, before COVID-19, the term "digital learning" was connected to the use of technologies in lecture halls or as a parallel service (provided typically in a learning management system), whereas now, "digital learning" in Austria is the prominent term for "distance learning with technologies" [2]. To sum up, "digital learning" in Austrian higher education institutions can now be seen as an e-service.

Nevertheless, even before the pandemic, we at the "Educational Technology" team at Graz University of Technology (TU Graz) have already changed the way technology-enhanced learning solutions and teaching settings were developed within the university. While the development of teaching concepts and methodologies used to be the task of higher education didactic centers in the 1990s, with the adaptation of technologies, other development methodologies were used and adapted. Instructional design in technology-enhanced learning builds upon the nine steps of Gagné, among others, starting by "gaining attention" and then a presentation of the learning objectives, followed by the stimulation of prior learning, etc. [3]. Especially, in the USA Merrill's [4], principles are popular, favoring problem-based assignments, application-oriented learning, and day-to-day issues. As a script for the development of e-learning materials and courses, the ADDIE model, an abbreviation of "analysis, design, development, implementation, and evaluation," describes how instructional design should be implemented [5]. While the development of learning technologies is of course influenced by the methodologies of software development, the attention for user experience and the need for good design received more and more attention. The use of experience from design and software development, that is, the knowledge of design principles regarding shapes and colors as well as strongly user- and prototype-oriented methods of design development comes to bear in the so-called "learning experience design" [6]. In our contribution, we want to explain the key processes and methods from our daily work within the educational technology team, where instructional, software, and graphic designers work together. In the form of a workshop report, this paper introduces learning experience design (LXD) and shows its implementation in three examples of materials that support teachers in developing good teaching concepts. Finally, the authors will highlight how LXD challenges higher education institutions and their traditional way of applying instructional design.

## 2. Processes and methods of learning experience design

Learning experience design is "the design of learning experiences that (also) use technology, with the help of design knowledge and methods" ([6], p. 3). This design discipline has been forming for several years and combines specific design knowledge and methods (from interaction design, user experience design, and graphic design, among others) with knowledge and experience from the field of methodological-didactic design of learning and teaching, as well as IT and application development [6–9]. The term "experience" does not necessarily refer to experiential learning (although some refer to it, see Ref. [10]), but has been borrowed from "user experience design": the focus lies on what individual learners experience while learning. The emphasis on (learning) experience also refers to designing the entire learning situation, not just the immediate interaction with a learning application [11]. There are different representations for the process of learning experience design, such as by Ref. [6, 12–14]. **Figure 1** illustrates the steps according to Kircher et al. [6].

Sequence A, empathizing with learners, means investigating the challenge or problem from the learners' perspective: What do they need and what is their interest in learning? This includes interviews with target group members; another typical method here is to develop a persona, a (fictitious) description of person

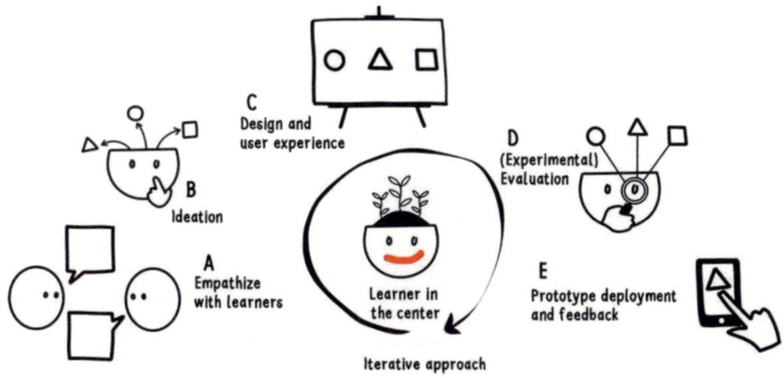


**Figure 1.**
*Process sequences in learning experience design. Source: Own illustration according to Ref. [6],* **Figure 4**, *p. 11, which is based on similar representations/overviews by Ref. [12–14].*

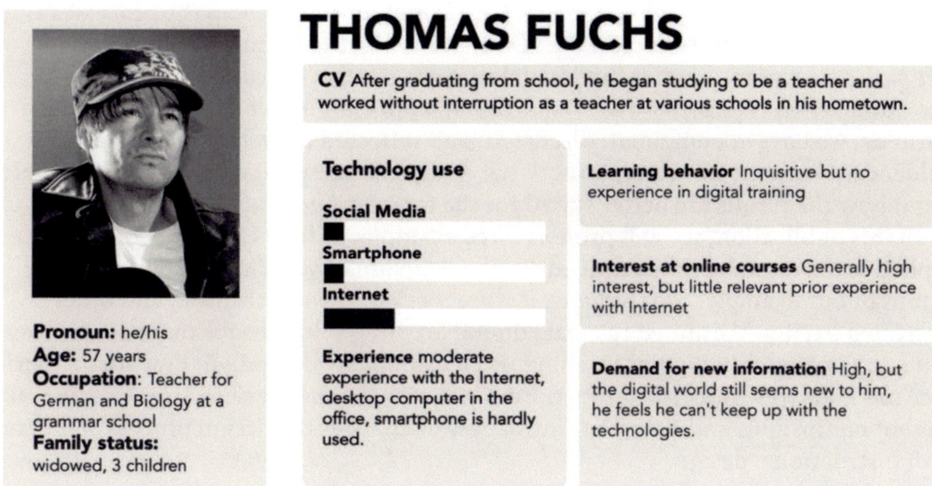


**Figure 2.**
*Persona developed and in use for the development of the MOOC platform, iMooX.at. Own illustration and shortened presentation. Source: Educational technology at TU Graz.*

representative of the target group. **Figure 2** shows such a persona that was developed for our national MOOC platform development.

Then in sequence B designers develop a set of ideas (called “ideation”). There are many well-known methods for generating many “original” ideas. For us, it is important not to focus solely on certain technologies in this phase yet but to develop visions of how a learning setting might look like to foster a positive experience afterward.

In sequence C, initial sketches are drafted, prototypes are built, and their usability is investigated (see [9]). For this, the developed persona can be applied and used as a tool to foster discussion on the needs of the target group(s).

First implementations, e.g., of learning methods or tools, are then tested in sequence D. Typically, mock-ups are used——which can be paper-based or simple digital mock-ups. Typically, two users are invited for a joint test, as we then understand better where adjustments are necessary or need to be considered.

After that, in sequence E, the first real application, for example in a (small) lecture, takes place, where the feedback——as in all previous steps——leads to revisions and renewed implementation of the previous steps.

Strictly speaking, iterative implementation is the rule. The sequence does not always have to be followed and individual steps may also be omitted. To achieve the best possible outcome, people from a wide range of backgrounds should be involved in the process——first and foremost the users, that is, learners, but also teaching staff or other stakeholders.

## 3. Methodology

The question we would like to answer is: How and with what outcomes and experiences is LXD used in the creation of resources for learning-related e-services? Within the tradition of participatory action research [15–18], the authors, who are part of the design team, have documented the processes, revised the process steps and artifacts, and discussed how the usage of LXD methods influences the processes and perspectives. We actively explored LXD methods together with graphic designers, software developers, and instructional designers and then tried to integrate them into our daily work. Based on several different applications, where we applied such methods, we have documented, discussed, and reflected upon how these methods influenced the work from an instructional designer's perspective. We did not explore if and how the results are better suited for the target groups.

In this publication, we will present three examples of how LXD methods were applied in the organizational unit educational technology at TU Graz. The target groups of our examples are students, lecturers of our own institution, and other interested parties. We aimed to create digital learning solutions for them or services that support their learning or teaching. Each example will highlight how user experience methods were integrated into the development of the service. After this, we will present our insights and how LXD influences or changes the design process compared with instructional design.

## 4. Examples of LXD development of teaching-related e-services for learners and faculty at our university

### 4.1 A dashboard for study progress: wished and codesigned by students

In a workshop on how to improve teaching, in March 2019, students of TU Graz expressed their wish to have a better and simpler overview of their study progress. Based on this impulse by users, the development of a student progress dashboard was then planned and implemented in the form of codesign and several feedback loops (see [19]). **Figure 3** presents artifacts of initial ideas, development, and the final product. First, from March to October 2019, an analysis of data structures and origins was conducted, and initial visualizations were sketched: In the summer of 2019, a codesign workshop with students was held for this purpose, and further meetings with students in the following months. Then, in spring of 2020, several meetings were organized with stakeholders, including student representatives, faculty, experts from the Vice Rectorate for Academic Affairs, members of the works council, and the legal department. At the same time, information material for

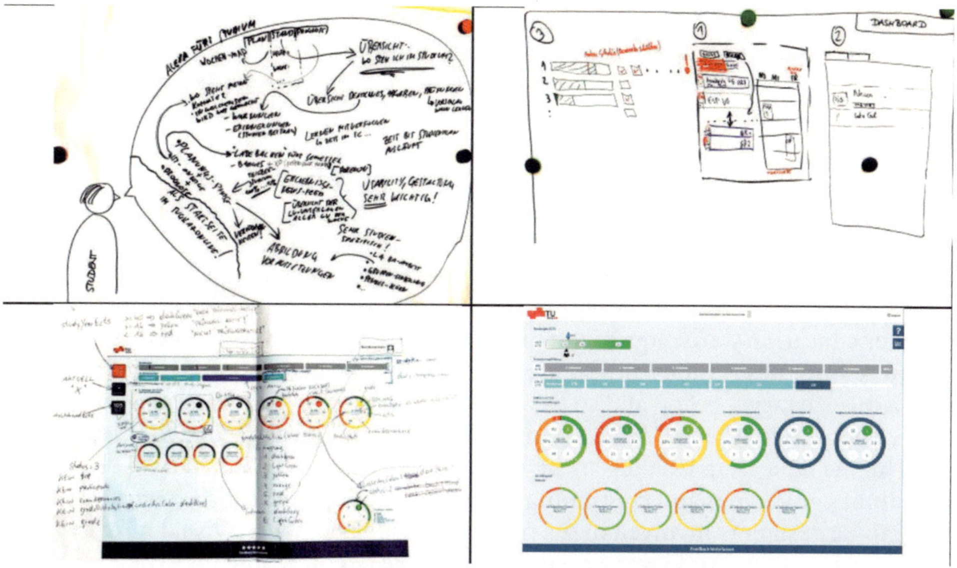

**Figure 3.**
*Artifacts from the codesign sessions with students and result of the development of the TU Graz student dashboard. Top left: Students' needs and initial ideas, top right: A first sketch, bottom left: Annotated paper prototype, bottom right: Final dashboard. (Source: Ref. [19],* ***Figures*** *5 and 7).*

students was produced (see [20, 21]). Eighteen months after the first vague ideas, the new study progress dashboard was implemented for all bachelor students of the Faculty of Computer Science and Biomedical Engineering in May 2020 (see **Figure 3**, bottom right image page). User feedback was then gathered for minor revisions. After a 6 month test phase, the service was made available for all bachelor students in December 2020, including various information materials and the development of a consulting services.

The study progress dashboard is intended to give students a helpful overview of their successes and activities. The data used was already accessible before, but students had to painstakingly gather it; now in the dashboard, it is visualized in such a way that your study progress is visible briefly (or with a few more clicks). Now students can see, colored appropriately, their achievements and the credits they have gained in comparison to the average of the other students. In addition, their own study progress, the progress in the various compulsory and elective subjects, and the official study recommendation are clearly displayed. By visualizing the learning data, students can now keep better track of their own learning process, which might ultimately lead to an improvement in their study success [19]. Student satisfaction with the dashboard is very high; there have been comparatively few complaints or ambiguities communicated via the feedback function since the system has been rolled out across the university.

### 4.2 The collection of texts for lecturers: TELucation becomes a low barrier

TELucation ("technology enhanced learning" and "education") is a service for teachers in higher education, offering them freely available information and step-by-step guides to improve their technology-enhanced teaching and stay up to date with developments in the field. TELucation was developed based on several internal workshops at TU Graz with teachers, an online discussion over 3 weeks, and a final round table discussion during the strategy development of TU Graz regarding digitalization, where teachers expressed the wish to have information on different concepts, tools, and implementations as a starting point for their own continuing education, and so that they know what to ask for if necessary. As a result, a website with TELucation articles in five categories was launched in 2021. As the topic of technology-enhanced teaching has received a lot of attention due to the closure of university spaces [1], the website had to be expanded and adapted accordingly. We chose to do this according to the idea of learning experience design.

The users' demands were crucial to the decision to adapt the website since teachers in higher education were requiring more step-by-step guides for digital teaching and wanted to find these guides on a single page. As a public institution, we also aim to reach a diverse target group and so the second focus of the adaptation was on accessibility, in line with the WCAG 2.1 standards [22] to guarantee a good user experience for all higher education teachers using the service. This phase included research into accessibility guidelines and continuing education on the topic for the instructional and graphic designers involved in the project. A colleague with a visual impairment and expertise in accessible web design was also able to contribute his expertise.

In the first step, requirements for the new website were identified based on users' needs: The TELucation website must be navigable by keyboard, a path must indicate where you are on the website, the color scheme should be changeable (for color-blind people), no light boxes should be used because they are not recognized by screen readers. At the same time, it was suggested to also introduce the team behind TELucation and explain who is behind the project to make the service feel more personal. Some design choices were deliberately kept from the previous website: categories of articles should still be easily distinguishable by color and by the icons used. All changes made should not interfere with the open license of the website, because TELucation was supposed to remain an OER.

As envisaged in LXD, these ideas were not only discussed and implemented but also shown to the target group with the help of sketches and mock-ups and adapted according to the user feedback. Different website templates were compared with each other and the one with the most positive feedback was chosen for implementation. Testing was not only done with accessibility test tools but also by users with a disability. In the meantime, the TELucation website has been fully revised and is now as accessible as possible. In addition, a "TELucation map" and a guide for authors, which can be downloaded from the website, make the editing and design process of the content transparent for teachers (**Figure 4**).

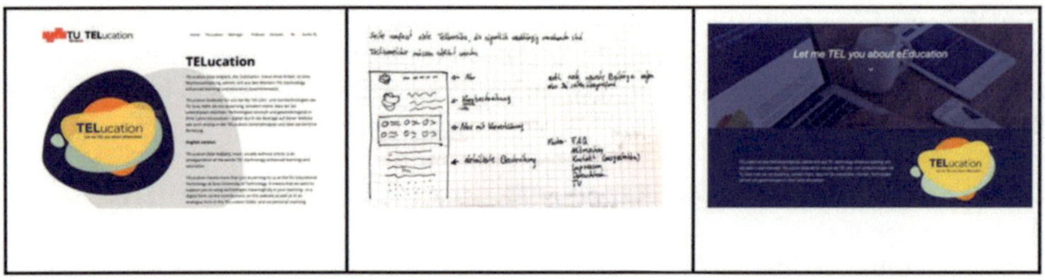


**Figure 4.**
*The TELucation folder: first online version (left), first sketches (middle), and accessible new version (right). Source: educational technology at TU Graz; screenshots of https://telucation.tugraz.at .*

### 4.3 OER canvas: modifiable working aid for OER projects

Our third application of LXD addressed users outside of our university: We planned to offer materials that we have developed for our teachers to others so that they can adapt them themselves. The material in question is the "OER canvas", a template that can be used in print or digitally for consultations or training on the topic of open educational resources (OER). The OER canvas guides through the planning and creation of openly licensed educational resources, for example with a checklist or relevant URLs. We had already learned from our experience with an "OER project canvas" that others like to adapt such tools: In 2018, we offered to send interested parties an Open Office file for translation in a short time and 17 translations of the canvas were created and published [23]. From a legal point of view, such modification and republication were allowed since the OER canvas itself was openly licensed.

In 2021, we planned to also make the OER canvas (**Figure 5**, middle) available so that modifications and translations can be made easily. We wanted to avoid using Open Office this time since we wanted to make the modification very easy and preferably have a document that can be edited online. After some consideration, we decided to publish the canvas as a Google Slides file. Without a Google account, the template can be downloaded in various formats —— including Microsoft PowerPoint and Open Office files. For people who have a Google account, creating a copy that can be edited is an even easier option. The template can then be edited in several languages and design variants in different formats. To ensure that everything is understandable and everyone will produce roughly the same results, instructions on how to proceed are included in the first slide. The canvas itself was presented at the global OERcamp 2021 (**Figure 5**, center). It was promptly translated into Telugu (**Figure 5**, right).

## 5. Result: a different view on teaching and learning with LXD

LXD methods require an engagement with the target group and its needs. This change of perspective is particularly challenging in higher education, where traditionally the focus lies strongly on a systematic transfer of knowledge and development of discipline-related competencies. The development and introduction of such knowledge are learning goals oriented and often chronologically follow developments in the discipline rather than focusing on the learners' interests and experiences while learning. LXD sets a clearly different focus here with its perspective on the learner

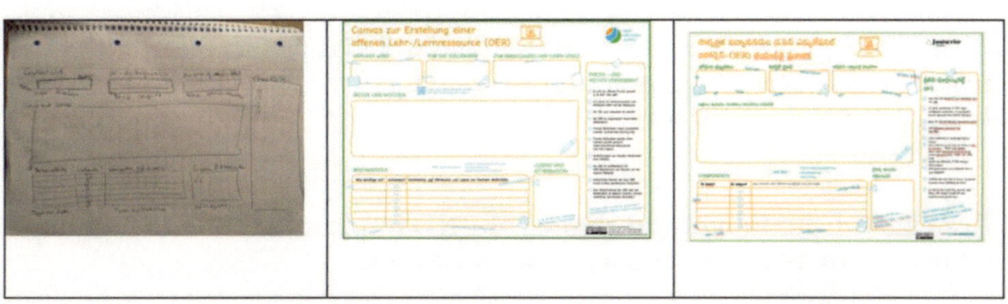

**Figure 5.**
*The first sketch of the OER canvas (left, source: educational technology at TU Graz), the modifiable original canvas version for Austrian teachers [24], [center], and a translation into Telugu [25], [right].*

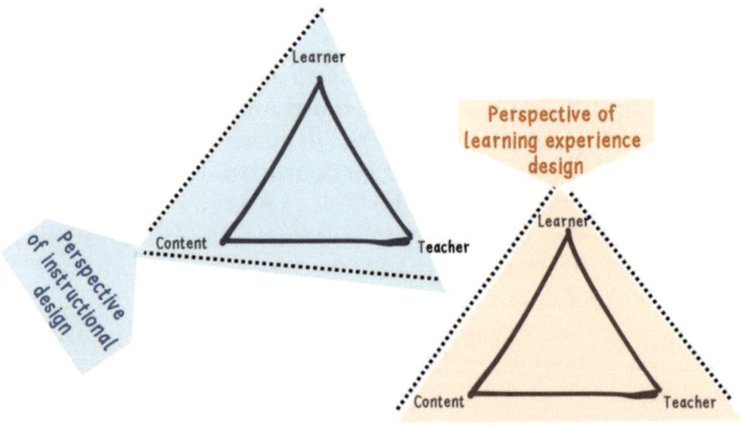


**Figure 6.**
*The different perspectives of instructional design in higher education versus learning experience design.*

and their perspective. For example, the focus is not on what a learners should already be able to do, but on what he or she can potentially do. The main question is how someone learns particularly well.

To illustrate these results, we use the visualization of the "didactic triangle" to show relevant aspects in the design of teaching arrangements [26] in **Figure 6**. Whereas in higher education the focus is typically on the arrangement of content and actions related to the competencies to be acquired, LXD has a clearer focus on the concerns of the learners.

## 6. Discussion

So, not surprisingly, all the examples mentioned here concern creations by the service unit educational technology; we do not know of a similar design of lectures with the help of LXD methods by university teachers' own initiative so far. We would like to add that the term LXD and the self-understanding of LXD are not yet clearly sharpened. We also learned that LX designers cannot take charge of the entire process of designing technology-enhanced learning experiences, as they continue to have only a specific view of the process and outcome. Collaborations with other disciplines are certainly still essential here.

For our educational technology team, the adaptation of LXD was not very "exciting" since user experience methods are well-known and common, especially in software development. We have now, however, transferred these to other settings and teams that do not primarily work on software applications.

## 7. Conclusion: challenge and chance of LXD implementation in higher education institutions and a recommendation

A challenge for LXD, perhaps specific to universities, lies in the fact that development methods for didactic-methodical designs are hardly a research object themselves and it is also not trivial to research them. Thus, the exchange about such innovations happens rather marginally, even in more research-oriented networks, such as technology-enhanced learning or development of teaching at universities. In any case, however, we expect that activities for the professionalization of LXD, that means its use in further education and also by teachers will increasingly lead to awareness of its development. Ultimately, it is important to us that we support good teaching with technology. This increased interest found resonance as a trend toward "quality online learning" in the current Horizon Report [27]. For us, LXD is a helpful wayto better realize this claim.

As we have shown, LXD puts the learner at the center of its work. In practical terms, this is what we might expect from instructional design in general, but where we have seen a less defined practical application. So, with what we have now learned from LXD, we would like to advocate also for learning situations that are not primarily about e-learning, or about digital services, to focus more on the actual user. This can be done simply by sharing and discussing plans and mock-ups with them. Furthermore, we have also learned that besides methodological considerations, early involvement of graphic designers and e-learning developers give everyone a better picture of the needs, backgrounds, and considerations of all parties involved. This may mean that the design process will not be shorter or less time-consuming per se, but unproductive "loops" or "mistakes" may be avoided.

## Acknowledgements

The developments of materials presented here, in particular the OER canvas, are partly funded by the Open Education Austria Advanced project (OEAA, 2020-2024) with financial support from the Austrian ministry BMBWF.

## Conflict of interest

The authors state no conflict of interest.

## Author details

Martin Ebner*, Sarah Edelsbrunner and Sandra Schön
Graz University of Technology, Austria

*Address all correspondence to: martin.ebner@tugraz.at

## References


[1] Ebner M, Schön S, Braun C, Ebner M, Grigoriadis Y, Haas M, et al. COVID-19 epidemic as e-learning boost? chronological development and effects at an Austrian university against the background of the concept of "E-learning readiness", Future Internet. 2020;**12**:94. Available from: https://www.mdpi.com/1999-5903/12/6/94

[2] Pausits A, Oppl S, Schön S, Fellner M, Campbell D, Dobiasch M. Distance Learning an österreichischen Universitäten und Hochschulen im Sommersemester 2020 und Wintersemester 2020/21. Bundesministerium für Bildung, Wissenschaft und Forschung: Wien; 2021. Available from: https://pubshop.bmbwf.gv.at/index.php?article_id=9&type=neuerscheinungen&pub=926. [Accessed: September 8, 2021]

[3] Gagné R, Briggs L, Wager W. Principles of Instructional Design. San Diego: Harcourt Brace Jovanovich College Publishers; 1992

[4] Merrill M. First principles of instruction. Educational Technology Research and Development. 2002;**50**(3):43-59

[5] Branch RM. Instructional Design: The ADDIE Approach. New York: Springer; 2009

[6] Kircher J, Burger E, Ebner M, Schön S. Learning Experience Design – zur Gestaltung von technologiegestützten Lernerfahrungen mit Methoden der Design-Entwicklung. In: Wilbers K, Hohenstein A, editors. Handbuch E- Learning. Expertenwissen aus Wissenschaft und Praxis – Strategien, Instrumente, Fallstudien, 93. Erg.-Lfg. Vol. 7-15. Hürth: Wolters-Kluwer; 2021. pp. 1-14

[7] Ahn J. Drawing inspiration for learning experience design (LX) from diverse perspectives. The Emerging Learning Design Journal. 2019;**6**:1-6. Available from: https://digitalcommons.montclair.edu/eldj/vol6/iss1/1. [Accessed: September 8, 2021]

[8] Sousa F, Nuno M. Learning experience design: instructional design applied to the onboarding of digital products. In: Martins N, Brandão D, editors. Advances in Design and Digital Communication, Digicom; Springer Series in Design and Innovation. Vol. 12. Cham: Springer; 2020. DOI: 10.1007/978-3-030-61671-7_5. [Accessed: July 11, 2022]

[9] Schmidt M, Tawfik AA, Jahnke I, Earnshaw Y, editors. Learner and User Experience Research. An Introduction for the Field of Learning Design & Technology. Brigham: EdTech Books; 2020. Available from: https://edtechbooks.org/ux

[10] LXD.org. What is Learning Experience Design?. 2021. Available from: https://lxd.org/fundamentals-of-learning-experience-design/what-is-learning-experience-design/. [Accessed: September 8, 2021]

[11] Interaction Design Foundation. Learning Experience Design – The Most Valuable Lessons. 2018. Available from: https://www.interaction-design.org/literature/article/learning-experience-design-the-most-valuable-lessons. [Accessed: September 8, 2021]

[12] Stone M, Kent KM, Roscoe RD, Corley KM, Allen LK, McNamara DS. The design implementation framework: Iterative design from the lab to the classroom. In: Roscoe R, Craig SD, Douglas I, editors. End-user

Considerations in Educational Technology Design. Hershey: IGI Global; 2018. pp. 76-98

[13] McCarthy K, Watanabe M, McNamara D. The design implementation framework: Guiding principles for the redesign of a reading comprehension intelligent tutoring system. In: Schmidt M, Tawfik AA, Jahnke I, Earnshaw Y, editors. Learner and User Experience Research. An Introduction for the Field of Learning Design & Technology. Provo: EdTech Books; 2020. Available from: https://edtechbooks.org/ux. [Accessed: July 11, 2022]

[14] Schmidt M, Earnshaw Y, Tawfik AA, Jahnke I. Methods of user centered design and evaluation for learning designers. In: Schmidt M, Tawfik AA, Jahnke I, Earnshaw Y, editors. Learner and User Experience Research. An Introduction for the Field of Learning Design & Technology. Provo: EdTech Books; 2020. Available from: https://edtechbooks.org/ux. [Accessed: July 11, 2022]

[15] Lewin K. Action research and minority problems. The Journal of Social Issues. 1946;**2**(1):34-46. DOI: 10.1111/j.1540-4560.1946.tb02295.x

[16] Adelman C. Kurt Lewin and the origins of action research. Educational Action Research. 1993;**1**(1):7-24. DOI: 10.1080/0965079930010102

[17] Adugu E. Contextualizing action research. International Journal of Adult Education and Technology. 2021;**12**(2):31-46

[18] Mertler CA. The Wiley Handbook of Action Research in Education. New Jersey: Wiley; 2019

[19] Leitner P, Ebner M, Geisswinkler H, Schön S. Visualisation of learning for students. A dashboard for study progress. Development, design details, implementation, and user feedback. In: Ifenthaler D, Sahin M, editors. Visualisation and LA. Cham: Springer; 2021

[20] TU Graz. Leitfaden: Grundlagen des Studierenden-Dashboards. 2020. Available from: https://tu4u.tugraz.at/fileadmin/Studierende_und_Bedienstete/Anleitungen/Studierenden-Dashboard_Funktionen_Leitfaden.pdf. [Accessed: September 8, 2021]

[21] TU Graz. Learning Analytics. 2021. Available from: https://tu4u.tugraz.at/studierende/mein-laufendes-studium/learning-analytics/. [Accessed: September 8, 2021]

[22] W3C. Web Content, WCAG 2.1. 2022. Available from: https://www.w3.org/WAI/standards-guidelines/wcag/glance/. [Accessed: July 11, 2022]

[23] Schön S, Atenas J, Ebner M. OER Canvas. In: Open Education Working Group; 2018. Available from: http://education.okfn.org/handbooks/oer-canvas/. [Accessed: July 11, 2022]

[24] Edelsbrunner S, Ebner M, Lari C, Schön S. Canvas for the creation of an open teaching/learning resource (OER)—OEAA version. Graz: TU Graz Educational Technology for Open Education Austria Advanced; 2021. DOI: 10.3217/szkrw-aew74

[25] Rao S. OER Canvas template_Telugu. 2022. Available from: https://www.oercommons.org/courseware/lesson/88624/student-old/. [Accessed: July 11, 2022]

[26] Kansanen P. Teaching as teaching-studying-learning interaction. Scandinavian Journal of Educational Research. 1999;**43**(1):81-89

[27] Pelletier K, Brown M, Brooks DC, McCormack M, Reeves J, Arbino N. 2021 EDUCAUSE Horizon Report, Teaching and Learning Edition. Boulder, CO: EDUCAUSE; 2021. Available from: https://library.educause.edu/-/media/files/library/2021/4/2021hrteachinglearning.pdfla=enhash=C9DEC12398593F297CC634409DFF4B8C5A60B36E. [Accessed: July 11, 2022]

Section 3

# Application of Digital Innovation

Chapter 8

# Perspective Chapter: Data Monetization Model for Sustaining Smart City Initiatives

*Mercy Samuel and Siddharth Gupta*

## Abstract

This chapter aims to create a G2B business model framework for data monetization under Smart City Mission (SCM) in India. It sets a premise to understand the urgency of a data monetizing model as a revenue option for sustaining the smart city initiatives. The sustainability of smart city makes it inevitable to look for a separate revenue stream for cities to fund the operations & maintenance of smart city infrastructure created under SCM. The chapter explores few attempts made by other ministries in India towards data monetization and the role of data privacy and sharing policy for protection from data exploitation. The first approach to the research includes analysis of cases of other smart cities and data monetization initiatives around the world. Further the paper also explores the kind of data generated under Smart City Mission India to understand the possibility of monetization and its value for different stakeholders. The limitation of this study is that data monetization has not yet been rigorously tested in practice in the government sector. Hence the current study attempts to explore the potential of the same as a financing option for sustaining smart city initiatives in India.

**Keywords:** data monetization, data exchange, smart cities, internet of things, self-financing cities, business model, data marketplace, government-to-business, urban data exchange, business model canvas

## 1. Introduction

Smart Cities Mission is the Government of India's urban regeneration and retrofitting project launched in 2015 to create livable and sustainable smart cities in India [1]. The Indian government through a competitive process selected 100 cities to be developed as smart cities in multiple rounds. The cities were required to submit their proposals in two categories viz. pan city and area-specific proposals. Different cities chose different services to plan and prepare their proposals with the help of consultants and participated in the competitive process. Finally, 100 cities were selected to develop themselves based on the proposal submitted. The government of India dedicated a whopping US$ 6.3 billion for smart city development. Most of the smart city projects revolved around applying smart solutions to the infrastructure, mixed land use in area-based growth, improving housing opportunities for everyone, defining

 IntechOpen

walkable areas, maintaining and enhancing open spaces, supporting a range of transit choices, etc. There was extensive tech deployment in the smart city project and technology was identified as an enabler for city management. Tech deployment generated data that could be converted to information for better planning and strategizing.

A total of 5151 ventures worth some 2,05,018 crore is to be completed in 5 years from the respective selection date of the cities under the scheme under the Smart Cities Programme, which was initiated in 2015 [2].

As of March 2019, under the Smart Cities Mission, integrated command and control centers (ICCCs) estimated at Rs 27.7 billion were made operational in 15 towns [3]. The ICCC identified as one of the projects in many cities were designed as the "nerve center" for operations management, day-to-day exception handling and disaster management. In addition, Rs 22.6 billion schemes are under development in 31 towns. The government has also initiated tenders in over 18 cities for projects worth Rs 25.5 billion [4].

The idea for a Smart City must provide funding strategy for the Project's full development cycle. The financial strategy should define internal (taxes, leases, permits, and usage fees) and external (grants, delegated sales, loans, and borrowings) streams of capital expenditure allocation and activity and maintenance over the project's life cycle. This financial strategy would include outlets for recovery of project expenses for a span of 8–10 years or more. O&M expenses which would also provide ULB's financial planning, capital management action plan [5].

When communities are planning to update their facilities with new technology, the large-scale deployment of advanced technologies raises a huge obstacle to compensate for such ventures. Cities are limited by small budgets and need to define market models that can help draw private investment to render and sustain the transition financially.

It is imperative for Smart Cities to identify a revenue generation model to specifically take care of all the tech devices engaged in data capture among other expenses Smart cities will have to continually search for ways to exploit the development infrastructure and network to create new revenue sources for smart cities. Throughout growing layer of the company model, suppliers and collaborators will consider innovative ways to produce income from the products and services they offer. Such opportunities could mimic the business models used in the digital economy as a whole.

It is particularly essential for India, as cities are trying to automate their delivery of public infrastructure by introducing interconnected Pan City Smart Technologies under the Smart Cities Project by producing huge volumes of data. Meeting digital infrastructure's operating and maintenance costs, measured at 15–20 percent of capital annually, would be a challenge unless the cities think of innovative mechanisms to generate revenue monetize city information [6].

The Economic Survey (2018–2019) proposed that the government intends to monetize the data of residents as part of a wider strategy to use data as a public good. There is no justification to prohibit the private usage of this data for benefit, in keeping with the notion of data as a public good. Although the social gains will well outweigh the government's expense, at least some of the data produced would be monetized to alleviate the burden on government finances. Datasets may be provided to analytics firms that analyze the results, produce insights and offer insights back to the private sector, who in effect will use these insights to forecast demand, find untapped opportunities or develop new goods [7].

Today data is called the "new oil" as it could prove to be a valuable resource. These days companies are using data analytics to grow and optimize business, by understanding customer patterns, which in long run adds value and helps to foresee the modification necessary to be made that can easily outrun their competitors, therefore data becomes the game changer in competition. This has led to the monetization of data by companies from B2B (business-to-business) that could be used to optimize self-processes, design strategy, and could be sold externally. Comparing to this monetization in private sector, data from G2B (government to business) is still in nascent scale across globe. This gives an opportunity to tap underlying potential of tremendous amount of data bank with the government which could be monetized and can generate revenue streams by G2B (Government to Business) model.

Selling the data or analysis derived from it, have been studied scarcely in business and academic literature. In academic literature, the phenomenon of big data and the utilization of it have been popular topics over the last few years. The interest in the subject of data monetization has also increased due to the rise of digitization and big data. The principle of monetization, providing new value and data earnings, is not new and yet the practice has not been thoroughly studied.

Changing the market landscape, on the other side, provides different data use opportunities, data monetization being one possibility for broader data use. This has created a research void, as businesses are increasingly using the data in new ways, while the academic literature does not cover offers extracted from such new data. The result of this research provides a probable business model framework of this new emerging data marketplace. Due to limited availability of data and to get a head start, the business model canvas by Alexander Osterwalder, a business theorist with works on business model is used.

## 2. Background

Data no longer acts as a secondary asset in the current world used for decision making or processing but is now taken the front stage where it in itself to could be productized to sell and use. This new role is referred to as "Data Monetization". But at the same time, various factors and risks are involved when a new product is ever launched in the market. First is overcoming the reluctance over its transparency when related to data sharing on different platforms and second is a platform where it could be safely stored to be shred, processed, or moderated with no harm to data as well data source owner [8]. At the same time, it is important to understand that data is not only about incorporating information technology or providing business intelligence.

Data in itself has formed an economy in which the extraction of data from IoT devices has given thrust. With the advancement in IoT, data is also exponentially growing. With the growth in data, its monetization would become more real. But there has to be certain standardization when it comes to monetization. For example, devices such as Wi-Fi, GPS, beacon, would produce data related to location or region and say sold to a cab service [9].

For example, the healthcare industry is a sector that has immense potential to generate revenue streams by monetizing their health care data. As a seller, pharmaceutical organizations could be seen as a strong customer base to buy the data from medical labs where the disease insights will be gained. Data on chronic diseases could be shared with healthcare partners or retail players producing health equipment or health food product. As a buyer, health insurers could provide data on the claims to the healthcare providers to improve their services and minimize their financial risk. Thus, data needs to be exploited at its fullest not only for revenue but to improve service delivery [10]. In developing countries, the responsibility to collect Health data regarding population, prevalent diseases, lies with common health workers (CHW). But the lack of incentives for these CHWs leads to challenges in the collection and aggregation of data. The most common hurdle is the technological challenges, i.e., difficulty in usage of computer or internet facility. Secondly, maintaining a similar pattern while collecting data, especially over larger nations where the accumulation of data in itself would be a challenge. Thus, overcoming these hurdles would be the first step towards making data monetization in healthcare possible [11].

It is not as simple a job to extract data and supply, but involves a team of participants who would create an entire data ecosystem through understanding both dynamics as well as structure. These participants include data manager, suppliers, custodian, aggregator, developer of the application, and a service provider. Setting the pricing, IP protection, and privacy concerns are the most highlighted concerns in data monetization [12].

A revenue model is what comes next after the formulation of the business model where data-driven service is sold by the start-ups to the consumer through four distinct business models. Subscription model, Usage fee, and gain sharing are the most common type that is generally taken up by individuals, small enterprise, and private office through limited access. The multi-sided model incorporates any previous three models with beneficial addition of extra data or helps to create revenue from one model to another [13].

Data not only serve as a revenue stream but the open data concept has created a lot of transparency in the system of people and government. Government data available on the public domain helps to define services that are offered. The datasets released by the government highlights the progress of the projects, census data, etc. which are all the core of any ecosystem or industry [14]. A suitable example is the monetization of the vehicle data ways by the government of India from the Ministry of Road Transport and Highways (MoRTH). The ministry has sold vehicle data and registration records to the various private and government entities worth more than 50 crores till date in duration 2014–2019. The buyers comprise of 30 public and private sector banks, 20 logistics solution providers finance organizations 18 insurance organizations, and 5 automobile manufacturers. Only the non-personal data of the vehicles for share and a total of more than 20 indicators of 50 crore registrations have been sold. Source.

The third case from the Indian urban data exchange with established under Smart City mission. The first urban data exchange of an Indian city is established by Pune Smart City also known as Pune Urban Data Exchange (PUDX) which has 850 data sets available on the detection website.

This is the initiative from the Ministry of Housing and Urban Affairs (MoHUA) and Indian Urban Data Exchange (IUDX), and Pune Smart City. This is to help citizens, academic institutions, entrepreneurs, government, industry, and cities. In their first stage, they have connected the Smart City administration, police, cab operators, cellular service provider, safety data aggregator, safety application provider, citizen mobile apps. In their recent initiative, they have launched the women safety application and this platform has integrated the data from the street lights, police, traffic, geographical location to serve better to the citizens in need.

Also, there are few bigger players in the industry in such as Amazon Web services (AWS), Dawex, Quandl, and Centre for Monitoring Indian Economy (CMIE). These companies are big players in the data exchange business for quite a long time and each has its own a diverse database but each operates on a distinct model.

Among these few companies have been compared and used as a benchmark to formulate the business model further in research.

### 2.1 Smart City data

Smart cities are constructed by connecting the city's public infrastructure with city application systems and passing collected data through numerous layers. City application systems then use data to make better decisions when controlling different city infrastructures [15, 16]. These application systems allow additional ICCC components to aggregate, consume, and process the information for deriving insights. Data collection and processing consists of modules for collecting and converting data from multiple structures, data repositories and diverse data formats [4].

The ICCC is the city's brain, making it smart, sustainable and ready for the future by monitoring all of the city's activities. Such centers are built to integrate knowledge through various applications and sensors deployed across the city, and then provide actionable intelligence with accurate analysis for decision-makers with the aid of sensors installed throughout the region [3]. The data collection under ICCC collects real-time data from sensor systems, data sources, static and real-time data streams for air and water quality control, light sensors for street light monitoring, metering tools, telematics and location-based apps, proximity sensors, surveillance and security cameras, sensors for disaster detection [2]. Hence, the data is distinct and non-perishable in nature making it a unique value proposition.

Smart cities had already started using data for good governance and taking strategic decisions. For example, the city of Ahmedabad in the state of Gujarat deployed Automated Fare Collection Service (AFCS), Automatic Vehicle Location System (AVLS), Passenger Information System (PIS), Vehicle Planning Schedule and Dispatch System (VPSD), Depot Management System (DMS) in their Bus Rapid Transit System. These are few of the IoT systems deployed in traffic system in smart cities which will later form a basis of study for targeted customers. All of these involved immense tech interventions and hence could generate real-time data for city transit service. Around 69 cities of the 100 cities have created Integrated Command Control Centers [17]. Data from each service is collected and analyzed uniformly in a command control center against key performance indicators to create more efficient and dynamic bus service operations, and a smarter, safer travel experience for commuters, across the ticketing, in-station, and in-journey stages [18].

The Bhubaneswar Smart City of the state of Orissa had deployed environmental sensors for, a sensor-based monitoring dashboard. The main environmental challenges that Bhubaneswar faces include rapid unplanned development especially construction, increasing pollution from vehicles and commercial establishments, road dust and other fugitive emissions, and significantly higher noise levels. The instruments transmit sensor data to the cloud platform through Ethernet / General Packet Radio Service connection, where it is stored and real-time analysis is done to make it meaningful. It is then visualized using a pollution-monitoring dashboard, where data is presented using interactive graphics and statistics for easy interpretation by citizens and administrators [19].

This data gives insights to the cities to take strategic decisions on several dimensions for better service performance. This creates an enabling ecosystem to makes the cities liveable. They are also used for monitoring citizen activities in public spaces making them also participate and be responsible for their conduct which is a crucial factor given the population and diversity in India.

Internet of Things (IoT) is revolutionizing the functioning of smart cities, especially in areas such as Efficient Water System, Smart Traffic Control, Accessible Public Transit, Energy-Saving Houses, Smart Parking, Productive Parking, Smart Street Lighting, Safe Environment, and Waste Management [20].

Indian government has succeeded in creating an Open Government Data (OGD) portal to promote transparent data. On this portal data is already being pooled to a data lake and refined for public use from a data warehouse. This website helps policy agencies to distribute their data sets for free public access, in a transparent format. Around 538,330 resources have been submitted to the website so far, and has received more than 31.64 million views. Many of those types of data can be personalized and optimized [21].

Thus far, from 100 Smart Cities the accessible data network has 12,547 data catalogs. Despite of having huge number of data catalogs the level and refinement of these data is not enough to get rich inferences for the cities. The data is being collated at macro level but still the analytics are weak and lead to suboptimal utilization of such real time data to take strategic decisions for the city. Wherein it can be observed that the private data platforms are able to sell their product due to the depth, richness and extent of information the data is able to generate for specific user segments. Many private entities like Google, Facebook and various e commerce companies are able to utilize the information obtained from their platform to sustain and grow their businesses or even arrive at data-based business models.

In contrast to that, being one of the complex and high maintenance systems involved in smart city missions, the data portal initiative needs to be taken to a level where it is capable enough to cater needs of data consumers and could support a part of expenses by revenues generated from it.

### 2.2 Smart City finance

The Smart City Mission being a Centrally Sponsored Scheme (CSS) the Central Government of India provides budgetary assistance to the Smart City Project to the amount of Rs. 48,000 crores over 5 years, i.e., an average Rs. 100 crore per region annually. The State / Urban Local Bodies (ULB) would have to spend an equivalent sum on a reciprocal basis; thus, almost Rupees one lakh crore of government / ULB funds would be required for the creation, operation and sustenance of Smart Cities.

The investment plan of each Smart City is different, based on the degree of commitment, model, implementing and repaying ability. Substantial funds are likely to be needed to execute the Smart City plan and to this end both the Center and the State must use policy grants to raise financing from internal and external sources.

The Government of India (GOI) grants and the States / ULB funding allocation would only cover a fraction of the expense of the initiative. Balance funds for operations are required to be collected through novel funding frameworks. Some of the smart cities are able to tap potential of municipal bonds, land monetization and other methods. The GOI encourages smart cities to come up with innovative financing methods to make Smart City systems more sustainable. With immense capital deployment under smart city mission the cities in India are in a dilemma to sustain the initiative as the operations and maintenance of smart city assets need to be fetched by the urban local body itself [7].

Although smart cities have been provided with some seed funding from the Centre and the state, with some to be created by their own budget, the financial necessity remains enormous as smart city strategy needs to support the whole city and not just the region specified for growth in the times to come.

### 2.3 Data as a source of revenue for cities

For example, "Terbine" is an enormous system of IoT data feeds to organizations involved with smart city research and pilot projects. This exchange offers sensor data sources that include electricity, water, wastewater, air quality, vehicular counts and movements from land/air/sea. Data researchers use deep web searching and customized Terbine tools to seek out publicly available machine-generated/sensor data from many sources. These include towns, cities, counties, and states, whole governments around the world, plus universities, research institutions, and more. Searchers then create highly descriptive metadata and submit them for entry into the Terbine system. Thus, bringing the data generated from the actual infrastructural elements found within and around municipalities into a single cohesive system, makes it discoverable and usable to researchers and project implementers alike [22].

With virtually every industry sector beginning to utilize Artificial Intelligence for internal processes, systems operation, supply chain and logistics, plus customer interactions, the requirement for AIs to discover, access and process data coming from machines is increasing rapidly. Smart cities in particular are key areas for implementation of AI-based functionality [23].

The technology revolution which is envisaged here would cost capital. Given that the private sector has the ability to harvest huge dividends from this information, charging them for its usage is common but there are limited cases where cities are monetizing data as a revenue model [7]. The financial position of cities in India is not encouraging enough to fund for the operations and maintenance of smart city projects. It is imperative for them to find a viable source for continuing with the initiatives taken under smart city mission reasonable.

The Ministry of Road Transport and Highways (MoRTH) experimented with monetizing vehicle data. The ministry came with a bulk data sharing policy to share data related to driving license and vehicle registration to various private and government entities. The buyers comprise of public and private sector banks, logistics solution providers finance organizations, insurance organizations, and automobile manufacturers. Only the non-personal data of the vehicles was shared and a total of more than 20 indicators of 50 crore registrations have been sold [24]. Though policy have been scrapped now, the agency monetized data to a considerable extent. However, in 2020 the policy was scrapped due to privacy issues arising out of triangulation [25]. This initiative if applied appropriately with better business models and backed by data privacy settings in accordance with the data privacy act (still in draft stages in India) can not only help government agencies generate revenue but also would be provide a sound base for researchers, private businesses, lending agencies to better strategies their offerings.

### 2.4 Data from G2B as a source of strategic competitive advantage

Information is a critical source to attain competitive advantage. Both established competitors and new entrants in most industries leverage with data-driven strategies to innovate, compete and capture value.

Vast data sets are being compiled and evaluated to identify trends for decision making and developing intelligent strategies to enhance the value proposition of the offerings. According to research carried out by the McKinsey Global Institute and the Market Technology Office of McKinsey & Company, the sheer volume of data produced, processed and extracted for insights has become economically important to companies, governments, and consumers [26].

Companies in current times could effectively monetize from data through enhancing their data storage and offer the data to other customers or companies. Data could be raw or purified based on the inventory and needs of the buyer. Vodafone sells mobile network data to TomTom to enhance their real-time navigating services. Similarly, Barclay's bank provides a platform for SME companies to compare their financial (key performance indicators) KPI's to others. But at the same time, the major setback would be the ability of the partner or purchaser to have the same system that would support data apart from the sensitivity of it [27].

Since the data in G2B is unique in nature, it can help generate potential development possibilities and completely different market areas, such as those aggregating and reviewing data from the sector. Many of these will be companies that are sitting in the middle of large flows of information where data can be captured and analyzed about products and services, buyers and suppliers, consumer preferences and intent [26].

As soon as businesses and policymakers realize Big Data's ability to produce higher efficiency, greater value for customers, and the next phase of innovation in the world economy, they will be granted a good enough motivation to move robustly to address the obstacles to its usage [26]. Like the targeted advertising which Facebook and other tech giants practice is a big business for them.

This is the kind of potential government can unlock out of their collected data. In doing so, they will open opportunities for new market competition, higher public-sector productivity that will make for improved infrastructure, and balance fiscal deficit to some extent.

### 2.5 Policy and regulatory framework

As of now regulatory framework Personal Data Protection Bill ("PDP Bill") and Information Technology Act, 2000 ("IT Act") empowers the government to manage and organize the data within government and non-personal data to various stakeholders. But the PDP Bill introduced various contentious concepts such as data localization and data mirroring, which caused much consternation among corporate stakeholders who would have had to restructure significant parts of their data flow architectures to comply with such requirements. The existing IT Act is a relic of its time and does not adequately cater to modern data protection requirements. Therefore, a comprehensive overhaul of all data laws in India is a positive step towards solving India's data woes in a holistic manner. Recently media reports citing that government sources have indicated that the Government of India will shortly commence work on a new law to replace India's IT Act. As part of this process, it appears that the Government may introduce policies on data governance and cybersecurity, a "Digital India Act" to replace the IT Act and new regulations to replace the PDP Bill [28].

In support to this the Ministry of Electronics and Information Technology, GOI released draft National Data Governance Framework Policy (NDRFP) empowering data to be harnessed for more effective Digital Government, Public good, and innovation by maximizing data led governance and catalyzing data-based innovation that can transform government services and their delivery to citizens, especially in areas of social importance that include agriculture, healthcare, law and justice, education, among others. This policy also launches a non-personal data-based India Datasets program and addresses the methods and rules to ensure that non-personal data and anonymized data from both Government and Private entities are safely accessible by Research and Innovation eco-system [2]. But considering the risks like triangulation and revealing the identity of individuals and assets it has to be handled carefully so that data sets from open sources and received under NDRFP combined should not lead to privacy issues like what happened with vehicular data from Bulk Data Sharing Policy under MoRTH.

## 3. Methods

Selling the data or analysis derived from it, have been studied scarcely in business and academic literature. In academic literature, the phenomenon of big data and the utilization of it have been popular topics over the last few years.

The changing business environment creates new possibilities for data utilization, data monetization as being one option for broader data usage. This has created a research gap, as companies are increasingly using the data in new ways, while the academic literature does not cover these new data derived offerings.

Therefore, the concept of data exchange is a nascent Indian ecosystem and is more practiced on B2B with high confidentiality on backend thus this is an under-researched theoretical topic in the Indian context, therefore, the qualitative methodology with support of case studies, documents and journals from various sources for data is used. Further, due to limited availability of data wherever suitable, the case studies, and practical practices would be used for the genesis of this exploratory research.

## 4. New perspective

### 4.1 Leveraging Smart City data

Smart Cities are deploying emerging technologies to capture real time data from cities in different sectors. Barcelona, Copenhagen and Singapore, as indicators of Smart Cities, are frequently cited being the front runners. There are examples of Big Data and its insights for enhancing the transport industry tremendously in a number of ways. It may be used to ensure that at any given moment, consumers are constantly made informed of the most appropriate / efficient mode of transport. Train operating companies now use Big Data to process live seat allocation data to say which carriages have the most seats available to passengers waiting on station platforms. Public transit is one of the main problems confronting today's communities. For example, in the transport sector big Data includes such data on bus and rail vehicle occupancy, real-time car parking data, local weather and air quality data, road speed and traffic count data, and real-time infrastructure status. Customer identification may serve to optimize customer satisfaction in addition to the improved customer experience resulting from improved awareness. The collection and successful review of the same customer's repeat grievances may result in a single, more efficient response. Smart Cities and Big Data will also enhance customer satisfaction by providing creative technologies that substitute both system and ticket utilizing mobile apps [5].

The more integrated and open our rail networks are, the greater the profits for travel companies and transporters. Improved information for consumers would contribute to a more effective usage of transport networks- time and resources optimization for passengers. Previously, the amount of time saved arising from the opening of Transport for London's accessible data was calculated to be around £58 m a year, with an average investment of less than £1 million. Additionally, the Big Data buying / licensing industry itself, and other associated businesses, would broaden and thereby boost economic development as a whole [5].

Smart City data also helps digital marketers to help target consumers with more tailored advertising they will more definitely like to see. Google, and now Facebook — the main digital ads players — have proven really good at developing and providing more non-intrusive advertisements. The explosion of mobile apps, especially smartphones, has provided a significant incentive for digital marketers to offer mobile unique advertising at the right time — in context — to the right people. It has been seen that hyper-localized ads improves consumer interaction and sales volume. This will also put forth actionable perspectives that guide strategic decisions and strategies [29].

### 4.2 Business model canvas

These data exchange work on specialized service delivery business models. For creating a simplistic picture, Business Model Canvas by Alexander Osterwalder is used. A Business Model Canvas is a strategic management tool to quickly and easily define and communicate a business idea or concept. It is a method that works through the fundamental elements of a business or product, coherently structuring an idea. In these, the customer segments which the entity is going to target base on the segment, value propositions based on the amount of value and USP we can provide to the customer, channels for delivering the service, type of customer relationships to be maintained with the customer, revenue streams that would generate income for the business, key resources required to run the whole business, key activities that need to happen to sustain business and operations, key partnerships that are required for business, the cost structure of all the expenses of the smooth functioning of the business [30]. These are identified to formulate in-depth insights and design a business layout as shown below in the **Table 1**.

| **Key partners** | **Key activities** | **Value proposition** | **Customer relationships** | **Customer segment** |
|---|---|---|---|---|
| | **Key resources** | | **Channels** | |
| Cost structure | | Revenue stream | | |

**Table 1.**
*Business model canvas.*

First to identify the right data sets few of the smart City IoT platforms have been listed such as intelligent traffic management, smart lighting, smart health, which collection, smart environment, smart water supply, smart meter, and smart parking. These platforms have been thoroughly evaluated and out of these data sets, the data collected under these platforms have been narrowed down.

## 5. Business model

The approach that has been followed to identify the right data sets for the right customers to provide the right value through the right channel and that makeup to the whole business model.

Based on the segmentation the mass market it turns out to the retailers, consulting firms, application developers, telecom services, advertising companies, research companies, hospitals, and the niche market belongs to car insurance company, payment wallet companies, credit card companies, transporters, shopping malls, real estate developer.

To carry on further study with an example out of all these companies two of the companies from the mass market in two of the companies from the niche market have been identified. For the chapter the case of advertisement agencies has been considered as a targeted buyer.

After identifying the companies and the target segment, further, the right value proposition for each of the companies has been evaluated.

### 5.1 Customer segment and value proposition: Value proposition canvas

Since the study aims to establish a G2B system, the value proposition for each of the businesses will vary as per their requirement since every business is unidentical and every business will have a unique set of requirements for their service to their clients. The value proposition will differ for each of the customer segments [30].

#### *5.1.1 Value proposition: Advertising companies*

The customer jobs of the advertisement companies are to look for an increase in awareness, wanted to have innovation in their products, to have the most profitable spaces, and retain customers also they wanted to stay up-to-date to stay ahead of their competitors and to capture potential target markets. The gains for the advertisement company would be to keep customer retention, innovation, to acquire new customers, and to have a strong network. The pains to achieve all this would be if the advertisement company acquire loss-making locations or if they had a hard time finding new markets. Also, extreme competition would be a pain and new entrants, wrong surveys, and time have taken processes to collect data is a pain.

The products and services that will be provided are area-based insights based on the data sets with an analysis tool through an interactive platform is to be provided for the assessment of areas by the company. This is assisted by backend services if opted for it. Gain creators would be analytics and tips to use analytics that for advertisement companies, the real-time data, the coverage area, and the pre-feed calculation modules will lead to gain and save time. On the other hand, pain relievers would be the product that would minimize the risk of failure, it is practical and visual and easy to use prefilled with applicable content accurate data and with real-time data collection.

There are also few unavoidable and addressable gains, customer jobs, and pains for advertisement companies like customer retention that is based on the competencies of the advertisement companies. Also is an extreme competition that they have to face on their own then the issue with a strong network and acquiring new customers also lies with the competency and the service provided by the advertisement companies to their customers.

Concluding the business model canvas, we can say value proposition is information as a service that is accurate, trusted, descriptive, and convenient for a customer segment that is advertisement companies that fall under mass segment as shown in **Table 2** below.

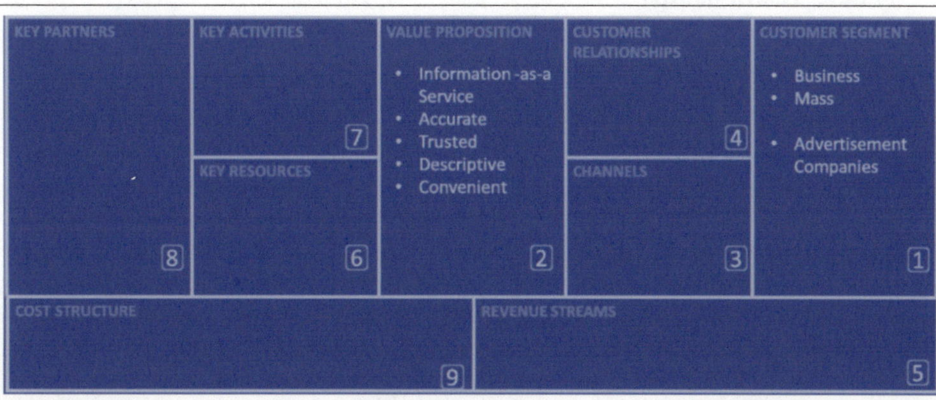


**Table 2.**
*Business model canvas: Value proposition for advertising agencies.*

Before going it must be realized that out of the data sets that will be provided to these companies, not all the indicators or attributes would be useful for the advertisement companies. To evaluate what are the data sets and indicators are for specific use for the advertisement companies, a few data sets have been shortlisted on how to weight the most useful indicators that would be e evaluated for the advertisement companies. Now there are a different number of indicators under each of the data set this like one IoT sensor collects a total of 12 indicators, Citywide Wi-Fi has a total of 38 indicators, electronic ticketing has a total of six indicators, smart poles have 38 indicators, multi-service digital caves have a total of 12 indicators. Based on this there are only a few indicators that would be packaged for the advertisement companies and the rest are of no use for the advertisement companies. The useful indicators make some portion of the total indicators in each data sets on evaluating that we would get the amount of leveraging the company or sell the advertisement company is getting over is data set. For example, under the first dataset, only 5 out of 12 data indicators are required, under city Wi-Fi only 3 out of 38 data sets are required, for electronic ticketing to out of 6, for smartphones 538, and for multi-service, digital gives 5 out of 12. This will help o.

Under this exercise we have determined the value proposition for the specific company and how your product can help this company to achieve its customer jobs also how much leverage that company is getting on our product.

### 5.2 Channels

Further evaluation of the business model, two types of channels is owned or it could be a partner channel or a combination of both. The own channel would be direct and on the other hand, the partner channel would be indirect. Under direct and we can have Salesforce, web sales on stores, and under indirect services, we can have partner stores or wholesales stores.

Show by comparing benchmarks of the services from AWS, Dawex, Quandl, and CMIE, all of these have their direct sales force and the product is sold through web sales since it is an intangible asset. It is not necessary to have physical resources concluding out the sales force would be there for the proposed business model with the help of web sales.

### 5.3 Customer relationships

There are distinct kinds of relationships that we could avail to our customers like personal assistance, customized dedicated personal assistance, self-service, automatic services like backend support from AI and ML or there could be blogs communities to help the customers. In AWS there is no dedicated personal assistance in the vertical of data exchange but they do provide rest of the services. In Dawex the only provision of personal assistance dedicated personal assistance to the large enterprises and self-services option for the most basic one and the rest are not provided. For Quandl there is an availability of automated service rest of the services are available based on the package type the customers are opting for. For CMIE only personal assistants and dedicated personal assistance are available for the customers. Concluding all the options since this data exchange would be in the critical and small stages it is recommended to have a personal assistance type of customer relationship also dedicated personal assistance to the large enterprise rest could be dropped. But in the future when scaling this data exchange, the rest of the type of customer relationships could be included in this data exchange.

### 5.4 Revenue streams

Revenue streams could be categorized in the sale of the assets, uses fees, subscription fees, renting for leasing of the platform, license to use the product, brokerage fees on the sales, or it could be through advertisement. Under the selected vertical in AWS, only the revenue is made on asset sale and the brokerage fee is also charged from the vendor that has to list its product on the platform. For Dawex do there is only use it brokerage fee for the big enterprises a subscription fee for the small and base packages to use the products. Also, there is a licensing fee to use the platform. In Quandl only subscription fees charged for the product used also the brokerage fees are collected from the vendors that are listing their products on this platform. In CMIE subscription fees are charged based on the type of user that could be categorized in companies or institutional packages.

Based on the above benchmarking it would be appropriate to charge only a subscription fee type of model in the earlier stages and later on added to the licensing brokerage fees when scaling up.

### 5.5 Key resources

Key resources could be physical, intellectual, human, and financial resources. In all the four cases all these aforementioned resources are required in all the cases, therefore, concluded that each type of resource is essential to make this business model viable.

### 5.6 Key activities

There are three types of activities that are production, problem-solving, or providing a platform or a network. Buy understanding of AWS it was found that all three key activities are there, i.e., production, problem-solving, and provision of the platform is there. In Dawex the only production of the data and platform network is present. Problem-solving is a key activity is not there since it is operating to provide data not prescriptive or predictive analysis. Quandl has all three key activities just like AWS and CMIE does not have a problem-solving feature. It only has the production and provision of a platform network to provide the service. Inference to that these business models, concludes the production. That would be provided over a network hence the activity would also include the provision and also the packaging is based on the prescriptive and predictive analytics therefore problem-solving component would also be included in this business model.

### 5.7 Key partners

This has a breakdown in 4 types of partnerships. The first strategic alliance between the non-competitors, and corporation that would be a strategic partnership between competitors. The third is joint ventures to develop new businesses and products. Fourth is the buyer–supplier relationship to sure reliable supplies of the product.

In AWS we have only a strategic alliance between competitors and buyer–supplier relationships. In Dawex to the buyer–supplier relationship does not exist, the rest of the options are present. In Quandl there is no corporation or strategic partnership between competitors rest of the options of key partnership types are present. In CMIE there is no sort of key partnership is involved. Inference in this there could be a strategic alliance between non-competitive sort of partnership in the early stages of the business model. Also, the buyer–supplier relationship to have the supply of raw data into the system. The rest of the options are not recommended based on the risk involved.

### 5.8 Cost structure

Aforementioned shortlisted the key resources that are physical, intellectual, human, and financial will account for a cost. For physical this could be the infrastructure required to run these operations on intellectual sides we need licenses permissions brand and the raw product. For human resources, there would be salaries and insurances. Also, there would be a maintenance cost of the digital platform, background services, and sales marketing.

Collating all the exercises that we have mentioned above we have concluded a business model for advertising consulting firms based on the concluded business model components as below in **Table 3**.

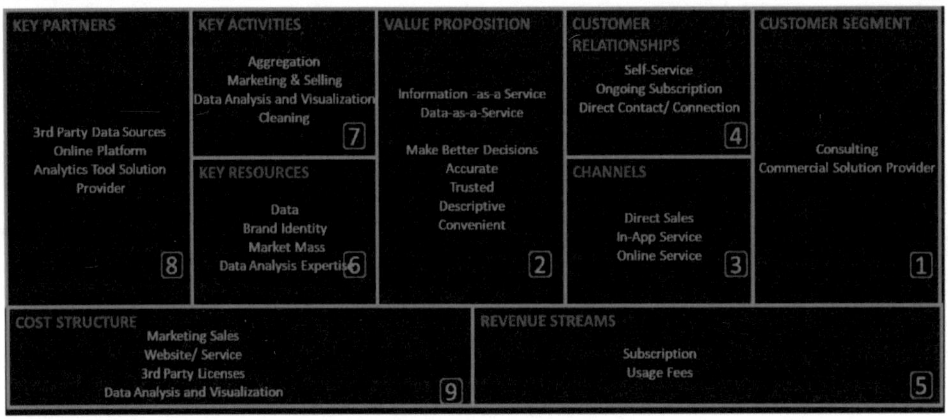

| KEY PARTNERS (8) | KEY ACTIVITIES (7) / KEY RESOURCES (6) | VALUE PROPOSITION (2) | CUSTOMER RELATIONSHIPS (4) / CHANNELS (3) | CUSTOMER SEGMENT (1) |
|---|---|---|---|---|
| 3rd Party Data Sources<br>Online Platform<br>Analytics Tool Solution Provider | Key Activities: Aggregation<br>Marketing & Selling<br>Data Analysis and Visualization<br>Cleaning<br><br>Key Resources: Data<br>Brand Identity<br>Market Mass<br>Data Analysis Expertise | Information -as-a Service<br>Data-as-a-Service<br><br>Make Better Decisions<br>Accurate<br>Trusted<br>Descriptive<br>Convenient | Customer Relationships: Self-Service<br>Ongoing Subscription<br>Direct Contact/ Connection<br><br>Channels: Direct Sales<br>In-App Service<br>Online Service | Consulting<br>Commercial Solution Provider |
| COST STRUCTURE (9): Marketing Sales<br>Website/ Service<br>3rd Party Licenses<br>Data Analysis and Visualization | | REVENUE STREAMS (5): Subscription<br>Usage Fees | | |

**Table 3.**
*Showing derived business model for advertising consulting firms.*

## 6. Conclusion

The data exchange businesses shall always be value-driven since data is an intangible asset the information shall hold the value for the customer. If data is not valuable and distinct to the customer then there is no unique selling proposition in the product. Data exchange is an expensive operation so most of the services can be outsourced as there is a cheaper option available outside to outsource the businesses rather than having again in house setup.

Creating industry specific data insights by leveraging the data capturing ability of the smart cities and further monetizing the same will be a win – win proposition for government and private entities. But caution needs to be exercised with respect to privacy breach. It is particularly essential for India, as cities are trying to automate their delivery of public infrastructure by introducing interconnected Pan City Smart Technologies under the Smart Cities Project by producing huge volumes of data. Meeting digital infrastructure's operating and maintenance costs, measured at 15–20 per cent of capital annually, would be a challenging task unless we identify a revenue model [16].

*DOI: http://dx.doi.org/10.5772/intechopen.108345*

This system will not only help government to increase its efficiency for public operations and ease on financial support but also will help business to optimize, generate and expand new services while staying ahead of competitors. The transformation of the new open-data model into a data monetizing system creates a tremendous opportunity for all the stakeholders and a motivation for city officials to collect and feed appropriate data into the system.

## Author details

Mercy Samuel* and Siddharth Gupta
CEPT University, Ahmedabad, India

*Address all correspondence to: mercy@cept.ac.in

## References

[1] Ministry of Housing and Urban Affairs Government Government of India. Making a City Smart: Learnings from the Smart Cities Mission. Smart Cities Mission, Ministry of Housing and Urban Affairs, India: Government of India; 2021. Available from: https://smartnet.niua.org/sites/default/files/resources/making_a_city_smart_mar2021.pdf [Accessed: May 28, 2022]

[2] Ministry of Electronics and Information Technology Governement of India. National Data Governance Framework Policy. India: Ministry of Electronics and Information Technology Governement of India; 2022. Available from: https://www.meity.gov.in/writereaddata/files/National Data Governance Framework Policy_26 May 2022.pdf [Accessed: May 28, 2022]

[3] Government of Uttar Pradesh. Smart Cities. Uttar Pradesh: RFP; 2015. Available from: http://localbodies.up.nic.in/DLBGO/RFP_Uttar PradeshSMART CITY.pdf [Accessed: May 28, 2022]

[4] tele.net. Core Control- Key ICCC projects under the Smart Cities Mission. 2019. Available from: https://tele.net.in/core-control-key-iccc-projects-under-the-smart-cities-mission/ [Accessed: May 28, 2022]

[5] Bonas W, Rayner T. Deriving Transport Benefits from Big Data and Internet of Things. UK: Womble Bond Dickinson; 2017. Available from: https://www.womblebonddickinson.com/uk/insights/articles-and-briefings/deriving-transport-benefits-big-data-and-internet-things-smart [Accessed: May 28, 2022]

[6] Ministry of Housing and Urban Affairs Governement of India. Financing | Smartcities. India: Government of India; 2017. Available from: https://smartcities.gov.in/financing [Accessed: May 28, 2022]

[7] Ministry of Finance Government of India. India Economic Survey 2018-2019. India: Government of India; 2019

[8] Buff A, Wixom BH, Tallon P. Foundations for Data Monetization. SAS Best Pract. White Pap., no. 402. Cambridge, MA: MIT Sloan Center for Information Systems Research and SAS Institute Inc.; 2015

[9] Opher A, Chou A, Onda A, Sounderrajan K. The Rise of the Data Economy: Driving Value through Internet of Things Data Monetization. NY, USA: IBM Corp; 2016. pp. 1-16

[10] Srinivasan AR, Narasimhan, and Rajaram. New Revenue Streams in Health Data Monetization. India: Tata Consultancy Services Limited; 2019

[11] Bram JT, Warwick-Clark B, Mehta K. Utilization and monetization of healthcare data in developing countries. Big Data. 2015;**3**(2):59-66

[12] Thomas LDW, Leiponen A. Big data commercialization. IEEE Engineering Management Review. 2016;**44**(2):74-90

[13] Schüritz R, Seebacher S, Dorner R. Capturing Value from Data: Revenue Models for Data-Driven Services. Proc. 50th Hawaii Int. Conf. Syst. Sci. Hawaii: University of Hawaii at Mānoa; 2017. pp. 5348-5357

[14] O'Hara K. Data Quality, Government Data and the Open Data Infosphere. AISB/IACAP World Congr. 2012 Inf.

Qual. Symp. United Kingdom: University of Southampton; 2012

[15] Deloitte. The Challenge of Paying for Smart Cities Projects. Deloitte; 2018. Available from: https://www2.deloitte.com/content/dam/Deloitte/global/Documents/Public-Sector/gx-ps-the-challenge-of-paying-for-smart-cities-projects1.pdf [Accessed: May 28, 2022]

[16] Sajeesh KN, Bibek D. Opinion | City Data Monetization Could Help our Development Road Map. India: LiveMint; 2019. Available from: https://www.livemint.com/opinion/online-views/city-data-monetization-could-help-our-development-road-map-1568830292070.html [Accessed: May 28, 2022]

[17] JournalsOfIndia. 6th Anniversary of PMAY-U, AMRUT & Smart Cities Mission – JournalsOfIndia. India: Manifest IAS; 2021. Available from: https://journalsofindia.com/6th-anniversary-of-pmay-u-amrut-smart-cities-mission/ [Accessed: May 28, 2022]

[18] Nec. Smart City Ahmedabad Gets IoT-Driven Buses. India: NEC Corporation; 2018. Available from: www.nec.com [Accessed: May 28, 2022]

[19] Bisht DS. Smart Cities: Testing Ground for Sensor-Based Instruments. India: DownToEarth; 2020. Available from: https://www.downtoearth.org.in/blog/urbanisation/smart-cities-testing-ground-for-sensor-based-instruments-71345 [Accessed: May 28, 2022]

[20] Grizhnevich A. IoT for Smart Cities: Use Cases and Implementation Strategies. Dallas Area, Texas: ScienceSoft; 2018. Available from: https://www.scnsoft.com/blog/iot-for-smart-city-use-cases-approaches-outcomes [Accessed: May 28, 2022]

[21] Catalog | Open Government Data (OGD) Platform India. 2022. Available from: https://data.gov.in/catalogs/ministry_department/nsdi-india-geo-portal-national-spatial-data-infrastructure-nsdi. [Accessed: May 28, 2022]

[22] Forst A. World's Largest IoT Data Ecosystem Opens to Smart City Developers. UK: Traffic Technology Today; 2019. Available from: https://www.traffictechnologytoday.com/news/data/worlds-largest-iot-data-ecosystem-opens-to-smart-city-developers.html [Accessed: May 28, 2022]

[23] Terbine. Terbine _ Terbine Opens World's Largest System of IoT Data to Smart Cities Players

[24] Barik S. SBI, Mercedes and ICICI Lombard among the 142 Entities That Bought Vehicle Registration Data from Government. India: MediaNama; 2019. Available from: https://www.medianama.com/2019/09/223-142-entities-that-bought-vahan-data/ [Accessed: May 28, 2022]

[25] Internet Freedom Foundation. MoRTH Scraps its Bulk Data Sharing Policy. India: InternetFreedom; 2020. Available from: https://internetfreedom.in/morth-bulk-data-sharing-policy-scrapped [Accessed: May 28, 2022]

[26] McGuire T, Manyika J, Michael C. Why big data is the new competitive advantage. Ivey Business Journal. 2012

[27] M. Laitila. Data Monetization: Utilizing Data as an Asset to Generate New Revenues for Firm. Finland: Aalto University; 2017

[28] Malik R. Revamping India's Outdated Data Laws. India: The Economic Times; 2022. Available from: https://economictimes.indiatimes.

com/small-biz/policy-trends/one-of-the-last-few-countries-without-modern-data-protection-law-why-india-needs-an-urgent-revamp/articleshow/91556170.cms [Accessed: May 28, 2022]

[29] Qubole. The Impact of Big Data on the Digital Advertising Industry. India: Qubole; 2014. Available from: https://www.qubole.com/blog/big-data-advertising-case-study [Accessed: May 28, 2022]

[30] Osterwalder A, Pigneur Y, Smith A, Clark T, van der Pijl P Business Model Generation: A Handbook for Visionaries, Game Changers, and Challengers. John Wiley and Sons; 2010

Chapter 9

# Understanding the Artificial Intelligence Implementation for Allocating an Order to a Seller among Multiple Sellers Who Sell the Same Product

*Md Imtiaz Ahmed*

## Abstract

E-commerce sectors are growing rapidly worldwide and it adopts the new technological innovation drastically, such as embracing artificial intelligence in e-commerce sectors. Machine learning adaptation in e-commerce sectors is the most and much news already published by giant e-commerce companies, such as Amazon and eBay. The aim of this paper is to find out how artificial intelligence helps the e-commerce platform to choose a seller from multiple sellers when the same products or listings are sold by multiple sellers. When a customer will place the order, then who will get the order of the customer as multiple sellers sell the item within the same product listings. In the research, it is figured out that machine learning techniques are normally used for the selection of the seller where the prior points used for finding the appropriate seller are feedback or ratings, seller products location or distance from the customer, advertising or PPC or campaign, discounts, etc.

**Keywords:** e-commerce, artificial intelligence, machine learning, order management, multiple sellers

## 1. Introduction

The e-commerce sector is growing drastically every day due to the customer's trust and easiness of the products ordering process. It can be said that e-commerce is one of the most identical evolutions of the twenty-first century and in COVID-19 situations worldwide [1]; its value or worth cannot be written in a sentence, which means the e-commerce sector's priority goes up dramatically. Many small businesses and large businesses use e-commerce platforms to operate their business and get sales from the platform. However, most of the people or companies who run or operate their business on large platforms, such as Amazon, eBay, and Google shopping, actually do not know how they actually get the sales from them.

How to get a sale from an e-commerce platform? Many people or companies have these questions normally in their minds. Then the methodologies that are popular nowadays are that one should use digital marketing or SEO or advertisements [2]. Many people or companies invest a lot of money into the marketing purpose to get sales on an e-commerce platform. If one uses their own e-commerce platform, then it is okay to invest a lot of money on sales and marketing purposes, as well as getting popularity of their own e-commerce platform; however, in the 1st world countries, most companies or people are moving to the giant e-commerce platform, such as the Amazon, eBay, Alibaba, Rakuten, and Google shopping, because they know that they can get orders from their platform if normally they list or create their stores on these giant platforms. How can one seller or a company or person get sales from a popular platform? This is one of the big questions nowadays.

One should say that these giant platforms invested a lot of money for building their popularity or getting attractions to the customers. Not only did they invest money in advertisements but also in the adaption of new technologies and methods for implementation in their platform. Artificial intelligence is one of the prime technologies that are being adopted in e-commerce by which many tasks are very light and can be used for prediction, forecasting, and allocation purposes [3]. Customer behavior to the platform and trusted customers or defaulted customers can be sorted out through the implementation of artificial intelligence [4]. How the products can be cycled and how the product's assortment helped in selling an item in e-commerce can be pointed out through artificial intelligence [5].

Nevertheless, it should be stated that artificial intelligence applications, such as machine learning, data mining, deep learning, and recommendations algorithms, are vastly used by a lot of giant e-commerce platform owners and they keep updating themselves with the use of these techniques [6]. The recommendation algorithms are very popular and are used by a lot of sectors or industries, such as Netflix, Amazon, eBay, and Google [7]. Recent news comes from Amazon is that they reduced packaging waste by the use of machine learning [8], so it can be noted that giant platforms keep updating themselves with the use of AI. In this paper, the key technologies that surround how one should understand that they can get sales from an e-commerce platform where multiple sellers sell the same product. Though it cannot be stated that every platform uses the same key technologies that are stated in this paper, however, sellers or companies will gain vast knowledge after reading the paper (**Figure 1**).

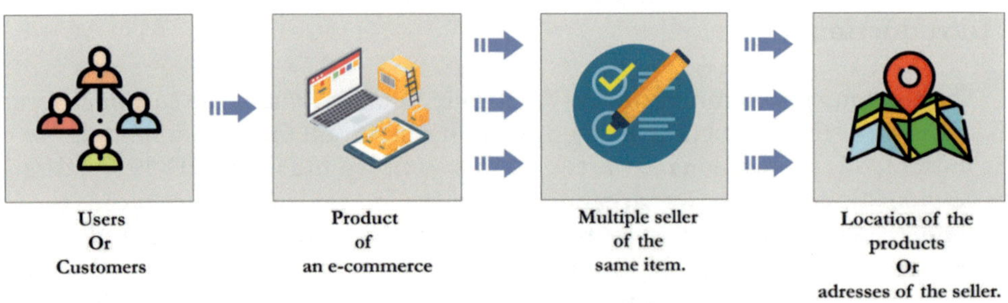


**Figure 1.**
*E-commerce ordering procedure for a product where multiple sellers sell the same product.*

## 2. Background

E-commerce sectors are growing rapidly, and in most cases, people are most likely to build B2C e-commerce sites. However, there are few e-commerce sectors that provide multiple sellers opt for specific products or brands. Some of the e-commerce platforms both served as B2C, B2B, and in all e-commerce sectors that provide an option for companies or stores to list their items on their platform are normally called C2B but have the option of B2C and B2B as well. The seller who is selling the items on the e-commerce must need to know how to use their platform and how to add images or products. In many cases, sellers are worried about the sales and want to generate sales by using advertising or campaign techniques. Without implementing or investing in marketing for the products, some sellers can easily get sales as well. This paper focuses on how sales can be generated from e-commerce by the e-commerce built-in methods or implementation of AI or machine learning methods.

Research carried out shows that it depends on the customer's rating and feedback [9]; however, many researchers find out the products need to be attractive [10] or products' popularity can be an eminence that can play a good role in the sales of a product. Product choices for selling purposes on e-commerce are similar, like before starting any company, one should think and survey the market and how the people are willing to absorb the new products and the similar product's current market worth or value [11]. People or companies need to know a basic understanding of how the platforms normally work and how the technology helps run an e-commerce platform to be more identical so that marketing costs will be less.

It can be stated that without any investment in the advertisement, one seller can get sales from a platform such as Amazon, eBay, and Etsy. Actually, no one knows how it will work, however, the key technology behind it is the recommendation algorithm, whenever a similar type of product will be searched on the platform, if the seller item is cheap and have a good reputation, then it will show on the search [12]. However, there are some other criteria that are on the air for getting better search activities, such as elaborative descriptions, features, good zoom quality images, correct product type selection, and informative keywords. A group of researchers already worked on the features finding as it plays a vital role in the sales of products and comes up whenever a product search occurs [13]. It seems that for the betterment of the products, looks, and sales, the above criteria are necessary.

We are living in a Era where we cannot think of a single moment without the help of artificial intelligence, rather day by day more implementations are adopted to our regular life as AI shortens the tasks and helps us improve our tasks. Data science and machine learning are currently widely implemented in e-commerce sectors for sales and attracting customers [14]. The machine learning approach is used for fraud detection in e-commerce sectors as well [15]. The machine learning support vector machine used on the product reviews helps people's choices or attraction or sentiment analysis [16]; in some cases, machine learning is used to predict sales of a specific store's products [17]. Knowledge-based means using data mining techniques and machine learning the recommendation system actually work as well [18]. At last, it can be said that every aspect of the e-commerce sector is updating rapidly with the use of artificial intelligence, machine learning, recommended systems, data mining, etc.

## 3. Observation

In this research, the identical observation has made through the use of a renowned e-commerce platform and the main observation was about the multiple sellers who are selling the same item. Example: Let us say, a product is a sunglass, which is from the company Ray-Ban, and that item can be sold by different sellers as the manufacturer authorizes those sellers to sell the same product on their floor and online. So if all the sellers want to sell this item on online platforms, such as Amazon and eBay, then they have to use the manufacturer-provided specific UPC. By using the same UPC, different types of issues can arise and it is found in a research paper [19]. As the same product can be sold by multiple sellers, then questions can be arising to the seller who will get the order when a customer will place an order. The shortest path algorithm to find the nearest product location from the customer can be a good solution that can be stated for selling purposes [20]. However, the background of the technologies is still hidden as everyone knows that e-commerce sectors are adopting new technologies and artificial intelligence vastly, so how the order procedure beyond one product with multiple sellers works is still hidden. In this research, the basic ideas with the proper example will be given step by step to figure out the key technologies or the techniques that are involved in getting an order for a seller.

## 4. Research gap

The main research gap for this research, which is conducted, is finding how the large vendor manipulates the orders whenever a list of sellers sells the same item. It can be very good for the seller who wants to sell in large vendors, such as Amazon [21], Ebay, and Google shopping. Because if they can understand the technology behind how they can get the orders from the large vendor as they seem that it is very competitive. However, if they want to sell only their products, then they can judge whoever will buy their products, how much sales they can generate from the e-commerce platform, and they need to do research based on similar products, but it can be very useful for the retailers. If one seller sees that a product is sold by 40 different sellers, they normally will lose hope to sell that item and that can be a negative effect on the e-commerce sector. However, when they will find out that the main technology behind the selling procedures is artificial intelligence where each of the sellers will get a minimum order, then they will definitely move to the large platform for selling their products.

## 5. Experimental procedure

After years of observation of the e-commerce sectors, it is very identical that a product can be sold by different sellers or companies. Like a shoe of the UGG brand can be sold by multiple sellers on an e-commerce platform like Amazon, where each seller is different as they listed the item with the same UPC (Universal Product Code). So, let us say a seller sells a shoe whose size is 8, and the same shoe size has 6 different sellers, then sellers seem to be worried about from whom the customer will buy. It is true that one customer can choose from a list of sellers; however, in research, it is figured most cases customers do not choose sellers (**Figure 2**).

The experiment was done using the largest e-commerce platform Amazon [21] and multiple orders have been tried from different locations in the USA to figure out

*DOI: http://dx.doi.org/10.5772/intechopen.105560*

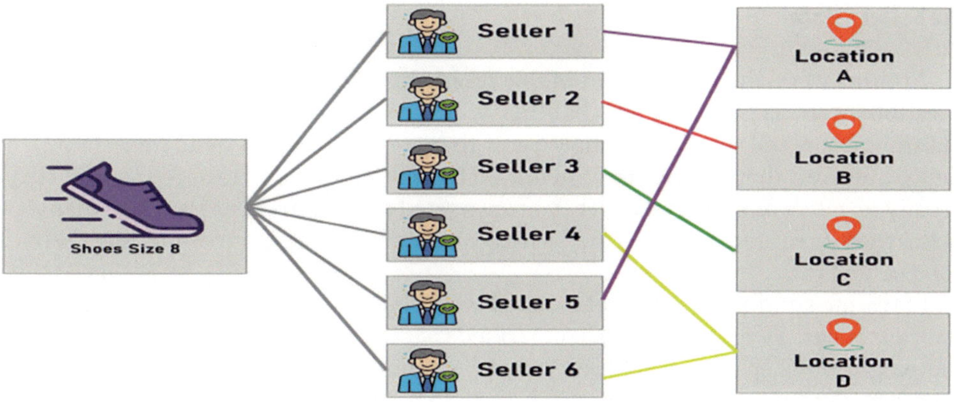


**Figure 2.**
*Multiple sellers of the same product and seller's location.*

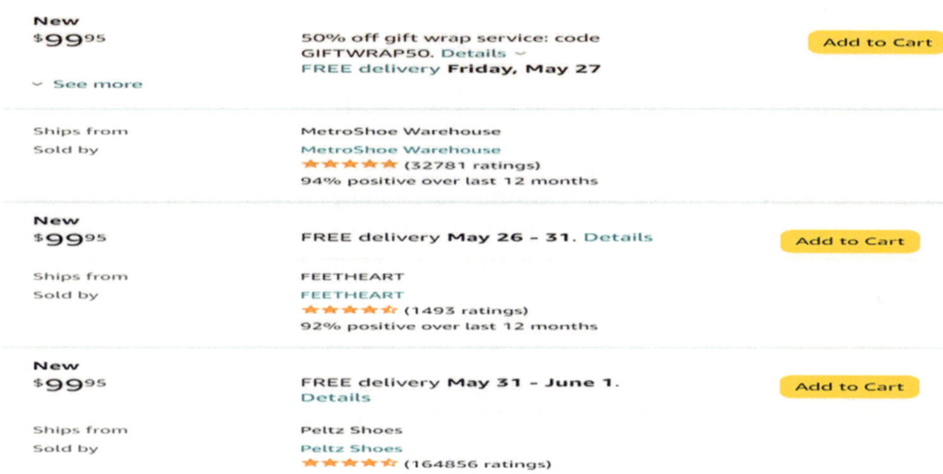


**Figure 3.**
*Twenty-seven sellers sell the same products and some of them are captured in the figure.*

which vendor is chosen whenever a customer from different states orders a product of UGG [22]. If one visits the product, then it will be found that around 20 plus seller sells the same product. In **Figure 3**, the images of the sellers are enlisted.

## 6. Data collection

### 6.1 Consumers data

In this research, feedback from 97 customers has been taken, where 75% of customers told that they do not choose the sellers, whereas 25% told that they sometimes but not always check the seller's name. A total of 25% of the customers also suggested that it is better to check the seller's overall scores, feedback, etc., so that they can normally think about the defect rate of the products or wrong shipment issues. Customers always look for prestigious sellers who are for a long time so that people have faith in them.

### 6.2 Sellers data

Around 40 sellers participated in this research, where they have been asked some questions, such as how they feel that they will get a chance to sell their products as multiple sellers sell the same item. Most of them replied that this is an uncertain thing, however, they always try to maintain their store's page attractively, and if they get any negative or bad reviews, they always satisfy the customer's issues. In many cases, they do refund and offer an exchange for the products for maintaining their good selling ratio.

In the questionnaire, it has been asked what they normally do for getting sales for their items. Twenty-nine of them replied that they normally do advertisements, campaigns, PPC (pay per click), discounts, etc. But in many cases, as the manufacturer bound them not to put discounts, then they cannot do it. Ten sellers told that they do nothing but they are getting orders. However, it is noted that those sellers who are doing advertisements, campaigns, PPC, etc., have better sales than the other sellers. So the question in mind is that how does the seller who does not do anything get sales as well?

## 7. Understanding the process of order distribution

It is figured out on the questionnaire that each seller can get sales from a platform whether they have good feedback (customer ratings) or no feedback (no customer ratings). However, if bad feedback (customer ratings) any seller has, then it will lower their chance of getting an order on an e-commerce platform.

### 7.1 Multiple sellers with good feedback

The key technologies of getting an order for the seller are normally evaluated by the system's hidden calculations that normally occur by artificial intelligence. Suppose that in machine learning we normally train the dataset that we have, then the algorithm predicts the results. So if we think of five sellers who have good ratings or feedback and sell the same item, then an algorithm can help allocate the customer's orders for them. If we draw with a diagram, then it can be easily understandable. Let us say, we have sellers 1, 2, 3, 4, and 5, where each of them has the ratings or feedback as follows:

- Seller 1 = 450 ratings
- Seller 2 = 200 ratings
- Seller 3 = 1010 ratings
- Seller 4 = 590 ratings
- Seller 5 = 900 ratings

So, if we train the dataset on a machine learning algorithm, then it can easily predict that seller 3 has the best rating, so the order should go to seller 3. However, a good system checks more basic points, such as the distance or location of the sellers as the buyer or consumers will always prefer the seller with less distance. So that the dataset-based distance algorithm can be an ideal technique for selecting a seller for the order [20]. Let us say that the five sellers have the distance from the customer as follows:

- Seller 1 = 300 km
- Seller 2 = 400 km
- Seller 3 = 1200 km
- Seller 4 = 350 km
- Seller 5 = 500 km

Now the system will calculate differently as the distance is another factor so that the system will allocate the nearest seller with average good ratings. So, in this case, the system will choose seller 4, though seller 1 has the lowest distance, however, seller 4 has a better rating than seller 1. So, the artificial intelligence applications help a seller for getting an order (**Figure 4**).

However, exceptions can be there if sellers use the system campaign or advertisements. Like seller 4 does not use the campaign, however, if seller 1 uses the campaign of the e-commerce platform, then the seller will be awarded for the order as the platform owner will get an amount of money for the order as the sellers are willing to pay for the pay per click (PPC) option (**Figure 5**).

### 7.2 Multiple sellers with no feedback

When an item has multiple sellers but none of the sellers owns any feedback or ratings, then the system will just check the distance from the customer to the seller for

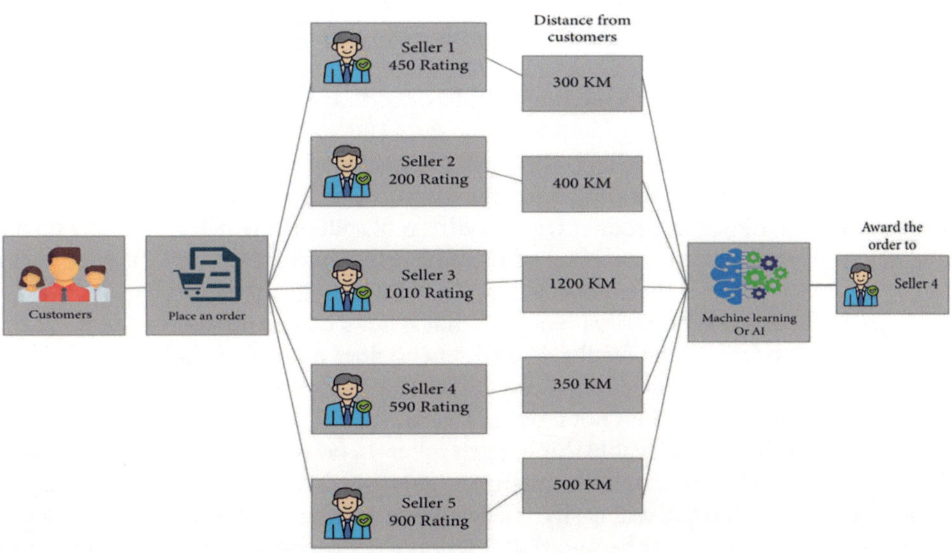


**Figure 4.**
*How machine learning and artificial intelligence allocate an order among the sellers.*

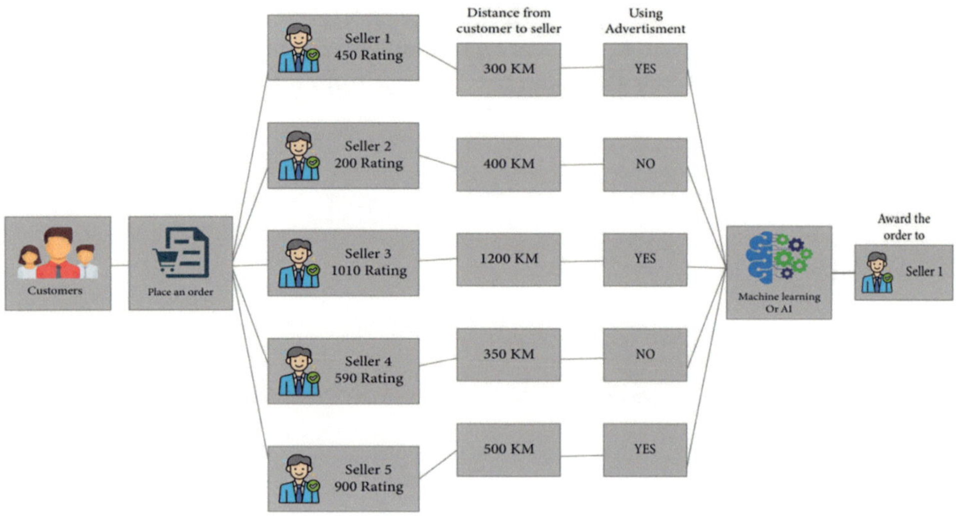


**Figure 5.**
*How machine learning and artificial intelligence allocate an order among the sellers when the seller uses.*

allocating an order to the seller. Let us say seller 1, seller 2, and seller 3 do not get any feedback yet, and then the system or application will check the distance as follows:

- Seller 1: No feedback: Distance from customers 400 km
- Seller 2: No feedback: Distance from customers 300 km
- Seller 3: No feedback: Distance from customers 500 km

Then the system will automatically select seller 2 for getting the order as the customer address are the nearest distance from the seller. However, if any of the sellers use the advertising, then their possibilities of getting the order will be more appropriate.

### 7.3 Multiple sellers with both feedback and no feedback

Whenever a product has sellers with both feedback and no feedback, then the system chose from both depending upon the distance, ratings, and advertisement purposes. Let us think of a product with six different sellers in which two sellers do not have any feedback or ratings and four of them have feedback or ratings. Three of them use the advertisement for their items to be sold, which are given in the chart below:

From **Table 1**, it can be easily identified that seller 5 has the lowest distance for the customer, however, it has no feedback, and seller 5 does not use any advertisement. It can be also identified that sellers 4 and 6 have the 2nd lowest distance, which is 300 km, however, seller 6 does not have any feedback but seller 4 has good ratings or feedback. There is one noticeable thing, both seller 4 and seller 6 use the advertising of the products, so both can win the chance to get an order. Depending on this case, the algorithm or technique will easily select seller 4 as it has both feedback and uses advertisement. But it cannot be said that it will not choose seller 6 for any order. There can be conditions like if the same approach occurs multiple times, then select seller 6 one time if the same thing happened 10 times. Otherwise, if the seller with no rating

| Seller no. | Gained ratings | Distance from customer | Using advertisement? |
|---|---|---|---|
| 1 | 500 | 800 | Yes |
| 2 | 600 | 450 | No |
| 3 | 300 | 550 | No |
| 4 | 800 | 300 | Yes |
| 5 | 0 | 200 | No |
| 6 | 0 | 300 | Yes |

**Table 1.**
*Dataset format when product sellers have both feedback and no feedback.*

doesn't get any orders on the platform, so it will lead the seller to lose hope to sell the item on the e-commerce platform.

### 7.4 Exception cases

There can be a lot of cases as an exception, which means the system described here cannot be potential for it because how the algorithm the developers will use in their policies. One of the identical exceptions is providing discounts on the products to get the attention of the customers, and customers always prefer to get discounts and willing to buy good products with discounts. The sellers who are giving discounts on their products will definitely get the priority of selling; however, in many cases, the manufacturer or the owner of the brand bounds the seller not to provide discounts. But in many cases, it is observed that many sellers do not follow the rules. So, this case can be an exception for getting an order. In some cases, it is observed that still in some orders, the seller does not get a discount because of their interruption and product availabilities. Like the discount exception, if a seller has items like 10pcs and another seller has 2pcs of the same product then, if the customer does not look properly at the discounted items then it will automatically be awarded to the seller with fewer quantities.

## 8. Discussion

The technology is beyond our knowledge of any e-commerce site where each platform owner implements their own technology. The popular technologies that are used to minimize the tasks of an e-commerce site are normally machine learning, data mining, data science, deep learning, and methods [23]. Research is already going on the theoretical understanding of products embedded in e-commerce by which researchers are trying to figure out how the machine learning techniques can be utilized properly in e-commerce [24]. This paper tries to figure out how an order will be distributed to a seller from a list of sellers of the same products.

The procedure and steps shown in this paper are normally investigated on an e-commerce site and there was a questionnaire section for both customers and sellers. So, both the seller's and buyer's perspectives on the e-commerce sector can be known. The research tried to figure out the hidden machine learning models that are occupied by the e-commerce sectors if e-commerce provides an option for selling the same product with the same UPC. It finds out the pattern by observing the platform and the questionnaires. The platform is observed for a year for the methodology finding and it can be stated that the e-commerce platform uses these techniques for selecting a seller whenever an order is placed by the customers.

It is true that there can be always exceptions; however, the e-commerce platform owners never open their ways of working into the air, but in this research, it was tried to figure out the technologies adaption and how the process actually is beyond a platform. In near future, more research will be carried out, and hope to work on the future with the platform owner so that real-time observation can be carried out by practically seeing the background system of any platform.

## 9. Conclusion

E-commerce uses are rising rapidly during the pandemic, and if a person thinks of business nowadays, then he/she first thinks of setting up an e-commerce platform. There are a lot of e-commerce platforms that already exist and give the option for the seller to list on their platform and in that case they take commissions from the sales. So that a lot of brands' products can have multiple sellers, and under one product page, a list of sellers can sell their inventory. So questions can arise about how the sellers will get an order as many sellers use the same platform. In that case, the research will help them find out how the sales will come or be appointed to the seller from an e-commerce platform. There can be exceptions that are elaborate in this research; however, the main summary has been sorted out that artificial intelligence is vastly used in e-commerce sectors, and choosing a seller from multiple sellers is one of the best examples of understanding the artificial intelligence uses. In the future, the research will focus on doing research physically with any of the renowned platform owners so that background codes and implementation can be understood more politely.

## Acknowledgements

I hereby acknowledge that there was no funding or grants for this research. I should mention the e-commerce platform company Amazon, as in many cases for the research, I checked their procedures and systems.

## Author details

Md Imtiaz Ahmed
Computer Science and Engineering, Prime University, Bangladesh

*Address all correspondence to: imtiaz.ahmed.ju@gmail.com

## References

[1] López Peláez A, Erro-Garcés A, Pinilla García FJ, Kiriakou D. Working in the 21st century. The coronavirus crisis: A driver of digitalisation, teleworking, and innovation, with unintended social consequences. Information. 2021;**12**:377. DOI: 10.3390/info12090377

[2] Sinha S, Singh T. Travel from traditional marketing to digital marketing. International Journal of Emerging Research in Management and Technology. 2018;**11**:173

[3] Feng Z. Constructing rural e-commerce logistics model based on ant colony algorithm and artificial intelligence method. Soft Computing. 2020;**24**:7937-7946. DOI: 10.1007/s00500-019-04046-8

[4] Vanneschi L, Horn DM, Castelli M, Popovič A. An artificial intelligence system for predicting customer default in e-commerce. Expert Systems with Applications. 2018;**104**:1-21

[5] Thomas JS, Jap SD, Dillon WR, Briesch RA. Investigating the role of product assortment in technology-enabled sales platforms. Journal of Interactive Marketing. 2021;**55**:31-51

[6] Prasad B. Intelligent Techniques for E-commerce. Journal of Electronic Commerce Research. 2003;**4**(2):65-71

[7] Sarwar B, Karypis G, Konstan J, Riedl J. Analysis of recommendation algorithms for e-commerce. In: Proceedings of the 2nd ACM Conference on Electronic Commerce. ACM, USA. 2000. pp. 158-167

[8] Amazon Reduces Packaging Waste with Machine Learning. Chain Store Age. Available from: www.chainstoreage.com/amazon-reduces-packaging-waste-machine-learning [Accessed: 19 January 2022]

[9] Liu G, Fei S, Yan Z, Wu CH, Tsai SB. An empirical study on response to online customer reviews and E-commerce sales: From the Mobile information system perspective. Mobile Information Systems. Vol. 2020, pp. 145-157

[10] Gupta A. E-commerce: Role of E-commerce in today's business. International Journal of Computing and Corporate Research. 2014;**4**(1):1-8

[11] Burt S, Sparks L. E-commerce and the retail process: A review. Journal of Retailing and Consumer Services. 2003;**10**(5):275-286

[12] Huang Z, Zeng D, Chen H. A comparison of collaborative-filtering recommendation algorithms for E-commerce. IEEE Intelligent Systems. 2007;**22**(5):68-78. DOI: 10.1109/MIS.2007.4338497

[13] Hariri N, Castro-Herrera C, Mirakhorli M, Cleland-Huang J, Mobasher B. Supporting domain analysis through mining and recommending features from online product listings. IEEE Transactions on Software Engineering. 2013;**39**(12):1736-1752. DOI: 10.1109/TSE.2013.39

[14] Saleem H et al. Data science and machine learning approach to improve E-commerce sales performance on social web. International Journal of Computer Science and Network Security (IJCSNS). 2019;**12**:401-424

[15] Guo Q, Li Z, An B, Hui P, Huang J, Zhang L, et al. Securing the deep fraud detector in large-scale E-Commerce

platform via adversarial machine learning approach. In: The World Wide Web Conference (WWW '19). New York, NY, USA: Association for Computing Machinery; 2019. pp. 616-626. DOI: 10.1145/3308558.3313533

[16] Jabbar J, Urooj I, JunSheng W, Azeem N. Real-time sentiment analysis on e-commerce application. Sensing and Control (ICNSC). 2019;**2019**:391-396. DOI: 10.1109/ICNSC.2019.8743331

[17] Jiahua Li, Tao Wang, Zhengshi Chen, Guoqiang Luo. Machine learning algorithm generated sales prediction for inventory optimization in cross-border E-commerce. International Journal of Frontiers in Engineering Technology (2019), 1, 1: 62-74

[18] Singh MK et al. Implementation of knowledge based collaborative filtering and machine learning for E-Commerce recommendation system. Journal of Physics: Conference Series. 2007;**1**:012032

[19] Ahmed MI. Web based seller support system: Amazon overview. In: 2020 IEEE Conference on e-Learning, e-Management and e-Services. 2020. pp. 104-109. DOI: 10.1109/IC3e50159.2020.9288418

[20] Ahmed MI. A novel dataset based algorithm for the fastest shipping by allocating nearest supplier. In: IEEE International IOT, Electronics and Mechatronics Conference (IEMTRONICS). 2021. pp. 1-6. DOI: 10.1109/IEMTRONICS52119.2021.9422656

[21] Amazon.Com: Online shopping for electronics, apparel, computers, books, DVDs and more. Amazon. Available from: www.amazon.com [Accessed: 26 March 2022]

[22] Amazon.Com | UGG Women's Fluff Yeah Slide Slipper | Slides. Amazon. Available from: www.amazon.com/gp/product/B078VDTCPH/ref=twister_dp_update?ie=UTF8&psc=1&redirect=true [Accessed: 4 April 2022]

[23] Rao H, Zeng Z, Liu A. Research on personalized referral service and big data mining for e-commerce with machine learning. In: 2018 4th International Conference on Computer and Technology Applications (ICCTA). 2018. pp. 35-38. DOI: 10.1109/CATA.2018.8398652

[24] Da X, Ruan C, Korpeoglu E, Kumar S, Achan K. Theoretical understandings of product embedding for E-Commerce machine learning. In: Proceedings of the 14th ACM International Conference on Web Search and Data Mining. New York, NY, USA: Association for Computing Machinery; 2021. pp. 256-264. DOI: 10.1145/3437963.3441736

Chapter 10

# UnIX-CARE: Universal Interface and Experience via Collaborative Archive Repository Express

*Sheldon Liang, Melanie Van Stry and Hong Liu*


## Abstract

It is feasible to simplify interface design for better user experience without web developing skillfully. CARE or collaborative archive repository express holds the answer to universal interface & experience (UnIX) through algorithmic machine learning. CARE in collaboration with DATA and wiseCIO as a whole establishes a CMD triad for content management and delivery that harnesses rapid prototyping for user interface and propels user-centric experience by cohesive assembly of Anything as a Service (XaaS). Basically, user-centric experience makes a user centered without often webpage swapping while browsing in hierarchical depth via "In-&-Out" interactivity, and exploring in contextual breadth via self-paced spontaneity. Furthermore, CARE incorporates express tokens for information interchange (eTokin) into the CMD triad to prepare integral content management and informative delivery. In particular, by exploiting eTokin, CARE promotes seamless intercommunications in-between and empowers users to be UNIX professionals cohesively, such as *ubiquitous* manager on content management and delivery, *novel* designer on universal interface, *intelligent* expert for business intelligence, and *extraordinary* liaison with XaaS without explicitly coding. More CARE uses algorithmic machine learning to coordinate instant online publishing, assemble efficient presentations via wiseCIO to end-users, and aggregate diligent intelligence over DATA for business, education and entertainment (iBEE) through robotic process automation.


**Keywords:** collaborative archive repository express, universal interface & experience, algorithmic machine learning, express token for info-interchange, algorithmic interactivity

## 1. Introduction

UnIX-CARE or Universal Interface & Experience has emerged from Collaborative Archive Repository Express through algorithmic machine learning that is involved in more and more aspects of everyday life through cloud-based content management and delivery (CMD) [1]. wiseCIO denotes web-based intelligent service engaging with cloud intelligence outlets [2], and DATA represents digital archiving via transformed analytics [3]. CARE is conceptualized as a "fastlane" that provides mathematical and



IntechOpen

computational solutions to distributed and cloud-based problems to bridge the gap between integral content management over DATA and informative delivery on wiseCIO.

CARE is central to collaborating DATA with wiseCIO into a triad that best serves cloud-based content management and delivery (CMD) for UnIX that makes a user centered without often webpage swapping while browning via wiseCIO and exploring over DATA via algorithmic machine learning that enables users to browse information in depth with hierarchically "in-&-out" interactivity, and to explore intelligence in breadth with contextually self-paced spontaneity to aggregate intelligence for business, education and entertainment (iBEE) in support of decision-making [2–4].

### 1.1 Collaborative triad for content management and delivery

Collaborative triad is a model created to guide policies for information comprehension among and direct fulfillment of multiple cloud-based components that refer to *digital archiving* for content management over DATA, *intelligent service* for informative delivery via wiseCIO to support enterprise decision-making, and *archival repository* express for instant publication via UnIX-CARE. The model is also somewhat helpful in resolving controversial agendas among web personnel [5]. In general, cloud-based distributed intelligent services are currently presented via a website, or enterprise websites that are quite subject to the management and influence of personnel, such as a webmaster, web designers, service maintainers and end-users. Taking a large collaborative enterprise IT team as an example, "controversial web personnel" often have objectives for the websites that fail to consider the services being offered and could lead to controversial agendas: the webmaster oversees and ensures that the technical aspects of a website are met; the web designer is usually responsible for the site's creative aspects; and the end-user is pleasant to discover useful and usable information for enterprise decision-making.

As a collaborative effort made to turn *controversial* agendas into *cohesive* advancement to propel large teams united and working together effectively, Collaborative Archive Repository Express (CARE) incorporates DATA and wiseCIO into a CMD triad via universal interface with better user experience (UnIX) for content management and delivery. As a borrowing term for the sake of emphasis on critical briefness, "DNA-like" ingredients are introduced for transmissible UnIX to promote collaboration among three parties of the CMD triad. "DNA" stands for deoxyribonucleic acid that contains units of biological building blocks as a vitally important molecule containing something that makes individuals unique [6]. In addition to UnIX that makes users centered while browsing web content and exploring information, the CMD triad provides novel solutions to controversial agendas via eTokin-express tokens for information interchange in support of seamless intercommunications among three CMD parties and semantic enrichment from "DNA-like" ingredients to human-computer interfacing that is presentable and rederable through highly robotic process automation [7].

Algorithmically, intelligent services are developed with mathematical and practical methods for advanced solutions to integral content management over DATA and informative content delivery on wiseCIO. As a result, the CMD triad empowers end-users to be cohesively UNIX professionals, such as *ubiquitous* manager on content management and delivery, *novel* designer on universal interface, *intelligent* expert for business intelligence, and *extraordinary* liaison with Anything as a Service without explicitly coding. In particular, DATA helps the end-user act like a webmaster to ensure that the technical aspects of web content management are met, CARE advances the end-user through web-based interface design without explicitly coding, and wiseCIO assists the end-user to be an intelligent expert to discover useful and usable information in support of decision-making.

### 1.2 Chance and challenge

By using "DNA-like" ingredients, both integral content under managed by DATA and informative delivery via wiseCIO are working cohesively without trivial information involved. It is the CMD triad through algorithmic machine learning [8, 9] that takes CARE in collaboration with DATA and wiseCIO to promote seamless intercommunications for interoperability via joint tasking of Anything as a Service among three parties of CMD triad. Express tokens for information interchange (eTokin) have been introduced in "DNA-like" notations to express (*via fast transmission*) digital archiving for content management and fulfill (*via online analytics*) intelligent services through universal interface & experience (UnIX). In a sense, UnIX simplifies instant content publishing in such a means that anybody could only need to input "DNA-like" eTokin in dictionary (Key-Value) pairs that are intelligently full of implicit syntactics and semantics in light of algorithmic machine learning; in a more significant sense, UnIX enables an ordinary user to be a webmaster, a web designer, and a database administrator with great ease. In light of "DNA-like" eTokin, In human computer interfacing, "DNA-like" eTokin's ability to innovate provides a key abstraction for UnIX differing abstractly from traditional web development in HTML/CSS/JS and/or PHP/Python.

The publishing express in dictionary eTokin pairs is capable of empowering universal interface & experience in the simplest means without explicit syntactics and semantics. This can shift the sophistication of interfacing design onto machine learning patterns without explicit coding required, but would result in highly brief description that is hard for a user to grasp, especially for a new-hand who might not be sure "what's going on" until the visual interface enabling algorithmic interactivity applied via operations. One of a "fake drawbacks" would become true that similar dictionary eTokin pairs may vary human computer interfacing when being associated with a variety of polymorphous and powerful patterns for machine learning. Web designers would have messed up web design with "wishy-sahy" agendas if they had lost understanding of original eTokin in depth.

Elastically, instant typing online publishing (iTOP) in dictionary eTokin pairs turns out immediately, the web designer can experience and enjoy visual renderability and actionable interactivity. Thanks to algorithmic machine learning, UnIX-CARE supports semantic enrichment transitioning "DNA-like" eTokin into analytical, interactive and responsive (AIR) across three parties of the CMD triad through elastic process automation.

### 1.3 Major contribution

UnIX-CARE in collaboration with wiseCIO and DATA utilizes "DNA-like" eTokin to achieve "cohesive UNIX" objectives as follows:

*Ubiquitous webmaster* across the CMD triad propels seamless intercommunication & interoperability among CMD parties to ensure technical aspects of web content management to be met (Section 2 ~ algorithmic CMD).

*Novel designer* utilizes eTokin to perform informative delivery via universal interface design and automate user-centric experience without explicitly coding required (Section 3 ~ innovative CARE).

*Innovative expert* aims to discover useful information and analytically harness intelligence for business, education and entertainment for enterprise decision-making (Section 4 ~ analytical iBEE).

*Extraordinary liaison* with universal interface for rapid prototyping of user-centric experience and cohesive assembly from Anything orchestrated as a Service, which will be discussed (Section 5 ~ Qinary XaaS).

## 2. CMD triad via algorithmic interactivity

Algorithmic interactivity represents information and operating technologies [10] applied to the CMD triad that is comprehended as UnIX-based Anything as a Service involving three correlated aspects: Collaborative Archive Repository Express promotes instant publishing to incorporate with integral content under managed over DATA, and informative delivery via wiseCIO to best serve cohesive personnel, illustrated in **Figure 1**.

With CMD triad diagrammatically illustrated in **Figure 1**, CARE to innovate uses iTOP for UnIX-universal interface & experience to bridge in between, DATA is evolved to cumulate "DNA-like" ingredients via digital transformation for integral content management (iCOM) through operating technologies, and wiseCIO is created to liaise with universal interface for informative content delivery (iCOD) through information technologies.

What is central to the CMD triad is computational thinking and machine learning [11]. The former empowers managers, decision makers and administrators to think laterally to generate a broader range of solutions, and the latter operationally automates a process of applying problem-solving from UnIX-CARE, through DATA, to wiseCIO. This chapter adopts the term of DNA as "DNA-like" ingredients that contain units of building blocks in the CMD triad for essential, vital, and sufficient information utilized for machine learning automata.

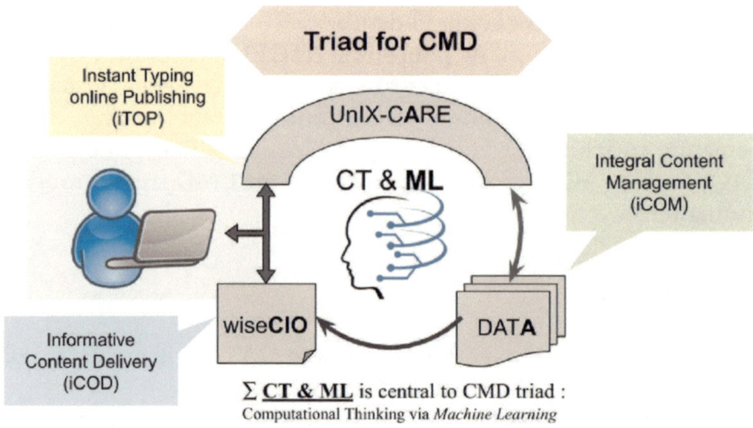


**Figure 1.**
*UnIX-CARE collaborated with wiseCIO and DATA into CMD triad.*

## 2.1 Integral content management via digital archives

Online analytics and procedural automation highly relies on integrity of content under management where archives are digitized to ensure content to be *formattable* for computational processing, *verifiable* for analytical processing, and *cohesive* for algorithmic machine learning without unnecessary redundancies. How to format information and/or digitize content denotes a means by which a chosen pattern is selected to arrange and store text on a computer. The digital pattern promotes integral content management through digital transformation to which algorithmic machine learning can be applied.

As well known, DOM (document object model) dominates traditional web documents in HTML/CSS/JSON, and some data retrieved in XML/JSON from a database that may have some digitized features for computing and processing. A traditional web document primarily serves the sole purpose on how to render content as a web page on the client device via retrieving and/or downloading. With DATA, "DNA-like" eTokin is introduced to express digitally-archived content to serve one of multiple purposes: significant content of integrity ensured without being trivial information in HTML/CSS/JSON.

**Table 1** discloses what "DNA-like" notations look like in expressing a **profile folder** as a single folder for George Washingtong, the first President of the United States of America, and how profoundly they serve multiple purposes. The profile folder or folder, a digital archive that is "DNA-like", intelligent and applicable via algorithmic interactivity, performs UnIX design with multimedia to play and virtual containers through fold-out / fold-up.

UnIX-CARE is embodied by digitally integral archives of excellent novelty, characterized as *actionability*, *interactivity* and *manipulability* (AIM) for bridging between DATA (management) and wiseCIO (delivery) via algorithmic interactivity. For instance, the little image button to the left of foldHead enables to play the folder-related multimedia, such as video, audio or other web service, and the arrow-button to the right fulfills fold-out (to open its body) and fold-up (to close).

As a result, all of the above mentioned activities will not cause webpage to swap but result in better user experience. Impressively, the "DNA-like" notation at least keeps integral content under management in utmost brief without redundancy, which will be in further discussions.

## 2.2 Algorithmic online analytics via machine learning

Online Analytical Processing or OLAP [12] is a core component of data warehousing implementations that enables fast, feasible, and flexible

| DNA-like notation | Actionable rendering in display and comments |
|---|---|
| **@FLDr(** `foldHead`<br>,) `imgURL`<br>,) `videoID`<br>,) `emBody..`<br>)@ | The DNA-like notation in brief is profound to express follows:<br>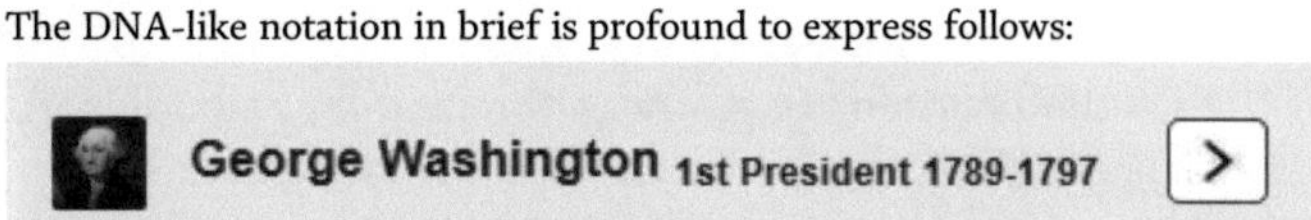<br><br>Where:<br>*foldHead*: George Washington archive ...<br>*imgURL*: the icon is *actionable* to play the video if exists<br>*emBody*: the folder body via "arrow" to extend or shrink beneath |

**Table 1.**
*An illustrative "DNA-like" notation to serve rendering with semantics.*

multidimensional data analysis for business intelligence (BI) and decision support applications. iOLAP represents innovative OLAP that makes CMD triad actionable, interactive and manipulable for intelligent UnIX service through algorithmic online analytics and machine learning. iOLAP aims to computationally examine facts and information for decision-making. For instance, **Table 1** illustrates an intelligent pattern of @FLDr that the archival "foldHead" is associated with a playable "video", which makes sense on how to drive machine learning to commit AIM for actionability, interactivity and manipulability.

Machine learning is about using historical search probabilities in order to generate expected search objectives, solutions, and applications given the user's input action, query, subject, vocabulary choices, problem, or question. Given lack of context, the response may be generic in scope. Whereas, given repeated uses by an individual or group, the specialization may ensue in order to better fit an intended outcome or focus. Jargon may skew the result culturally or possibly even sub-culturally. This could lead to positive results: quicker utilization and responsiveness; negative results: stereotypical discrimination; irrelevant results: similar nomenclature, but unconnected material; bad results: silo dead ends. Ultimately, machine learning must not be in a vacuum. It must be done with context and in connection to these other features within the utilization of an archival system.

Consequently, iOLAP has applied machine learning on deep learning that fulfills online service with abilities to learn without being explicitly programmed, as illustrated in **Figure 1**. Feasibly, computational thinking can be applied to UnIX among CARE, DATA and wiseCIO for better user experience through algorithmic machine learning [13]. Most importantly, UnIX-CARE makes it possible that an end-user could be a webmaster, a web designer, or an ordinary user who enjoys and engages with web exploration.

**Table 2** as derived from the previous table, describes multiviews of @FLDr pattern with AIM at wiseCIO of actionability for informative delivery, DATA of manipulability on integral content management, and CARE of algorithmic interactivity for UnIX characteristics.

Cloud-based collaborative archive repository express takes good CARE for CMD between DATA and wiseCIO via machine learning whose AIM is clear to be actionable, interactive, and manipulatable for cloud intelligent service, as discussed below.

### 2.3 Informative content delivery for decision-making

Informative content delivery represents digitalization or digital transformation from integral content (under managed as DATA) to informative delivery (as intelligence on wiseCIO). Better user experience signifies information useful to and deliverable for end-users to act and interact with the remote service (decision-making) [14].

One of the significant values in a practical approach toward UnIX is fold-out / fold-up of the detailed content (e.g. under the profile) as bodies. An end-user at his/her first glance at the profile is the foldHead the most attractive to explore, the secondary the image-related video (or some other multimedia) to play, and last (not least) folder body to open, all of which embodies user experience for readers' curiosity to be satisfied with spontaneity that enables individualization, interactivity, and independence.

User-centric experience aims at encouragement of exploring in contextual breadth (self-paced spontaneity) and browsing in hierarchical depth (in-&-out interactivity). It is easier to understand the interactive hierarchy without page-swapping while browsing the profile folder (**Table 2**).

<table>
<tr><th>DATA</th><th>@FLDr( foldHead ,) imgURL,) videoID,) emBody )@</th></tr>
<tr><td>UnIX-CARE</td><td>#>FLDr ⇒ *[ ;) foldHead ,) items, ... ]*</td></tr>
<tr><td></td><td>#>FLDr is the key for machine learning<br>multiple profile folders via iterative bracket: *[ ;) ... ... ]*<br>;) foldHead is the secondary key for each single folder</td></tr>
<tr><td>wiseCIO</td><td>AIM-actionability, interactivity and manipulability as follows:
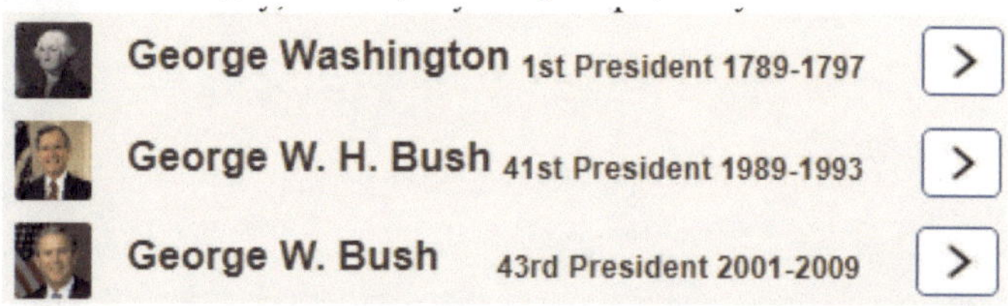
</td></tr>
<tr><td>AIM for UnIX (fold-out/fold-up)</td><td>Algorithmic interactivity via fold-out / fold-up as follows:
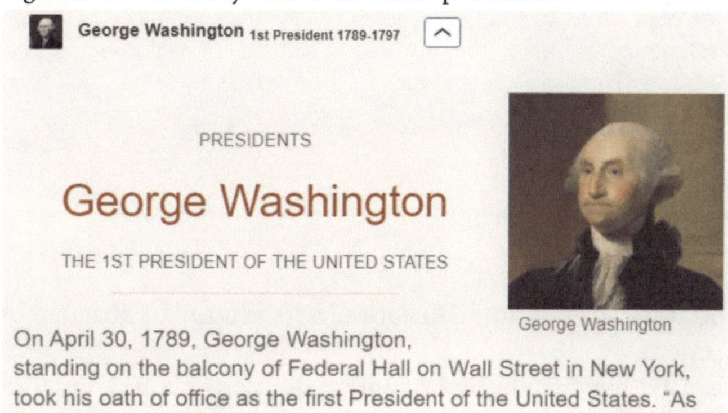
</td></tr>
<tr><td colspan="2">DATA ←wiseCIO ← CARE → DATA → wiseCIO</td></tr>
</table>

**Table 2.**
*Further illustration for "DNA-like" notation to serve rendering with actions.*

On the other hand, contextually self-paced spontaneity encourages individualization while a user's exploring in breadth. A good example is a group of multi-news presented in collaboration with each other. Both universal interface (without explicitly coding) and user-centric experience are applicable through the following example in **Figure 2**.

**Figure 2** discloses that excellence of UnIX is applicable on how to group multiple profiles for contextually self-paced spontaneity in breadth while exploring without a fixed order. UnIX promotes user-centric experience that has been successful through both hierarchical interactivity and contextual spontaneity. In practice, UnIX has been successfully applied to advanced instructional delivery (AID) for the sake of hybrid learning engagement, and surely applicable Anything as a Service in business, education and entertainment.

As a matter of fact, traditional web content delivery could commit some unfriendliness, and it would be against psychological observations in terms of user interface that causes poor user experience: (a) too much information on a given web page that would be destructive to users' attention according to Dr. George A Miller [15]; (b) monotony in the mind causes boredom to mental fatigue by repetition and lack of interest in the details of presented works online that require continuous attention paid to. According to "Eight Reasons Why We Get Bored" [16], too much of the same thing

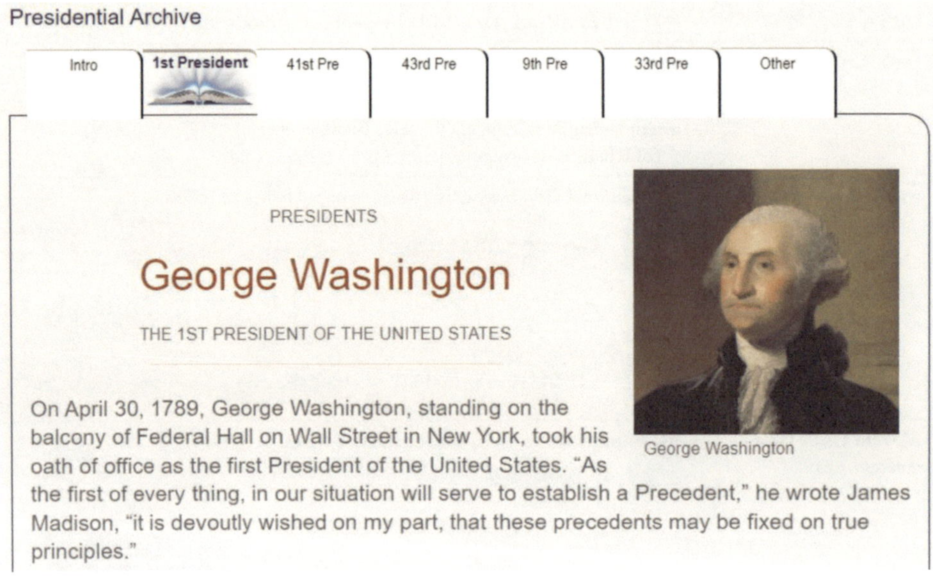


**Figure 2.**
*Contextually self-paced spontaneity for individual interests in breadth.*

and too little stimulation can cause in its victim an absence of desire and a feeling of entrapment.

wiseCIO has fulfilled informative delivery via universal interface for better user experience that is user-centric via hierarchical interactivity, and user-friendly via contextual spontaneity. Browsing in depth through hierarchical interactivity enables fold-out (to disclose hidden information) when desired to go into, and fold-up (to hide from too much information) from the first glance, which greatly assists the magical number of ($7 \pm 2$) applied to better user experience. The self-paced interests are satisfied by contextual spontaneity in breadth without a fixed order to explore, which wisely promotes avoidance of boredom in light of monotony in the mind [15, 16].

Further discussions will be conducted on how UnIX through Collaborative Archive Repository Express automates ideal informative delivery without explicit coding required.

## 3. CARE for UnIX via archival repository express

Cloud-based collaborative archive repository express aims for bridging DATA for integral content with wiseCIO for informative delivery where express tokens for information interchange (eTokin) are creatively introduced for universal interface & experience through elastic process automation. Similar to popularly used data formats such as XML and JSON [17] for C/S Architecture, eTokin is collaborative, text-based and more advanced (than XML/JSON) to support seamless intercommunications among the CMD triad.

It is "DNA-like" archival express (eTokin) that propels semantic enrichment during seamless intercommunication, as illustrated in **Figure 3**.

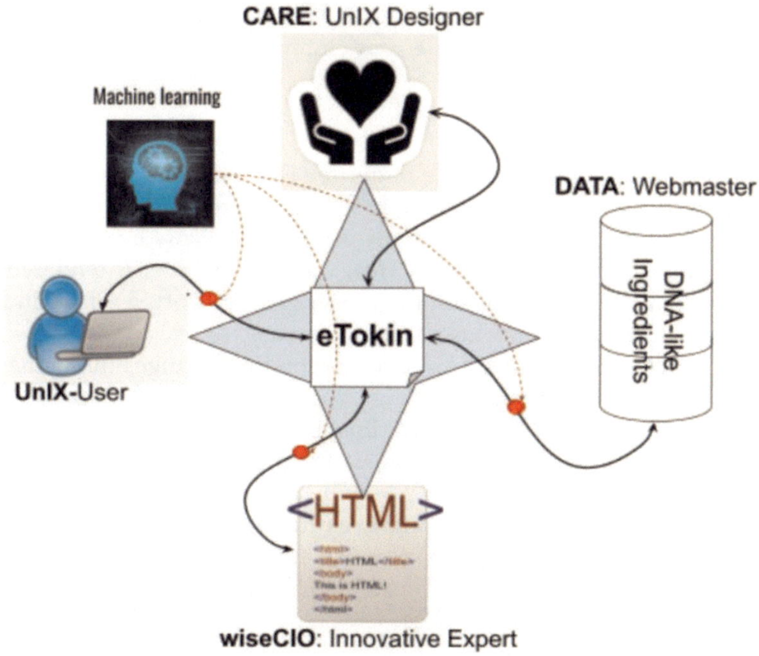


**Figure 3.**
*Collaborative archive repository express among CMD triad via eTokin.*

**Figure 3**, from the perspective of a UnIX Designer, discloses CARE for eTokin-oriented CMD triad through seamless intercommunications (arrows pointing toward) and semantic enrichments (away from eTokin) among three CMD parties: CARE, DATA and wiseCIO. Intercommunications toward eTokin perform implied elimination of trivial information without redundancy to guarantee integral content management, and semantics away from eTokin propels enriched activation of functional AIM for actionability, interactivity and manipulation without explicit coding required for informative delivery. Both trivial elimination and tactical enrichment are intelligently relying on deep learning experience, and automated elastic processes via machine learning (as denoted by dotted arrow lines).

### 3.1 "DNA-like" archival express for universal interface

"DNA-like" archival express enables universal interface & experience (UnIX) with which ordinary users can be made cohesive professionals to play multiple roles, such as UnIX Designer, Innovative Expert, and Webmaster via machine learning through elastic process automation, shown in **Figure 3**. The webmaster ensures technical aspects of a website over DATA, and the expert aggregates iBEE on wiseCIO, and the designer proposes CARE for universal interface & experience.

By using "DNA-like" archival express, cloud-aided DATA via machine learning acts like a webmaster for integral content management with high-speed accessibility to virtual containers, folders, and URL-related multimedia, so as to feed wiseCIO for informative delivery without unnecessary page swapping. Let us take a folder as an example: a profile folder (stated in **Tables 1** and **2**) usually represents a composite item with a caption and an arrow button that can be clicked to open with its body extended beneath, or to close with it shrinked. This embodies user-centric experience browsing in hierarchical depth via "in-&-out" interactivity. E.g.,

**@FLDr(** foldHead ,) imgURL ,) videoID ,) emBody **)@**

The @FLDr(... )@ denotes a profile folder in "DNA-like" archival express that is well archived with a group of ingredients specified as a **foldHead**, an **image** button that enables to play the multimedia underneath, and an **arrow** button that controls extension / shrinkage of the folder body. How the profile folder is rendered remains unspecified until machine learning automata is triggered (dotted arrow lines in **Figure 3**) to enrich semantics for informative delivery.

Collaborative archive repository for information interchange among the CMD triad involves text-based content that is digitized and stored in "DNA-like" eTokin to represent folders, containers, URL-related images and multimedia, and semantic patterns. "DNA-like" archival express is capable of digital archive with integrity endured for the sake of *transmissible* retrieval with *minimal* bandwidth, and *elastic* process automation for online analytics. Transmissible retrieval means applicable, optional and operational fulfillment of cryptography depending on the level of enforced security; elastic process automation represents algorithmic interactivity to accommodate universal interface & experience (UnIX).

### 3.2 Express tokens in collaboration within CMD tirad

Collaborative archive repository express introduces "DNA-like" archival express, or express tokens for information interchange (eTokin) to provoke seamless intercommunications among the CMD triad in comprehensive collaboration so that three CMD parties, such as CARE, DATA, and wiseCIO, can feed to and/or retrieve from each other. By instant typing online publishing (iTOP) "DNA-like" eTokin is utilized to describe "what to do" for the sake of seamless intercommunications, but leave "how to do" unspecified in light of semantic enrichment that highly relies on algorithmic machine learning.

So CARE for universal interface & experience helps to make an ordinary user a webmaster capable of managing integral content, an innovative expert able to aggregate and deliver useful information, and a novel designer to create the universal interface for better user experience without explicitly coding required. "DNA-like" archival express (eTokin) for information interchange between CMD parties is context-neutral, text-based and cryptographic when describing *instant* publishing, *integral* management, and *informative* delivery until applied rules have been chosen for machine learning specifically at runtime. The applied eTokin "implants" feasibility and flexibility for UnIX to become reasonable and possible through elastic process automation.

One of the strategies of choosing "DNA-like" eTokin for information interchange is SnR: sufficiency and no redundancy—*sufficiency* means good enough to fulfill semantic enrichment for aggregating information on wiseCIO; *no redundancy* minimal as necessary to support online analytics over DATA with consistencies. For instance, a series of folders described in dictionary eTokin pairs:

#> Presidential Archive :> values for the section
;] 1st President :> values for the profile
;] 41st President :> values for the profile

;] 43rd President :> values for the profile
;] Others :> values for the profile

Where

#> triggering machine learning for semantic enrichment with AIM for actionability, interactivity and manipulability
;] leading a profile folder in dictionary eTokin pairs iteratively
:> split into a Key-Value pair, and "values" set
in a list with more or less parameters applied to the profile.

The above dictionary eTokin pairs represent the "DNA-like" archival express with flexible sizes for rows (folders) and columns (more or less parameters). The dictionary pairs look like general data formats (XML/JSON), but are much more advanced than XML and/or JSON in light of machine learning automata implanted for UnIX through elastic process automation. The dictionary pairs are highly intelligent with AIM for actionability, interactivity and manipulability—under a specific context, the runtime situates machine learning rules in the context to fulfill semantic enrichment for informative delivery via wiseCIO, or integral content for online analytics over DATA. More importantly, text-based eTokin is the utmost core underneath in support of both seamless intercommunications and semantic enrichment among the CMD triad, as discussed afterward.

How a specific machine learning rule is situated under a given context will be thoroughly discussed next.

### 3.3 Collaborative intercommunications among CMD triad

Collaborative archive repository takes good CARE of Anything orchestrated as a Service via algorithmic machine learning, which establishes seamless intercommunications among three parties so that interoperability via joint tasking is made automated, interactive, and responsive (AIR).

Instant publishing takes initial CARE to prepare integral content under managed over DATA, and integral content enables wiseCIO to promote informative delivery. Furthermore, wiseCIO propels interoperability over joint tasks via innovative online analytical processing (iOLAP) for better user experience with DATA. As previously discussed, eTokin is text-based, and created as express tokens for information interchange to promote elastic process automation through Seamless intercommunications between distributed parties of the CMD triad incorporating data transmission with joint tasking .

The basic strategy applied to express tokens is to *suffice* with AIM at actionability, interactivity and manipulability, and *minimize* data storage without redundancy, *encrypt* networking transmission via cryptography. Text-based eTokin for seamless intercommunications has some similarities to, but is much more advanced than JSON, and/or XML [17]—intelligent ("DNA-like") ingredients are related to algorithmic machine learning without explicitly coding required. Consequently, CARE is expressed in text-based eTokin to incorporate AIM for actionability, interactivity and manipulability on UnIX.

One of the obvious examples is to situate a specific machine learning rule for a smartphone of a narrow screen, or a laptop of a wide screen, respectively. A smartphone may prefer a bulleted list (V-layout) to a multi-tab array (H-layout) for multiple profile folders in light of the width of the device screen.

| iTOP | eTokin for UnIX Design | Interfacing in UI Dictionary |
|---|---|---|
| In-between mappings | **Grouping title :> ...**<br>;] Key#1 :> folder values<br>;] Key#2 :> folder values<br>;] Key#3 :> folder values<br>;] Key#4 :> folder values<br>;] Key#5 :> folder values | 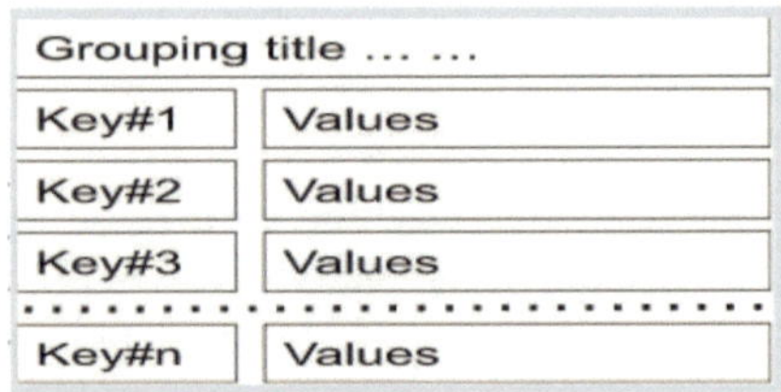 |
| V-layout (bulleted list) | AIM at multiTab layouts (actionable, interactive, and manipulatable) | |
| 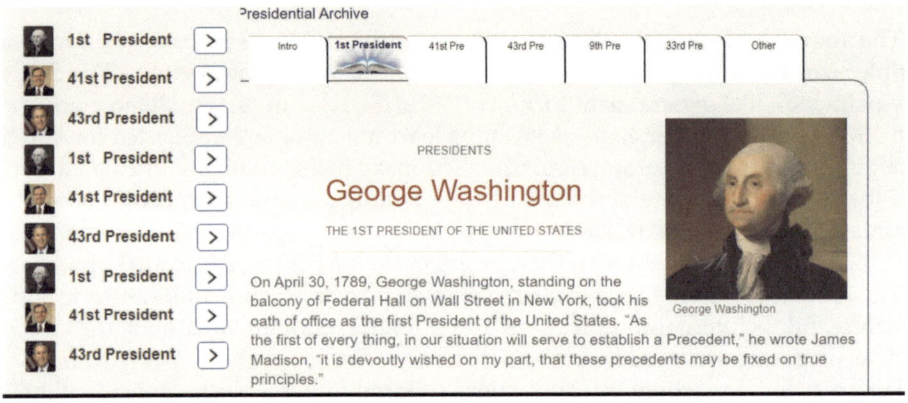 | | |

**Table 3.**
*Contextual spontaneity in breadth for self-paced interest in browsing.*

**Table 3** shows ideas of how "DNA-like" eTokin (that is text-based across the CMD triad) turns out to be *context-sensitive* via semantic richments for informative delivery on wiseCIO, *context-innovative* via integral content management for online analytics over DATA, *context-neutral* via for seamless intercommunication for instant publishing by UnIX-CARE. The text-based eTokin and its equivalence UI Dictionary play a key role in human-computer interfacing for user-centric experience through elastic process automation without explicitly coding required. However, algorithmic machine learning is *context-specific* at runtime where iTOP embodies CARE in some ways by which instant typing online publishing supports: (a) text-based eTokin for content management in storage, online analytics, and machine learning rule-driven automation as well, (b) interactive editor in UI Dictionary without markups required so that everybody can perform UI design, and (c) bidirectional conversions between text-based eTokin and UI Dictionary.

## 3.4 Machine learning-activated semantic enrichments

UnIX-CARE, conceptualized as bridging between DATA and wiseCIO, has three "i" objectives in mind to advance *instant* publishing in "DNA-like" archival express, accumulate *integral* content, and aggregate *informative* delivery as a whole across the CMD triad. Machine learning helps to activate semantic enrichment from "DNA-like" archival express (eTokin) to wiseCIO for Anything orchestrated as a Service.

Superficially, "DNA-like" eTokin looks like traditional XML or JSON, but they would be in vain without intelligent service. "DNA-like" archival express in eTokin is not just utilized in data formats, but empowered by algorithmic machine learning where semantic enrichments orchestrate Anything as a Service with AIM for following characteristics:

*Actionability*—wiseCIO is created for informative delivery and actionability represents an ability to turn web document into a live website from deafness (no or less action) to dedication to servicing the users to act—an end-user to browse, a webmaster to administrate and/or a web designer to create cloud-based content under managed over DATA.

*Interactivity*—universal interface is automated on wiseCIO to enable users to communicate with the remote server to request, and/or to be prompted to react—the interactivity here is more than just to swap the current page to a new page via anchored tags, such as buttons, hyperlinks, etc. Algorithmic interactivity is made for active collaboration, friendly incorporation and rapid assembly or integration of Anything as a Service.

*Manipulability*—DATA is built up by accumulating various data in "DNA-like" archival express and manipulability aims for back-end operating, processing and, for instance, control over joint tasks for interoperability that composes smaller servicing parts into a larger service. Manipulability utilizes operating technologies (OT) on the remote server to support online analytics, and supply computing resources, and synthesize "Anything" as a Service—applied information technologies to intelligence for business, education and entertainment (iBEE).

Semantic enrichments through algorithmic machine learning provide AIM for automated UnIX that is to be actionable, interactive and manipulatable. Let us recap the profile folder for the 1st President of the USA: George Wahshington, then evolved from the simplest @FLDr( ... )@ that represents a well archived folder to multiple folders (**Tables 1** and **2**). Each one of the profile folders is extensible and shrinkable by clicking the arrow button, which embodies successful semantic enrichment from @FLDr( .... )@ to be actionable, interactive and manipulable. With "DNA-like" archival express that is context-neutral, wiseCIO becomes smarter than ever to lay out in a bulleted list (V-layout) or multi-tab layout (H-layout), illustrated in **Table 3**.

The "DNA-like" eTokin-enabled semantic enrichments from a single profile to multiple folders maintain the core AIM for actionability, interactivity and manipulative, but as the number of folders is increased, both V-layout (for narrow screen) and H-layout (for wider screen) will not work properly, so the AIM should be empowered with new actionability, interactivity and manipulability by semantic enrichments, shown in **Figure 4**.

**Figure 4** addresses a much more intelligent solution to UnIX for the complex archival express through semantic enrichments. A foldable list is defined as a large number of profile folders and derived from both bulleted list and multiTab layout. The use case is about how to archive all 46 Presidents of the USA from the 1st President George Washington to 46th President Joseph R. Biden, Jr. Either V-layout (too high to scroll) nor H-layout (too wide to fit) would work well. A foldable list only occupies the screen space, the same size of a single folder, but the number of items in the list can be flexible, pretty large.

As a good example, a foldable list can be described by "DNA-like" eTokin that is context-neutral and empowered by semantic enrichments with AIM for actionability, interactivity and manipulability where algorithmic machine learning

**Figure 4.**
*"DNA-like" archival express empowered with a number of of profile folders.*

play a key part in seamless intercommunication and semantic enrichment among the CMD triad.

## 4. iBEE via online analytical processing

Collaborative archive repositories express promises to take CARE of integral content management (over DATA) and informative delivery (via wiseCIO) of intelligence for business, education and entertainment. Innovative online analytics has been utilized to support decision-making via machine learning patterns [18], as illustrated in **Figure** 5.

**Figure** 5 shows UnIX-CARE that acts as double bridging between DATA for integral content management and wiseCIO for informative delivery, and between users and intelligence-driven Anything as a Service. Machine learning is central to context-neutral description in the "DNA-like" archival express that "implants" feasibility and flexibility for UnIX to become reasonable and possible through elastic process automation. The implanted flexibility makes it possible for wiseCIO to vary universal interface & experience without explicitly coding required, and the feasibility enables semantic enrichment with AIM for actionability, interactivity and manipulability. Furthermore, "DNA-like" archival express (eTokin) collaborates with DATA for integral content management and wiseCIO for informative delivery among the CMD triad as a whole as an activator of machine learning to orchestrate Anything as a Service.

### 4.1 Innovative online analytics via elastic process automation

A web-based cloud intelligent service may involve very complex scenarios in order to support a large variety of specific situations. The elasticity of automation represents a flexible and feasible process that is able to adjust and cover through specific scenarios while staying within the mainstream. Algorithmic processing, as part of machine

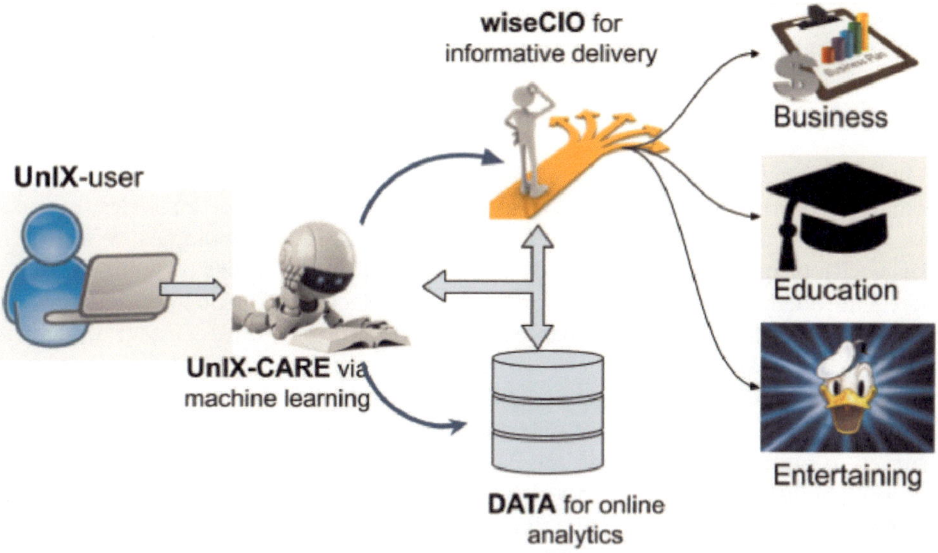


**Figure 5.**
*CMD triad serves the user with UnIX for iBEE.*

learning, fulfills online analytics that computationally examines information to find useful patterns [13, 14, 18], so how to recognize the context under a specific situation is quite dependent on "DNA-like" archival express that becomes the foundation of innovative online analytics.

A pattern with parameters implies a particular way by which a piece of algorithm can be derived to get some job done and some content organized. Parameterization enables elasticity for procedural automation. **Table 3** explicitly illustrates a good example of elastic process automation as follows:

```
@FLDr( foldHead0 :> imgURL ,) videoID ,) emBody
;]foldHead1 :> imgURL ,) videoID ,) emBody
;]foldHead2 :> imgURL ,) videoID ,) emBody
;]foldHead3 :> imgURL ,) videoID ,) emBody
;] ... ...
)@
```

Where

**@FLDr** stands for a pattern providing a means in which a folder is presented.
**Parameters** videoID denotes some elasticity of particular ways to play multimedia as embedded parts. wiseCIO is smart to play such multimedia as video, audio, traditional website, and anything via a URL that a browser can open.
**More significant elasticity** is "trade-off" between V-layout, H-layout, and Foldable List of grouping profiles via algorithmic interactivity according to the view resolution.

Innovative online analytics through algorithmic interactivity represents parameterized solutions to content management and delivery via machine learning with patterns. Semantic enrichment via algorithmic interactivity helps to vary for universal interface & experience as "One-Size-Fits-All".

### 4.2 Business intelligence via automated processes

Business intelligence is to utilize business data to drive decision making, which has become one of the significant objectives of intelligence via online analytics for business, education and entertainment (iBEE). In information technologies, wiseCIO takes CARE of intelligence to embody innovative online analytics through elastic process automation over DATA. In order to make decisions for business success trustworthily and dependably, reliable data is required to be IDEA (integral, digestible and elastically available).

"Business Intelligence" (BI) may be a generalized term, and it could be specialized for instructional / educational, or entertaining (business) intelligence, all of which is assumed to support decision making. Basically intelligence represents thinking ability, reasoning ability to understand and learn well in order to form judgments and opinions based on reason. The CMD triad propels computational thinking of "DNA-like" archival express for intelligence through elastic process automation.

According to the operational definition of computational thinking [11–13], computational thinking can be fulfilled in a feasible, operational and optimal approach. The CMD triad considers it done to get computational thinking through algorithmic problem-solving processes (shown in **Figure 5**) with operational activities such as: (1) by formatting problems "DNA-like" eTokin enables a computer to help solve those problems, (2) by analyzing data, "DNA-like" archival express establishes a transformational foundation over DATA, (3) by representing data through models and simulations, UnIX-CARE acts as a "fastlane" through elastic process automation, (4) by identifying, analyzing, and implementing possible solutions DATA aims for the goal of achieving the most efficient and effective combination of steps and resources, and (5) by generalizing a problem-solving process, wiseCIO transfers the liaison with UnIX to a wide variety of problems.

**Figure 6** Computational thinking via CMD triad is *feasible* via algorithmic interactivity to liaise with UnIX. It is also *operational* through elastic process automation and *optimal* for intelligence-driven decision making for Business, Education and Entertainment (iBEE). The highlight in terms of major contribution of CMD triad is applicable orchestration of Anything as a Service for decision-making, as detailed in Section 5.

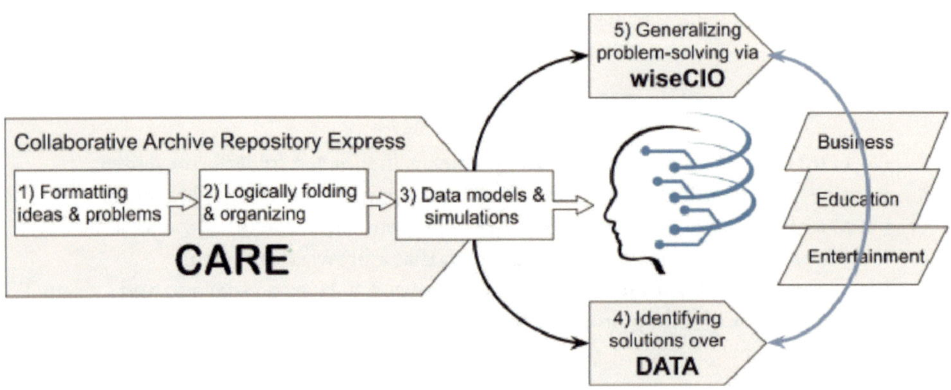


**Figure 6.**
*Computational thinking is feasible, operational and optimal via CMD triad.*

### 4.3 Educational excellence via collaborative efforts in learning

EXCEL—educational excellence via collaborative efforts in learning is considerably a specialized "business" that helps to excel education for student success. Generally instructional content under managed over DATA represents courseware design with aims for hybrid learning purposes, and instructional delivery via wiseCIO as intelligence to assist an instructor and/or students to make decisions on where, when, and how to browse in-depth hierarchy, or glance in-breadth context, and in-detail access, all of which assists to target educational excellence via collaborative efforts in learning (EXCEL).

UnIX-CARE strongly associate educational excellence with CIA-directed courseware presentation [14] of *Contextuality*, *Interactivity* and *Accessibility*: spontaneous contextuality enables exploring in breadth, sequential interactivity encourages browsing in depth, and sustainable accessibility enacts visitation in detail, which decisively promotes instructional engagement for student success, illustrated by **Figure** 7.

**Figure** 7 presents a CIA-aided courseware via a cloud-based intelligent service to promote educational excellence for student success. The courseware of CIA propels comprehensive engagement in a hybrid instructional approach throughout: (a) contextuality in breadth to meet the spontaneous needs of individuals to overview the content, (b) interactivity in depth to dedicate students sequentially through learning process by one after another, and (c) accessibility in detail to incorporate sustainable advancement with individual coursework published as profiles,

CIA-aided courseware is organized and discussed in following aspects:

*Spontaneous contextuality* is embodied by the top-folder bar that organizes multiple aspects beneath via a multiTab so that individuals can spontaneously explore with self-paced interests—a student may first glance at what is about the course he/she

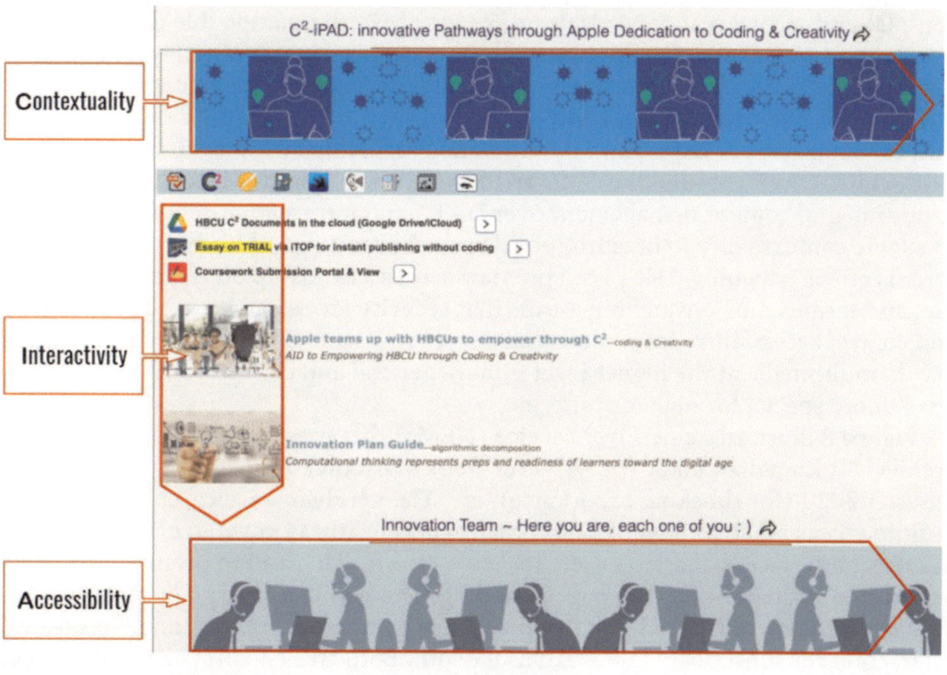


**Figure 7.**
*CIA to excel education via contextuality, interactivity and accessibility.*

is to take. Individual users' spontaneity helps to get rid of "monotony" by allowing the individual to go on self-paced interests without any boredom.
*Sequential interactivity* aligning on the left layout presents major learning modules sequentially so that both instructors and learners can follow with lectures & labs, and coursework as the class goes on. Algorithmic interactivity with each learning module serves learners in browsing in depth via fold-out (going down into) and fold-up (getting out of)—collaboratively only one module is allowed in fold-out at a time, and the other will automate in fold-up.
*Sustainable accessibility* is reflected by the bottom-folder bar with an intermediate media where all students have their own profile-boxes for coursework submission—a student may access to his/her own profile folder, or utilize instant typing online publishing (iTOP) to submit coursework according to the sequential learning paces; an instructor has the privilege to view, grade and interact hybridly with individuals for review & revision, and advancement ($R^2$A-rising to grade A).

CIA-aided courseware acting like a "mirror" reflects educational intelligence to assist hybrid learning with collaborative efforts to engage for student success: educational excellence is embodied in self-paced interests via spontaneous contextuality, in-depth learning via sequential interactivity, and in-details via sustainable accessibility between instructor and learners.

### 4.4 Netflix-like movie entertaining reactivator

Netflix is an American subscription streaming service and production company based in Los Gatos, California. Netflix can be accessed via web browsers or via application software installed on smart TVs, set-top boxes connected to televisions, tablet computers, smartphones, digital media players, Blu-ray players, video game consoles and virtual reality headsets on the list of Netflix-compatible devices. As a simulating service case, Netflix-like movie entertaining reactor (netFlyer) basically acts like Netflix to offer a film and television series library through distribution deals as well as its own productions. UnIX-CARE is presented here to provide users with the universal interface & experience by ultimately archiving all kinds of multimedia. With UnIX-CARE through the CMD triad as a whole, a Netflix-like reactivator performs integral content management over DATA and informative delivery via wiseCIO to enable contextuality in breadth for self-paced preview, and hierarchy in depth for serious movie watching. Self-paced preview acts as a heads-up on what a user wants to see, and serious movie watching means that security levels can be applied to manage and control accessibility for commercial purposes. As a vivid example, the hierarchical depth, multimedia at the higher level is more general and cheaper, and at a lower level, more special for higher profit, etc.

**Figure 8** illustrates a netFlyer service (NEMs) that presents a well-categorized archive: Multimedia Center (preview for free), Cartoon 2022 (for kids pleasure), c) Disaster 2020 (for shocking experience), etc. The netFlyer is well archived with multimedia as much as possible, but organized as neatly as novel to offer a set of universal interface that assists users to "*learn once for all*", and to prompt user-centric experience without often web page swapping. The netFlyer may go in such scenarios as a user explore: self-paced preview for free in contextual breadth, and "in-&-out" interaction for subscribers in hierarchical depth. Both free explorers and subscribers will enjoy previewing, watching videos, playing games, and so on, which demonstrates individualization and orchestration of Anything as a Service under netFlyer.

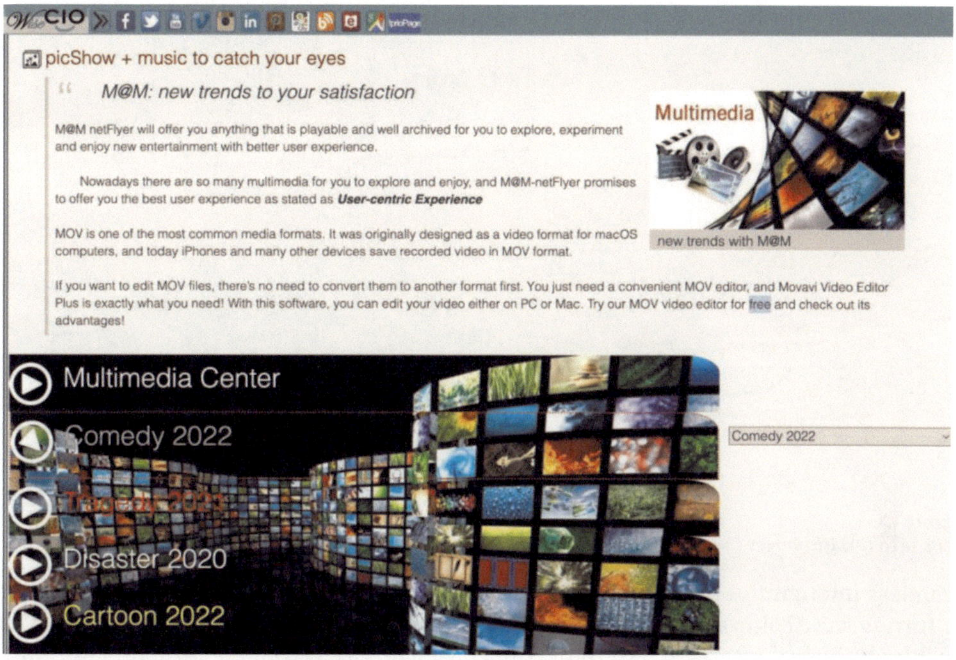


**Figure 8.**
*netFlyer entertaining service for UnIX via contextuality and interactivity.*

More intelligently, a dynamic dropdown list is an algorithmic companion to the banner (say, Comedy 2022) as the user opens it to watch or preview items of multimedia, which automatically assembles a dropdown list that enables rapid accessibility without needing to re-open the same banner. Furthermore, it best embodies user-centric experience that the user opens and/or closes banners alternatively without leaving the current context, which is really beneficial to users. In particular netFlyer works perfectly for the user to enjoy by exploring a "oceanic" number of multimedia.

UnIX-CARE provides a fastlane for new multimedia to be published dynamically in "DNA-like" archival express to DATA and to explore via wiseCIO. Innovative online analytics is applied to netFlyer via machine learning as illustrated in **Figure 5** in which machine learning plays a key role in elastic processes automation for business intelligence to support decision making.

## 5. Quinary XaaS orchestration

Universal interface & experience (UnIX) represents a novel model for content management and delivery (CMD), and collaborative archive repository express (CARE) incorporates DATA into wiseCIO to orchestrate Anything as a Service. Quinary UnIX suggests quinary cases of Anything orchestrated as a Service based on the CMD triad as a whole to promote *instant* publishing, *integra*l management, and *informative* delivery. Quinary UnIX provides quinary (five) servicing templates with aims at queryability, ubiquity, interactivity, novelty and availability.

**Figure 9** addresses Quinary Servicing Templates described in the "DNA-like" archival express as context-neutral in wise Dictionary and/or UI Dictionary in light of

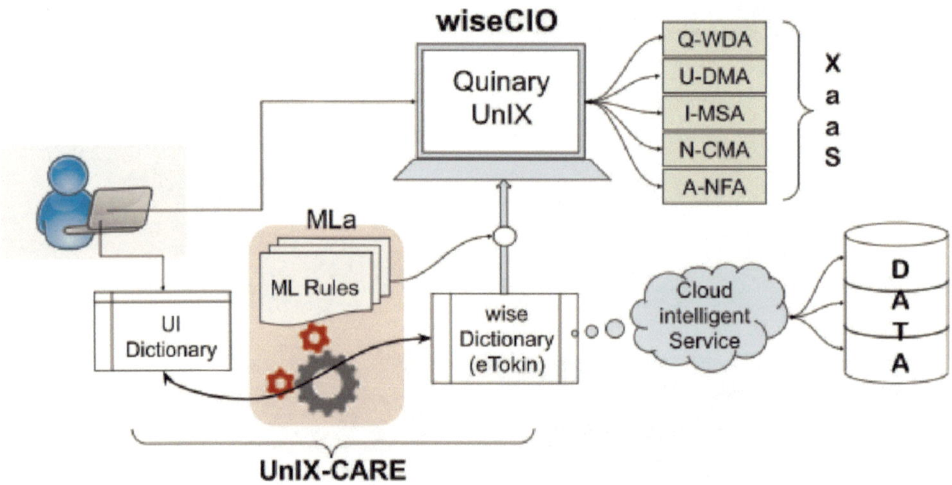


**Figure 9.**
*Wise (eTokin) dictionary takes CARE of web development over DATA.*

seamless intercommunication. Algorithmic patterns [16] apply semantic enrichment to turn wise (eTokin) Dictionary into context-sensitive Quinary UnIX. Deep learning enables universal interface design of context-sensitivity through elastic process automation. Consequently, context-sensitivity results from context-neutrality via algorithmic interactivity of REAP- retrievable (from the remote server), executable (on the client device), analytical (elastic automation), and pass-along (between wise eTokin and UI Dictionary).

Machine learning, according to IBM Cloud Learn Hub [8, 9], is a branch of artificial intelligence (AI) through computational thinking, which focuses on the use of data and algorithms to imitate the way that humans learn, gradually improving its accuracy. In this article, thorough discussion will be conducted with heuristics that are used to initiate machine learning through following characteristics, respectively.

**Queryability:** word-driven aggregation (5.1)
**Ubiquity:** digital music avocation in composition (5.2)
**Interactivity:** montage-selected animation (5.3)
**Novelty:** computing machinery assembler of programmability (5.4)
**Availability:** customizable name-featured activation (5.5)

### 5.1 WDA: word-driven aggregation for queryability

WDA represents the first XaaS template that initiates heuristics of word-driven queryability for universal interface & experience (UnIX) on **comprehensive aggregation**. WDA promotes queries to draw users' attention to categorized words: synonymous or opposite, which strategically encourages flexible queries [19] by applying heuristic wording to facilitate the extraction of relevant word-related DATA for presentation.

**Figure 10** illustrates how WDA heuristics can be applied to query for variously relevant words, such as LOVE, AGAPE, LIKE, HATE, ... For instance, associating LOVE with a category of loving movies, a user drags the letter "L" lower than "E", which may lead less love ("LIKE") to series of multimedia. On the contrary, the letter "L" becomes higher than "E", which may lead to sacred love ("AGAPE") series of

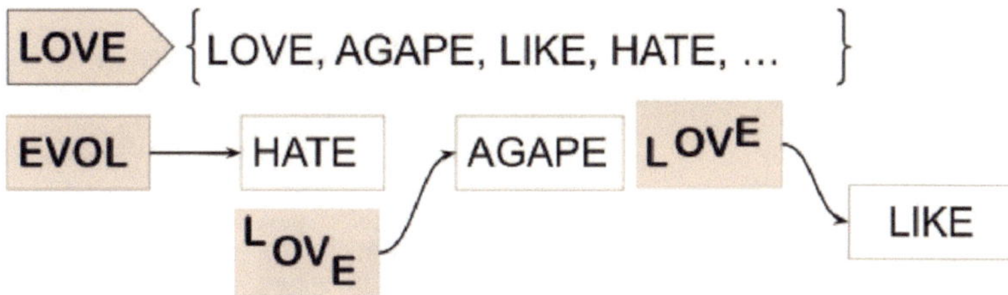


**Figure 10.**
*Heuristic queries aggregated by WDA for wording guess.*

multimedia. Inversive "LOVE" is "EVOL", which may lead to the "HATE" (opposite) series, etc.

**Queryability** expresses something unsure of "what to explore" while a user is browsing a new / complex website. Therefore the wording guess heuristically encourages the user to ask for more information specific in his/her mind. Query heuristics can help the user into a specific field to explore, say APAGE series of multimedia. Machine learning is nothing to do from scratch, but provides a means of solving problems by discovering things itself and learning from its own experience. So an initial wording guess is a great heuristics to enable the user in proceeding with further exploration.

WDA showcase serves with a heuristic wording guess, then engages the user to go further and explore in more depth. In facing a giant number of entertaining resources, the wording heuristics becomes especially effective while exploring entertaining multimedia.

In cloud-based applications, WDA encourages queryability through active exploration to discover things that are interesting to the user from his/her own experience for individual pleasure in contextual breadth and enjoyment in hierarchical depth.

### 5.2 DMA: digital music avocation for ubiquity in composition

DMA represents the second XaaS template that initiates heuristics of digitally-advocated ubiquity for universal interface & experience (UnIX) on **creative composability**. DMA prepares ubiquitous compositions anywhere with an iPAD or a laptop available and it does not matter with or without a musical instrument at hand. In general composability is a business principle that refers to the ability to combine modular business elements as needed [20, 21]. A simple DMA will do the trick on an iPAD or a laptop to foster early-age musical education for little kids to recognize music notes and perform music composition for fun. It is also helpful for them to discover their talent in composing music through coding and creativity Vividly a kid does compositions of a "song" by selecting and putting musical notes into a queue and he/she can also make chords (playable at the same time) by putting two or more musical notes into the same position in the queue so as to play simultaneously.

**Figure 11** illustrates how DMA orchestrates Anything as a Service includes "Songs" to play, "Chords" to make, and "Keyboard" to play the musical songs. The XaaS composer for DMA initiates with musical notes that can be play individually by clicking the key on the Playable Keyboard, and a kid can also click the speaker (button) to play a reserve song, or make a chord by grabbing two or notes to add on to the base notes so as to play simultaneously, and so on. A little kid would be pleased to learn how to compose a song by purchasing a piano, but it is apparently so expensive before his/her parents could find out whether or not the kid is interested in musical

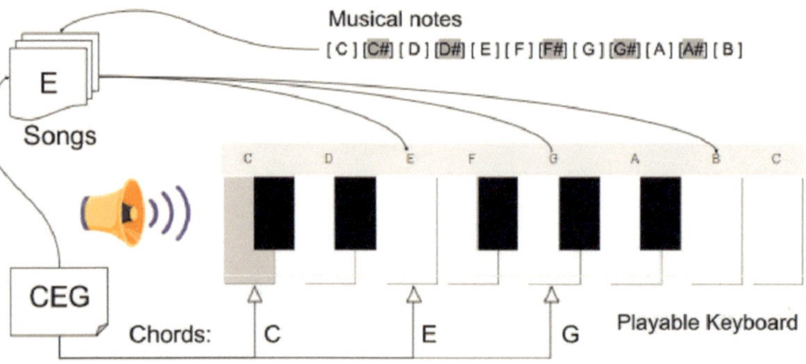


**Figure 11.**
*Ubiquitous composer dashboard with songs, chords, and notes.*

composition. Obviously, a simple DMA on iPAD or a laptop will be helpful to foster the kid in musical composition.

**Ubiquity** in composing makes "piano" everywhere available for musical composition that particularly embodies potential production or creation of music, poetry, or formal writing. Ubiquity via DMA aims to foster coding and creativity through computational and compositional activities.

DMA showcase serves Anything as a Service with a web-based keyboard that is made anywhere available to foster little kids to taste by composing songs, making chords with super ease. The heuristic virtual keyboard would be the first teacher to help kids recognize musical notes, try chords in direct experience of what a chord really means. It can also help code in practice, test in performance, and revise in progress to inspire creativity through programmable composition.

### 5.3 MSA: montage-selected animation for interactivity

MSA represents the third XaaS template that initiates heuristics of montage-selected interactivity for universal interface & experience (UnIX) on **vivid and friendly animation**. MSA promotes both manual and robotic operatings for human-computer interfacing. Manual operations serve the user who gives it a try to test and preview animations, and robotics automates a process of multimedia to play and as it goes, the user can intervene the animation to stop and then enter the montage related content. A selected montage frame provides a means to control an animated asset that enables combinational animation sequences into a single asset. In a looping mantaged series, the user can view it like a movie until he or she breaks it up into sections for playback [22]. An animated montage series is conceptualized for operating interactivity to express human-computer interfacing automation.

**Figure 12** illustrates how a montage series plays slowly until the user finds his / her interest in the category of multimedia to play and browse in more depth. Let us use Mickey Mouse as an example. A little boy is watching the slowly-playing montage series from "Kung Fu Panda" to "Thomas Train". He could try to click the montage "Donald Duck", then he would be taken to the category underneath and stay to watch more he likes. He can also be back up to the montage series by clicking "Duck" via "in-&-out" interactivity.

**Interactivity** is animated to engage the user in the exchange of information between cloud-based Anything as a Service, and client devices, e.g., smartphone, tablet, laptop, and/or computer. The exchange of informative montage series is

**Figure 12.**
*Animated montage series promotes operating interactivity.*

animated to control robots, play multimedia theater through robotic process automation, and so forth. In particular, MSA helps to enrich interactivity via wiseCIO to engage users with their exploration of entertaining services without boredom.

Everytime, when rendering a traditional website on the client screen, the view is almost the same as navigating header and/or footer, then a user has to scroll up/down to find a section of his/her interests in. The MSA prepares heuristics and/or visual "montage" via tab-based multi-sections to present preview animatedly until the user hits the section for better user experience.

The MSA supports human-computer interfacing via UnIX with heuristic scenarios to direct the user to preview primary categories of content, and which one to choose is quite customized.

### 5.4 ACM: assembled coding machinery for novelty in programming

ACM represents the fourth XaaS template that initiates heuristics of computing machinery-assembled novaly for universal interface & experience (UnIX) on **computational thinking and programmability**. ACM is a simulator of coding to promote programmable user interface design, similar to, but different from MSA. While montage series in play may be sequential, Assembled machinery plays a series in programmable order, and maybe with choice-making. It utilizes an assembly-like language to create new apps in a visual approach, so an instruction is encoded as an actionable token that consists of at least three elements: (a) a number (code), (b) a wording description (action), and (c) a visual illustration, such as an animated GIF, a video, or an audio. ACM encourages users to create their own instruction set from which they can program fun stories or scenarios in a programmable (sequential and selective) approach.

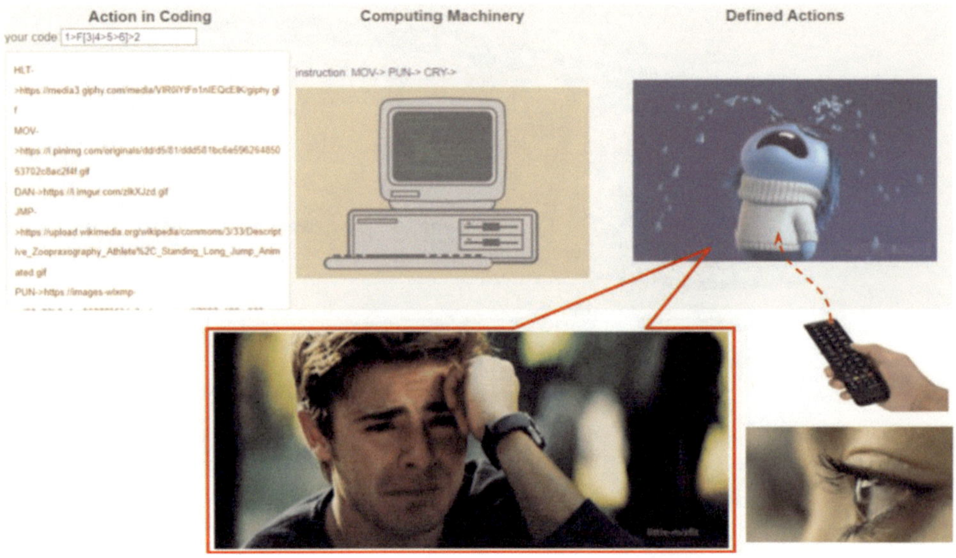


**Figure 13.**
*Programmable series promotes operating novelty.*

**Figure 13** illustrates how a programmable series plays slowly until the user finds his / her interest in the category of multimedia to play and browse in more depth. The upper part represents ACM, and the lower part extends the illustrative picture related folder. Let us use Crying Posture as an example. A user programs a series, tests and performs the slowly-playing programmable series according to the program at the running. The user could try to catch an illustrative picture or description of "CRY", then by clicking he would be taken to the category underneath and stay to watch more he likes. He can also get back up to continue the programmable series via "in-&-out" interactivity. The ACM program is developed in an actionable tokens that relates visual illustrations dynamically, so program executing will produce a cartoonish movie that is runnable, presentable, playable, and programmable (rPPP).

**Novelty in programming** of data path processing is a universal feature in virtualized networks [23]. A given instruction series is executable through sequential (*one step after another*), and/or selective (*one or the other*) order for the sake of instructional teaching through computational thinking of programmability. Furthermore, the user can enhance the existing instruction set, or create a fully new instruction set for the coding machinery.

Theoretically, ACM showcase serves as a virtual coding machinery that supports coding algorithms by using the instruction set, which encourages coding and creativity to problem-solving in programmability.

Also ACM can enable rapid prototyping and responsive assembly from the well-categorized multimedia to help users explore various scenarios for kids, adults, and so on.

### 5.5 NFA: name-featured activation for availability in customizing

NFA represents the fifth XaaS template that initiates heuristics of name-featured availability for universal interface & experience (UnIX) on **customization or**

**individualization**. NFA prioritizes customizable availability based on individual names, which denotes heuristics to encourage users to explore entertaining multimedia, such as audios or videos without boredom. By inputting the user's name the customizable availability gets started—the name becomes a key in ASCII to trigger a group of multimedia for preview until the user chooses to intervene.

**Figure 14** illustrates how a customizable series is made available to relate users' interest in the category of multimedia to play and browse in more depth. The upper part represents the NFA section that allows the user to input the name and whose ASCII series is used to draw specific background color, and the lower part denotes multimedia list to play. Based on a user when he / she input the name, the random availability is triggered toward a group of multimedia (list) for preview.

**Customizable Availability** represents adjustment making responsively to accommodate a users' individual needs for the sake of better user experience engaging the user with something new via cloud-based Anything as a Service. Most traditional websites start with a search port in addition to header and footer for further explorations in breadth. It is very beneficial for a new-hamd user to start with what to search and where to start. As initial heuristics, letters of a given name in ASCII are combined to bring out the customizable content for the user to get started with great ease.

Psychologically NFA showcase provides a customizable preview on the primary category of grouping content. According to Psychology Today—Hello, My Name is Unique [24], "Some parents want names for their children that are unique but not too trendy. Other parents seem to love alternative spellings. How important is a name to our self-perception?" A unique and special name will heuristically lead to pleasant experience while a user exploring entertainment through multimedia.

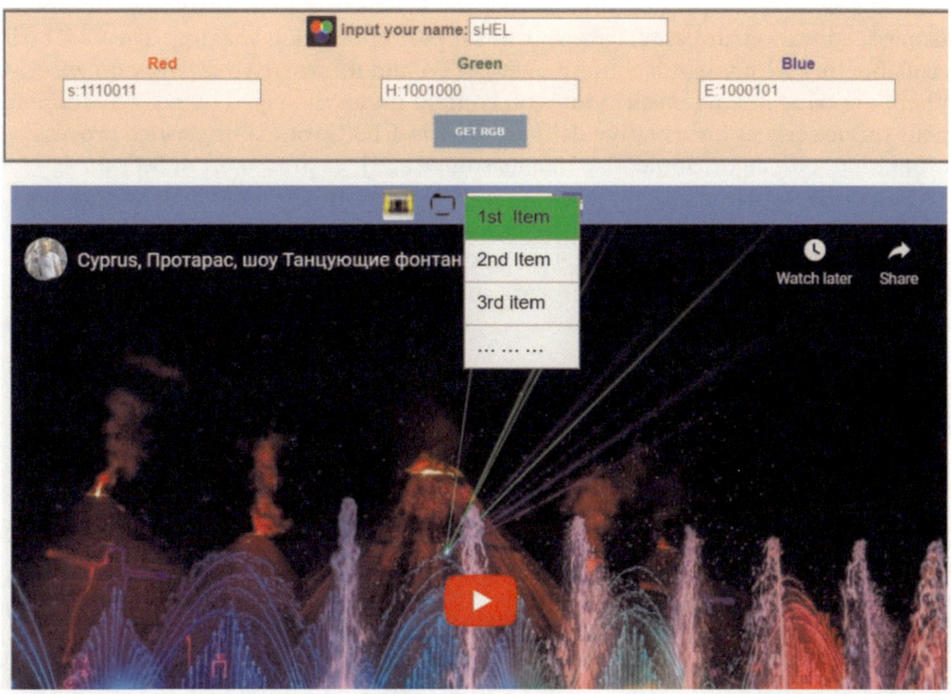


**Figure 14.**
*Name-featured activation promotes customizable availability.*

NFA aims for responsive adjustment over multimedia grouping to accommodate a customer's particular needs for better user experience that encourages engagement without boredom.

## 6. Conclusion

UnIX-CARE or Universal Interface & Experience has emerged from Collaborative Archive Repository Express (CARE) that collaborates integral content over DATA with informative delivery via wiseCIO through algorithmic machine learning. Conceptualized as a "fastlane" into the CMD triad, CARE provides mathematical and computational solutions to achieve following UNIX objectives:

*Ubiquitous Manager* is everywhere across the CMD triad to harness *comprehensive* information for business, education and entertainment (iBEE), and to propel *composite* assembly of anything as a service (XaaS). With which the "controversial" agendas among IT personnel [5] have been resolved so that an ordinary end-user can be made a webmaster, a web designer and/or an extraordinary user while browsing in hierarchical depth via "In-&-Out" interactivity, and exploring in contextual breadth via self-paced spontaneity [14] without overwhelming, as discussed in Section 2.

*Novel Designer* takes CARE for universal interface design and user-centric experience by instant typing online publishing (iTOP) via express tokens for information interchange (eTokin) differing from traditional XML and JSON [17]. In which iTOP, assisted by algorithmic machine learning, presents universal interface design that advances the aims at user-centric experience without explicitly coding required, as deeply studied in Section 3.

*Intelligent Expert* represents one of the CMD goals to aggregate intelligence for business, education and entertainment in support of decision-making. The CMD triad is collaborated with integral content over DATA and informative delivery on wiseCIO. Where digital archiving ensures integral content under managed by DATA, and intelligent service serves informative delivery by wiseCIO throughout elastice process automation with algorithmic machine learning [8, 9], as presented in Section 4.

*Extraordinary Liaison* facilitates human-computer interfacing via eTokin to simplify collaborative communications without rendering related redundancies, but semantic enrichment that suffice to orchestrate Anything as a Service with machine learning patterns through elastic process automation [18], as discussed as Quinary XaaS in Section 5.

## 7. Visible accomplishments

This article presents following critical advancements technologically and practically through multiple best efforts to pave comprehensive roadmaps toward the above accomplishments:

**Novel Triad** provides comprehensively innovative solutions to cloud-based distributed problems for Anything as a Service that involves Automated interfacing Design (AiD for various users) via UnIX-CARE, Proactive online Analytics (PaA) over DATA, and User-centric Experience (UcX) via wiseCIO for the sake of capability of intelligence for Business (Section 4), Education (4.3-CIA) and Entertainment (4.4-Netflix-like Movies).

**Challenges (versus Chances)** on serving "controversial personnel" [5] turn from *controversial* agendas into *cohesive* advancement on the basis of seamless intercommunications (*context-neutrality*) among the CMD triad and semantic enrichments (-*context-specialty*) through algorithmic machine learning, which propels large teams united and working together effectively. Algorithmically with practical methods implemented as intelligent services, the CMD triad assists to empower users to be cohesive professionals: like a webmaster over DATA, an interface designer via UnIX-CARE, and an intelligent expert on wiseCIO to discover useful and usable information in support of decision-making.

**Archival Express via eTokin** for information interchange among CMD triad succeeds with a firm foundation for interoperability, the top level characteristics of networking applications, that enables orchestration of Anything as a Service. As an essential backbone, seamless intercommunication upgrades three CMD parties up to interoperability to ensure Anything-orchestrated as a Service, thoroughly discussed in Sections 4 and 5.

## 8. Future work & practice

In addition to feasible and visual accomplishments, there will be more efforts to make as future work in comprehensive practice as follows:

a. *Algorithmic Deep Learning* (ADL) will be applied to discover learning patterns and usable rules in support of algorithmic machine learning with more active prompts for test-driven "sensors" or monitor to enable thorough analysis on archival express via eTokin to advance semantic enrichments, instead of confused execution without a clue to fix potential issues because of highly-express tokens that would be too brief (?) for success through information interchange.

b. *Sophisticated App Templates* (SAT) will be developed practically for domain-specific intelligent service (DSIS) and tested thoroughly with a full set of sampling data provided for deep learning on simple imports, execution and testing for algorithmic customizations. Sophisticate templates would be stable (*not to cause "earthquake" on the service basis in light of modifications*), flexible (*to encourage enhancement and enrichment of intelligent service with great ease*), and feasible (*algorithmic solutions are achievable*).

c. *Advanced Research Machinery* (ARM) will be conducted on algorithmic sophistications to enhance computational thinking and programmability for machine learning that minimize explicitly coding but more through elastic and robotic process automation. In general, elasticity means flexibility of "multiple birds with one stone"—one solution to a family of problems, and robotics enables procedural automation over DATA encouraging self-fulfillment without much explicitly coding required.

d. *Portable Online Intelligent Service* (POIS) will be discovered to reflect and represent Anything as a Service and put into practice with a strengthened "brain" in machine learning—through practice, we can gradually collect ourselves and learn how to be more fully with what we will do. POIS encourages

XaaS across platforms (iOS, Linux, Windows), and browsers (Chrome, Safari, Firefox, Microsoft Edge, and Opera, etc.)

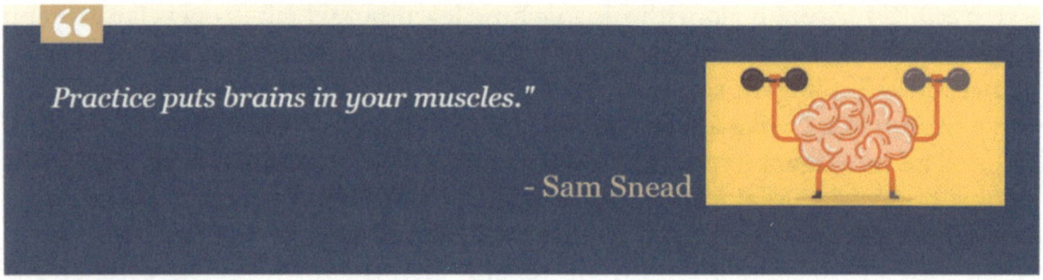


## Acknowledgements

This work is partially supported by Department of Education-MESIP Award P120A180072 subaward 161206PMJ157 to M.V.S., National Science Foundation HRD 201138, and Apple- HBCU C2—Any opinions, findings, and conclusions or recommendations expressed in this material are those of the authors and do not necessarily reflect the views of the Department of Education or National Science Foundation. Our sincere thanks to HBCU $C^2$ Partnership with Apple and Tennessee State University, *Dr. Robinson Blackman-* Senior Program Executive Director, HBCU C2 Project), *Dr Aminah F. Gooch-* Director of Lane Summer STEM Research Academy and Summer Interns: *Armon White, Innocent Munezearo, Jayleel George, Malcolm Little, and Mohamed Fall* for their contribution included in the article. Special thanks to *Dr Patricia LaGrow* (former Associate Provost of the University of Central Oklahoma, Edmond, OK) for her inspirational encouragement when needed and descriptive wording and writing. Last but not least, I am deeply thankful to Angela Hua for her always-encouragement and love of wiseCIO (!).

## Author details

Sheldon Liang[1]*, Melanie Van Stry[1] and Hong Liu[2]

1 Lane College, a HBCU Institution, Jackson, Tennessee, USA

2 Embry-Riddle Aeronautical University, Daytona Beach, Florida, USA

*Address all correspondence to: sliang@lanecollege.edu

## References

[1] Jamest J, Rajendra V, Zhang Y. Content Management and Delivery. Assignee: Microsoft Corp; 2012. Available from: https://pubchem.ncbi.nlm.nih.gov/patent/CN-104854842-A

[2] Liang S, Lebby K, McCarthy P. wiseCIO: Web-based intelligent services engaging cloud intelligence outlet. SAI 2020: Intelligent Computing. 2020;**1**:169-195. DOI: 10.1007/978-3-030-52249-0_12

[3] Liang S, McCarthy P, Van Stry M. DATA: Digital archiving and transformed analytics. Intelligent Information Management. 2021;**13**:70-95. DOI: 10.4236/iim.2021.131004

[4] Liang S, Mak L, Keele E, McCarthy P. iDATA-orchestrated wiseCIO for anything-as-a-service. FICC 2021: Advances in Information and Communication. 2021;**1363**:401-424. DOI: 10.1007/978-3-030-73100-7_29

[5] Iggy. Top 5 Web Design Debates That Cause the Most Riots. 2009. Available from: https://line25.com/articles/top-5-web-design-debates-that-cause-the-most-riots/

[6] National Library of Medicine. Cells and DNA—What is DNA? 2021. Available from: https://medlineplus.gov/genetics/understanding/basics/dna/

[7] SailPoint. Robotic Process Automation (RPA) Technology. 2020. Available from: https://www.sailpoint.com/identity-library/robotic-process-automation-rpa-technology/?utm_id=414626189

[8] IBM Cloud Learn HUB. What is machine learning?. 2022. Available from: https://www.ibm.com/cloud/learn/machine-learning

[9] Wolfewicz A. Deep learning vs. machine learning—What's the difference?. 2022. Available from: https://levity.ai/blog/difference-machine-learning-deep-learning

[10] Tripathi S, Luellwitz L, Egge K. Use Information Technologies and Operating Technologies to get the most from your Enterprise Asset Management System. 2020. Available from: https://www.ibm.com/blogs/internet-of-things/use-information-technologies-and-operating-technologies-to-get-the-most-from-your-enterprise-asset-management-system/

[11] Computational thinking—Be empowered for the AI age. Available from: https://www.computationalthinking.org/

[12] IBM Cloud Education. What is OLAP—Cloud Architecture. 2020. Available from: https://www.ibm.com/cloud/learn/olap#toc-what-is-ol-cEW94rVb

[13] DIMACS, NSF. An Operational Definition—What Is Computational Thinking?, Rutgers, the State University of New Jersey. 2020. Available from: https://ctpdonline.org/computational-thinking/

[14] Liang S, MacCarthy E, Hall C. Advanced Integral Digitalization to Digital Archiving and Transformed Analytics, SGCI Gateways. 2021. Available from: https://www.youtube.com/watch?v=YtqVBr-vi38

[15] Miller GA. The Magical Number Seven, Plus or Minus TWO: Some Limits on Our Capacity for Processing Information, The Psychological Review. 1956. Available from: https://pure.mpg.de/rest/items/item_2364276_4/component/file_2364275/content

[16] Heshmat S.. Eight Reasons Why We Get Bored. Psychology Today. 2012.

Available from: https://www.psychologytoday.com/us/blog/science-choice/201706/eight-reasons-why-we-get-bored

[17] Microsoft Docs. Windows Communication Foundations (WCF). Mapping between JSON and XML. 2021. Available from: https://docs.microsoft.com/en-us/dotnet/framework/wcf/feature-details/mapping-between-json-and-xml

[18] Misev A. Algorithmic Patterns—Data Structures and Algorithms in Java. 2012. Available from: https://perun.pmf.uns.ac.rs/java/workshops/Algorithmic-patterns.pdf

[19] IGI Global Publisher of Timely Knowledge. What is Flexible Querying. 2022. Available from: https://www.igi-global.com/dictionary/flexible-querying-techniques-based-cbr/11253

[20] Jon Radoff. Composability is the Most Powerful Creative Force in the Universe. 2022. Available from: https://medium.com/building-the-metaverse/composability-is-the-most-powerful-creative-force-in-the-universe-e82e3dd83ccd

[21] Digital Adoption Team. Composability: A Game-Changing New Paradigm for the Business World. 2021. Available from: https://www.digital-adoption.com/composability/

[22] Unreal Developer Network. Animation Montage Overview. 2022. Available from: https://docs.unrealengine.com/4.26/en-US/AnimatingObjects/SkeletalMeshAnimation/AnimMontage/Overview/

[23] Fang J, Karl F, Böhringer KF. Assembly Programmability for Architecture of Network Systems. 2011. Available from: https://www.sciencedirect.com/topics/engineering/programmability

[24] Psychology Today. Hello, My Name is Unique. 2016. Available from: https://www.psychologytoday.com/us/articles/200403/hello-my-name-is-unique